W9-AAF-081

He Did Deliver Me from Bondage

Using the Book of Mormon and the
Principles of the Gospel of Jesus Christ
as They Correlate with the
Twelve–Step Program to Overcome
Compulsive/Addictive Behavior
and Other Problems

Revised Edition

Colleen C. Harrison

WINDHAVEN
PUBLISHING & PRODUCTIONS
PLEASANT GROVE, UTAH

WINDHAVEN
PUBLISHING & PRODUCTIONS
PO Box 282
PLEASANT GROVE, UT 84062
WWW.WINDHAVENPUBLISHING.COM

Copyright © 2002
by Colleen C. Harrison and Windhaven Publishing and Productions
Printed in the United States of America

ISBN: 1—930738—01—3

All rights reserved. No part of this book may be used or reproduced in any
manner whatsoever, including but not limited to reproduction by electronic,
mechanical or other means, including photocopying and recording, or by any
information storage or retrieval system, without express written permission from
an authorized representative of Windhaven Publishing and Productions, except
for the inclusion of brief quotations in a review. Quotes used in personal journal
writing may also be used without written permission as long as they are framed
in quote marks and the full title of the book, *He Did Deliver Me from Bondage* is
included. The order form printed at the end of the workbook may be freely copied
and distributed as desired.

The Twelve Steps have been reprinted and adapted with permission from
Alcoholics Anonymous World Services, Inc. The opinions expressed are not to be
attributed to Alcoholics Anonymous. Information from various Heart t' Heart
printed materials have been reprinted and adapted with permission from the
General Service Board of Heart t' Heart, Inc.

Cover Art: ©2000, Julie Ann Cooper. Used with permission.
Design & Typesetting: Professional Pre-Press, Pleasant Grove, Utah.

This book is designed to provide you with information on Twelve Step recovery
so that you can deal more effectively with compulsive/addictive behaviors in
yourself or those you love. However, results from applying these principles will
vary with the individual. As a result, this book is sold with the understanding that
neither the author nor the publisher is engaged in rendering specific
psychotherapy or other professional counseling services to any individual.

ACKNOWLEDGEMENTS

I would like to acknowledge the hand of God in creating this book and give Him credit for the following miracles:

— The love and support of precious twelve-step sponsors and friends, who are also LDS, who encouraged me in the writing of these materials.

— The editing work of several gifted people, and particularly the final professional edit, done free of charge by one of the most caring, dedicated-to-Christ educators I have known. He struggles valiantly to teach me to write good... I mean, well.

— The hours and hours of typesetting that have been donated by one of my dearest sisters in Christ. I have often stretched her love and long-suffering far beyond human capacity. I know it is God's own patience manifest through her.

— My family, both past and present, who have been instruments in God's hands to teach me humility, patience, and charity. I am only sorry I have been such a slow learner.

— The gift to live every day of my life with a sure witness of the living Christ—that He is more than sufficient to be my Savior and yours. That knowledge gives me the freedom to relax and to trust and to enter into His rest.

One Last Acknowledgement:

— I realize that prophetic text cannot be reduced to any single "private interpretation." In other words, no one individual can say, "This is the *true* meaning of this scripture or quote" or "This is the *only* way this scripture or quote can be applied." In fact, the Spirit of God often opens the very same reference to me differently at different times in my life. The material in this book represents my personal thoughts and reflections on the scriptures and principles covered.

TABLE OF CONTENTS

FAITH IN THE LORD JESUS CHRIST—NOTHING LESS

REPENTANCE—HEART DEEP

GOOD WORKS
BASED ON HEART—DEEP CONVERSION

and oneness with everyone, including those I have hurt or been hurt by.

9. BLESSED ARE ALL THE PEACEMAKERS (3 Nephi 12:9) 117
The establishment of Zion begins with a mighty change in my own heart, and then extends to others as I act to amend all past wrongs.

THE GIFT OF THE HOLY GHOST—
CHRIST'S OWN WORDS

10. RETAIN A REMISSION OF YOUR SINS (Mosiah 4:12) 129
The mighty change of heart does not bring me to a state of perfection but rather to a state of continual repentance and abhorrence of sin.

11. COUNSEL WITH THE LORD IN ALL THY DOINGS

The mighty change of heart brings me an awareness of Christ's living presence in my life through the gift of the Holy Ghost as I learn to receive and believe the voice of the Lord in my own mind.

12. I [WAS] DESIROUS THAT MY FAMILY SHOULD PARTAKE

The mighty change of heart causes me to feel an irresistible desire to share with others the truly good news of Christ's reality and availability.

APPENDIX

HOW TO USE THIS BOOK AS A STUDY GUIDE

In the years since its introduction, this book has been used to aid people in recovering from a myriad of problems—addictions, compulsive behaviors, trauma in childhood and adulthood, as well as coming to a sense of peace and reconciliation with what can't be changed. The material has been implemented in three ways:

First: As a valuable course of study for individuals who have read it and worked through the scriptural exercises in the privacy of their own homes.

Second: As a study guide for use in a workshop or class setting. Usually the course of study takes thirteen weeks, with a two hour class held at a regular time each week, facilitated by a professional or priesthood leader.

Third: As foundational study materials for LDS Twelve Step recovery groups including LDS Family Services Substance Abuse Recovery Services (SARS).

Please note the following clarification for using the scripture study references:

In many books that encourage reader involvement to internalize the concepts discussed, the suggested activities found at the end of each chapter summarize and reinforce the previous chapter's contents. **In this workbook, however, the study questions found at the end of each chapter prepare you for the discussion of the principle to be covered in the next chapter.**

For example, on pp. 9–12, you will find seven suggested scripture references with thought provoking questions and comments which are intended to establish a scriptural foundation for the chapter that begins on page 13. Although it may be tempting, please do not pass over these exercises. If you must, read the book straight through and then come back to do the scripture study and journal writing these exercises suggest. If you do this, you will find your journals can be far more than you ever dreamed possible. In fact, like the writings of Lehi, Nephi, Mormon and Moroni, they can become "Another Testament of the Lord Jesus Christ."

In addition to the supplemental reading included in the appendix of this book, there are other articles suggested for reading from their original sources. They are:

- "Born of God," by President Ezra Taft Benson (*Ensign*, July 1989)

- "Beauty for Ashes, the Atonement of Jesus Christ," by Bruce C. Hafen (*Ensign*, April 1990)

- "A Practical Approach to the Atonement: Believing in Christ," by Stephen E. Robinson (*BYU Today*, November 1990)

- "Beware of Pride," by President Ezra Taft Benson (*Ensign*, May 1989)

FOREWORD

You promise you'll never do it again. You promise you'll never overeat again, never hide food again, never bounce checks again, never yell at the kids for no reason again—never, never, never! You promise God and anyone who will listen that you'll never repeat your destructive behavior. And you are sincere—heartbreakingly sincere. But repeat them you do. And you do. And you do. And day after endless day, your life repeats itself. You are caught in a cycle of repentance and relapse. You are in bondage.

Does any of this sound familiar to you? Have you ever found, or do you now find yourself in bondage too? Are you swept up in a similar cycle of bad habits, self-defeating behaviors, self-destructive and insane behaviors—compulsive, addictive behaviors? Do you ever wonder if there is a way out?

Several years ago, I took a good look at my life and realized that I was in a spiritual shambles. No matter what my good intentions were, no matter how I longed to change, and no matter how strongly I willed myself to change, it just wouldn't happen. I was a mess of "socially acceptable" compulsive, addictive behaviors and it was killing me. I had lived what I believed to be the gospel of Jesus Christ and I was still miserable. And I was almost hopeless.

I remember reading the *Book of Mormon* and thinking that there was an important message hidden in those words of wisdom and I just wasn't getting it. After weeks of pleading with the Lord for guidance, I was introduced to the Twelve Steps. I found some recovery in the fellowship of a Twelve Step group, but true recovery began when I turned back to the *Book of Mormon*. After learning the concepts and the principles in the simple, everyday language of the Twelve Steps, I returned to the *Book of Mormon*, and its mysteries opened up to me. The Twelve Steps were everywhere within its pages. That was when the power of the gospel of Jesus Christ really began to work in my life, and I began to be freed from the chains of emotional bondage, one link at a time.

I continued my fellowship in a Twelve Step group for some time, all the while wishing I were free to share the extra light that the gospel and the *Book of Mormon* shed on the principles behind the Twelve Steps. Fortunately, I wasn't alone. This same desire in the heart of another led to the publication of this workbook, *He Did Deliver Me from Bondage*.

He Did Deliver Me from Bondage illustrates the true principles that underlie the Twelve Steps with passages from the Book of Mormon. I have found that the Twelve Steps are nothing more (or more accurately, nothing less) than a bare-bones, step-by-step guide back to the Lord, Jesus Christ—the same step-by-step path found in fullness and glory in the *Book of Mormon*. I believe the Twelve Steps are a set of "baby steps" that lead to the "giant steps" found in the gospel. *He Did Deliver Me from Bondage* bridges the gap between the two.

I am very grateful for the recovery and the deliverance from bondage the Lord has orchestrated in my life thus far. Only He can lead us to that "mighty change of heart" of which Alma speaks. I pray that you will find Him and that this workbook may help you along the way.

— Karlene B.

AUTHOR'S "FOREWORD"

Hi, my name's Colleen; I'm an addict. In other words, I'm a mortal struggling with the effects of the fall. Without conscious contact with a power far greater than my own, even the Spirit of Truth, the Lord, Jesus Christ **(D&C 93:9)**, I cannot maintain anything resembling sanity or serenity.

Today, thanks to the twelve principles discussed in this book, learned first at *Overeaters Anonymous*, and later enhanced and magnified by corresponding scriptural validation, I have found that peace which passeth understanding, which only Christ can give **(Philippians 4:7)**. In him I have found a perfect brightness of hope that shines through even the deepest darkness. I have sanity and serenity because of His living presence in my life.

When I remember Him and keep my eye single to His glory, and to the glory of the Father who sent Him to be my Savior and closest Friend, I experience a remission of lies in my mind and of sin in my life. I lose my desire to do evil; to do that which separates me from God. I lose my desire to turn to the things of this world for counterfeit solace and comfort. I stop eating extraneous food; I lose weight. I stop spending money I really don't need to spend; my checkbook stays balanced. I stop trying to fix others; my relationships calm down. I stop fearing; I start hoping and trusting. My depression disappears.

When I apply these true principles in my life I am free—free of the lie of pride, free of the lie of self-sufficiency, free of the lie that any sin, either my own or another's, is more powerful and permanent than God's power to heal and atone. When I use these principles or steps in my life on a daily basis, I am not empty, and I am not alone. I am filled with a sure witness of Jesus Christ and of His personal love for me. Using these principles or steps, I am able to draw near unto Him, and unfailingly find that, as He promises in

D&C 88:63, He draws near unto me. I feel His encircling arms of love **(D&C 6:20)**; I recognize His words conveyed to me through the Holy Ghost **(2 Nephi 32:3, 5)**; and I know that according to His own will, I may see His face **(D&C 88:68)**.

When *He Did Deliver Me from Bondage* was originally written in 1991, there was no recovery support group for Latter-day Saints who were struggling with the more "socially acceptable" compulsive, addictive behaviors such as overeating, overspending, workaholism, perfectionism, and so forth. Nor was there a group in which I could introduce myself using the religious terms I have used in this foreword. Today there are such groups, based firmly in a combination of the Twelve Step concepts and the principles of the gospel of Jesus Christ. These groups were not created to compete with the Church or with other Twelve Step groups; rather they complement them all. This study guide, which was originally written for use in the Heart t' Heart Twelve Step program, is also used by several other programs, including LDS Family Services Substance Abuse Recovery Services program (SARS).

The most exciting result to come from the development of LDS programs using the Twelve Step model of recovery is we are free to study the Restored Gospel of Jesus Christ in harmony with and support of the principles in the Steps.

— Colleen H.

PREFACE: FIRST EDITION (1991)

In 1981 I tipped the scale at over 300 pounds. Believe me, I was the most miserable "active" Latter-day Saint I knew. Of course, I didn't know many people, Latter-day Saint or otherwise, because of the isolated, imprisoned lifestyle I lived. I walled myself in with cleaning, cooking, canning, sewing, even with children and husband and, of course, with eating. I'm not saying there's anything wrong with cooking and cleaning— they are the necessities of life. Sewing and canning are worthwhile activities too. They are good basic skills that every person should know to be prepared for hard times when life might be scarce instead of abundant. The only problem was that I *made* my life scarce doing those very things. While my children languished around me, I sewed and canned and crafted my way through 16 years and 11 pregnancies. I made my energy and time so scarce that there was a "famine in the land" emotionally, while I obsessively tried to fit into the Mollie Mormon mold.

And my husband and children? In my obsession to make everything perfect, I created a prison out of something as potentially exalting as my *family*. I used their lives as an excuse to never get around to my own life. Even their cleanliness came before mine. I went to bed when they went to bed (11:00 p.m. because of someone's just remembered school project), stayed awake until they fell asleep (12:00 midnight with my husband), got up when they got up (3:00 a.m. with the baby), and started the day before they did so *their* foundation got properly laid (6:00 a.m. to fix breakfast, conduct scripture study).

And what was I doing to sustain this concentrated pretense of perfection? Was I pursuing a course of daily personal prayer and scripture study to receive God's direction and power in my *own* life? Heavens, no! After all, I had no life outside my husband and children—cleaning for them, cooking, sewing, canning; thinking, planning. And besides, I'd been to Gospel Doctrine class. I wasn't a *total* scriptural illiterate. I knew that it was *only* after *all* that I could do to be perfect that I should turn to God, and I knew that if I ate just *one* more batch of cookie dough or one more helping of dinner I could *do* more. If and when I ever got through doing all I could, then I would rightfully seek God and worthily receive His input.

I mean, put yourself in my place. I didn't want to ask prematurely, as Oliver Cowdery did, and get rebuked (**D&C 9:7**). What if I turned to God and instead of comfort received chastisement? What if, instead of direction, I got recriminating memories about temple and visiting teaching assignments I either missed or did with a weary, grudging heart? Thanks, but no thanks. A doughnut or four extra dinner rolls promised to help me forget, if even for a few moments, instead of remembering anything more I needed to do to be "busily engaged." Eating was the one thing I consistently did for myself. Mother, the supreme nurturer and caretaker, finally got around to nurturing and taking care of herself at midnight by consuming food she had deliberately hoarded and hidden earlier.

It's pretty obvious that I had a problem—a *serious* problem. It's obvious to me today, but it wasn't then. Back then I didn't have time to recognize any problems in my life. All I needed was another Twinkie and I could make it; I could be there for *one* more act of service or hour of self-sufficient sewing or canning.

Didn't I ever diet? you might ask. Certainly! Constantly! At least constantly between that "last supper" of hoarded goodies at midnight and about 10:00 a.m. the next morning when the leftover pancakes from breakfast needed to be cleared. After all, how could I justify eating the eggs or fruit my food plan called for when I could feed them to the children tomorrow? How could I let these perfectly good pancakes go to *waste*! Hadn't I just attended a homemaking lesson in which one sister demonstrated three dozen ways to use the lint from our dryer screens to avoid wasting it?

I was in deep trouble, and digging myself deeper with every effort to get out. Even diets that lasted any length of time were only getting me into a worse mess metabolically. No matter how healthy the written plan of eating was, I could, with my perfectionistic, all or nothing, black or white thinking, pare it down to a third of its author's original intent and lose twice as much *twice as fast!* And I would! I would lose a *lot* fast. Who wouldn't on 500 calories of cottage cheese and lettuce leaves a day? Ten pounds in ten days. Wow! At this rate I would be a size ten by Christmas—and I could even overeat on my birthday in September, Halloween in October, and Thanksgiving in November if I just fasted three days after each traditional binge.

Again and again, I would sit and mark a new calendar with each new resolve, projecting weekly weight loss. I'd chart and rechart my miraculous transformation-*to-come* with bar charts and graph paper, filling little boxes with "x's" for each hour of my success. I would even fill in the boxes for the nighttime hours weeks in advance—after all, I would be sleeping between 1:00 and 6:00 a.m., right? Unless of course I was up at 2:00 a.m. with the baby for a nighttime feeding.

And thus I "dieted" my way *up* the scale instead of down, ending up in the summer of 1981 at about 315 pounds. I never knew for sure, because when the bathroom scale went all the way around the dial and started past the top number a second time, I stepped off forever.

I stepped off the scale and dropped to my knees. It wasn't that I had never done that before either. In fact that was the most agonizing part of this struggle. The entire fifteen years of my insanity—and it *is* insanity to be on such a course of self-destruction—was riddled by times of desperately weeping and wailing to God. Time after time, in the temple and out, I had pledged to God that I would conquer this terrible destructive behavior. Education Week after Education Week sent me home determined to be good for the prescribed 18 (or was it 21?) days that it took to eliminate a "bad habit." Sometimes I even made it through those lengths of time, but inevitably my devotion to my best self would fade, my old emptiness would return, and I would begin to overeat again. This was more than a habit. No amount of white-knuckled willpower gave me security against that first compulsive bite, which sooner or later led to another binge and complete self-degradation.

This time, in this prayer, though, there was to be no weeping and wailing on my part, no whining and justifying and rationalizing and bargaining. I was down for the count, and I knew it. I knew it because I had *finally* done all that I could do. I had sewn, canned, cleaned, quilted, made babies, served husband and children past a righteous balance **(Proverbs 11:1)** and had held four church positions at the same time. I had stayed up late and gotten up early. I had gone to Education Week classes, read books, made charts, made pledges, gone to every "quick-weight [money] loss" program I could afford. There was nothing left. Nothing. I couldn't even pray—at least not out loud. I felt much like Joseph in the grove, oppressed under a great cloud of darkness; only mine had not appeared in seconds—mine had taken years to build up.

I literally crawled to my bedside and crumpled there, and the tears finally came—tears of complete surrender to God. No words, no excuses, no pleadings, no answers— just tears. These were not tears of "poor-me" or "why-me." Instead, these were tears of "not my will—but Thine be done." Today, I know those tears were, at least in spirit, mingled with blood—Jesus Christ's own atoning blood; for from that hour my deliverance began. If I had known then how close divine help actually was, I might have heard a spiritual witness, as did Daniel of old:

> **Fear not,** [Colleen]: **for from the first day that thou didst set thine heart to understand** [instead of dictate], **and to chasten** [purify] **thyself before thy God, thy words were heard and I am come for thy words. (Daniel 10:12)**

I didn't realize that at that moment of complete surrender, I was about to enter a whole new life, *a life turned inside out.*

After I was finally through crying, I dragged myself up and sat on the side of my bed. Feeling the impression that I needed to invest more than I ever had before, I decided to call a weight-loss clinic I had heard about that offered absolute control over your meals, preparing and delivering them to you, for a formidable price. At least it used to be *formidable* to me. Now a new spirit had come over me. I was now willing to go to any length, to pay any price, to do whatever God wanted me to do. I wasn't running the show anymore, bargaining with life for a penny. I had to be willing to give all, or I would die, and I knew it.

I reached for the phone and phone book. Finding the appropriate number, I dialed. The line rang and rang. Tears sprang to my eyes again. Wasn't I humble enough, desperate enough, willing enough? Here I was in a state of total surrender, ready to be led in all things, and even go *bankrupt!* I didn't think there was a greater depth of humiliation and willingness.

Little did I know then that the course God was about to set my feet upon would require me to admit a bankruptcy far deeper than financial, develop a willingness to do God's will that would require every day of the rest of my life and would catapult me into a life so filled with friends and truly unconditional love that I would even start to feel some love for myself.

The next impression that came was to reach out to a friend, to someone who loved me, who would listen to me.

The friend I called had no answers for me, but that was okay, because God did. I was to realize later that from the moment of my admittance of personal powerlessness, of my absolute need for Him, He had taken over. All my friend could suggest was that she could put me in touch with a neighbor of hers who had been attending a weight-loss program of some type and having a lot of success, and it didn't cost too much.

A quick call to this other person, Latter-day Saint though she was, was another increment of complete humility for me. I, who was usually terrified of interaction with strangers, found myself already being lifted and sustained by a power far greater than my own.

The lady didn't say much but offered to take me to a meeting the next morning. I couldn't believe it when I heard myself accept her offer. Me? Three-hundred and fifteen pound me was going to walk out in the broad daylight tomorrow morning and get in a car with a complete stranger? And not only a stranger, but one who had had lots of recent success at losing weight and was looking great besides! I ate my last pan of brownies that afternoon, trying to suppress the fear of the unknown and of the change I felt. But changed I was—somewhere on the *inside* something was different. Even the pan of brownies couldn't deter it. It was going to be years later before I read President Benson's words: **"God changes men from the inside out"** (*Ensign*, **July 1989, p.4).** That day I was living his words.

The next morning came, and it was the proverbial first day of the rest of my life. I walked into my first Overeaters Anonymous (OA) meeting that day and was introduced to a program based on twelve simple steps of recovery. I was praying constantly about this strange new world I had entered. People were mentioning the word "God," and not all of them were LDS. I began to feel anxious. Maybe I was in some sort of danger here. Then I remembered I had been endowed with the gift of the Holy Ghost, and it could teach me the truth of all things **(Moroni 10:5)**; that Moroni had assured me if anything taught me to do good and to love God and to serve God, then it was of God **(Moroni 7:13)**; that the 13th Article of Faith declared my religion to include seeking after "anything virtuous, lovely, of good report or praiseworthy;" that Christ Himself, through the Prophet Joseph Smith, charged me to seek wisdom out of the best books **(D&C 88:118)**; that Brigham Young had once declared that we, as Latter-day Saints, could claim truth no matter where we might find it and should not be afraid to seek it *anywhere* **(*Journal of Discourses*, 13:335).** Still I felt concerned. After all, maybe having all these things come to my remembrance as I sat there in that first meeting was a ploy of the adversary to get me into some kind of cult or something. Maybe I should get up and leave!

Fortunately, God had other ideas. He had me stay long enough to buy an Alcoholics Anonymous "Big Book," the basic text for every Twelve Step group. There are many such groups, and for good reason—they work.

I took that "Big Book" home, and began to read. As I read I found how true it is that God is no respecter of persons. I read of Bill Wilson (the founder of AA) and his desperate need for a power greater than himself to solve a problem that he could not solve alone. I heard and felt echoes of Joseph Smith's own deep need which had been answered for him when he read **James 1:5**. It was as if I were hearing the scripture for the first time, caught between a prophet's witness on the one hand and a derelict alcoholic's on the other.

If any of you lack wisdom, let him ask of God, that giveth to ALL men liberally, and upbraideth not; and it shall be given him. But let him ask in faith, nothing wavering. (James 1:5–6; emphasis added)

"Nothing wavering"—at about the same moment those memorized words passed through my mind, I found myself reading these words on page 13 of the AA text:

There I humbly offered myself to God, as I then understood Him, to do with me as he would. I placed myself *unreservedly* under His care and direction. (Italics added)

And then the next sentence wrung out my heart as it echoed the very words of LDS scriptures:

I admitted for the first time that of myself I was nothing; that without Him I was lost. (AA "Big Book," p. 13)

I had to turn back to the title of the little book in my hands to make sure I wasn't reading **Mosiah 4:11, Alma 26:12** or **Moses 1:10**. No. This was the AA "Big Book," and these were the words of Bill Wilson.

I stayed and read and listened. Gradually I began to realize why this program had such a high success rate in its early years. It is totally focused on turning us to God and developing our relationship with Him. (See **Moroni 7:13** again.)

And what have I found in my years of involvement in Twelve Step program since then? Well, first I found that the Twelve Steps and Twelve Traditions reflected twenty-four of the most basic "true principles" ever captured and arranged into a program of action to overcome destructive behaviors. At every meeting I attend, I watch people beginning to recognize their absolute need for and their own nothingness without God. I see them learn to relax their stranglehold on life and on others they've tried to control. I watch them come to trust God. This trust gives them the courage to tackle a fine-tooth comb repentance process for themselves. As I watch this inner cleansing and heart-deep change, accompanied by changes in attitude and behavior, Joseph Smith's words go through my mind: **"I teach them correct principles and they govern themselves."**

Second, I have found and joined a fellowship of good people, people who have come to know, as I have, that:

> **Crushed by a self-imposed crisis that we could not postpone** [any longer]**, we had to fearlessly face the proposition that either God is everything** [to us] **or else He is nothing. (AA "Big Book," p. 53)**

It's been good for me to realize that while we as Latter-day Saints do have a corner on priesthood authority and sealing ordinances, we don't have a corner on God's love or truth.

Third, I have lost 140 pounds and have maintained that weight loss for over ten years, through several of the most devastating events life could bring my way, including the death of my oldest daughter. I know that the ability to live in these terrifying last days began when I finally accepted counsel like this: **"You** [are] **100% hopeless, apart from divine help." (AA "Big Book," p. 43)**

Needless to say, years later, when I heard President Benson's words—**"If you will put God first in your life, everything else will either fall into its proper place or drop out of your life entirely"**

(*Ensign*, **May 1988, p.4**)—I could only smile and nod as I thought of those 140 pounds. And the greatest blessing of all is that I know that I didn't do this alone. I know it was by the grace of God that He lifted my broken and bleeding soul from the bedroom floor that day and led me to a program that would turn my face to Him and not teach me self-mastery or self-sufficiency or that I just had to do more. Instead, it taught me that what I have to *do is believe* more, *ask* more and *receive* more.

— *Colleen H.*
Fall 1991

PREFACE: REVISED EDITION

In 1981, I discovered I was an addict. Though I had never used alcohol or illegal drugs, I came to realize that I was indeed an addict in every sense of the word when I read *Alcoholics Anonymous* (also called the *"Big Book"*) and the *Twelve Steps and Twelve Traditions of Alcoholics Anonymous*.

As I read this literature from Alcoholics Anonymous, I found myself identifying with every nuance, every turn and twist of Bill W.'s story. I could relate to Dr. Bob's experience and to the experiences of most of the other faltering mortals who contributed their stories to the volume from which the AA fellowship took its name. The shocking revelation was that while I could so closely identify with the stories of these addicts, I was also a "tee-totaling, card-carrying" member of the Church of Jesus Christ of Latter-day Saints.

I attended church every Sunday, sat on the second row in the chapel with my "quiver–full" of children and equally "faithful" spouse. We each held several callings in our ward. We bought food storage, attended "Know Your Religion" lectures, went to BYU Education Week for our annual vacation, practiced as little birth control as we could,... My list could go on and on to the point of exhaustion. Suffice it to say, being good Latter-day Saints kept us so busy we had no time to admit or contemplate the reality that there was a dark and shameful side to our publically exemplary life.

> **Satan has a powerful tool to use against good people. It is distraction. He would have good people fill life with "good things" so there is no room for the essential ones. Have you unconsciously been caught in that trap? (Richard G. Scott, "First Things First," *Ensign*, May 2001, p. 6)**

Distracted from what? From those portions of practicing our religion that bring personal spiritual experiences. We were too busy, too distracted, to acknowledge or participate in personal revelation, personal insight, honesty, wisdom and honor of the truth.

And so, in July of 1981, I read *Alcoholics Anonymous* for the first time and realized I was as self-destructive with my "socially acceptable" behaviors as these first AA members were with alcohol. I saw, also, that although my life was filled to the brim with external religious behaviors, I had never experienced the coming of God into my heart and mind—at least, not to the extent necessary for Him to relieve me of the "desire" or disposition to "do evil."

For the first time, I saw my self-defeating behaviors as "evil." In fact, these behaviors were not just self-defeating. They were self-destructive. They were robbing me of serenity, and at times it seemed my very sanity was slipping away also. How did I try to save myself, my serenity, my sanity? Like a true addict, I turned deeper into the very behaviors which created the crisis to begin with. I would eat. I would rage and scream. I would spend money or participate in any number of other "socially acceptable" but self-destructive behaviors, knowing full-well I was destroying myself and my family around me. I lived a cycle of addiction just as surely as Bill W., Dr. Bob, and all of the other addicts described in *Alcoholics Anonymous*.

By 1983, I had achieved two years of abstinence and *some* recovery. True to my former idea of success, however, I had focused on the outward behaviors and subsequent appearance of being better. I attended lots of meetings. I gave lots of service in Overeaters Anonymous. I remained abstinent—often hanging on with white knuckles to the support and example of others. I lost over 150 lbs. I looked like a new woman, acted like a new woman and tried to feel like a new woman, ignoring the fact that on the "feeling" level, deep inside, things weren't much different. The whirlwind of being thin and admired was pretty heady stuff. Addiction revisited.

The following three years I learned about relapse by doing it. It wasn't fun and it wasn't pretty, but it did serve to convince me that I wanted *and needed* more. Looking "sober" wasn't enough. I wanted to feel sober, to be sober "on the inside."

I gained back 80 lbs. while trying some "controlled eating" programs (diet plans). They obviously weren't the answer. When I finally "cracked the books" again in 1985 and began to study the AA literature, I opened the scriptures along with them. Eventually, I read and worked through the powerful workbook, *The Twelve Steps: A Way Out* and became aware of its companion book, *The Twelve Steps: A Spiritual Journey* which incorporated verses from the Old and New Testament. (Both workbooks are published by RPI Publishing, Inc: San Diego, CA.) As I began to apply the Twelve Steps to my life, everything changed. But this time, the change wasn't about behaviors or appearances; it was about changing my inner life, my spiritual being.

Over the next four years, I listened to the testimony of the prophet at that time, President Ezra Taft Benson. Over and over again, he stressed the gift of the *Book of Mormon*, calling it the most perfect book ever written, containing the power to bring us closer to God than any other book. He pled with us to sup from its pages daily. He chastened us with the truth that as a people we were under the condemnation of "vanity and disbelief"—the only solution to which was reading the *Book of Mormon* and living by its precepts.

I believed our prophet. I heard and took his counsel personally, as a single member of the "us" and the "we" of the church. I began a personal study of the *Book of Mormon* and was staggered at how perfectly its "precepts"harmonized with the "precepts," or principles in each of the Twelve Steps. I began marking and color-coding my scriptures, particularly the *Book of Mormon*, for each of these twelve powerfully true principles.

By 1989, addiction in several terrible forms had eaten away the heart of my family's potential for safety and salvation. Sexual addiction, drug abuse, alcohol and the lies so many members of my family told to hide these choices took all the light and hope and strength out of our midst. Finally, the ultimate horror of every mother struck. One of my children died in an alcohol related accident.

Over the next two years, "after shocks" continued to ravage what was left of our family unit, as child after child began to exhibit behaviors typical of survivors of the worst forms of abuse. The facade of "just fine" Sunday appearances began to crumble. By 1991, with the witness of the Spirit of Truth in personal revelation and the painful, but honest approbation of my bishop, I fled the horrifying abusiveness of my marriage by filing for divorce. I felt numb. Marriage, home and family was everything to me. I felt abandoned and alone... except for the unwavering witness that Christ lived and loved me and would never leave me.

In the midst of all this personal trauma, I clung to the *Book of Mormon* and used the Twelve Step model to sort out its precepts. Conversely, I used the *Book of Mormon* to magnify the concepts in the Steps with the glorious power of the Restoration. A vision began to dawn in my heart: how wonderful it would be if other members of the Church could understand the Twelve Steps as a powerful guide to study of the principles of the Gospel! I began to pray for an opportunity to share this idea.

I became a member of the Church in the early 1960's and brought so much addictive and compulsive bondage with me, right through the waters of baptism. I could only imagine how much more of a struggle to break the bondage of all kinds of addictions, new converts, today, had to face. And then there were the "active" families, like my own—only one generation removed from unacknowledged addictive tendencies—whose lives were being undermined by addiction in one form or another. Maybe, if a study guide could be provided that combined the Twelve Step model of recovery with the power of the *Book of Mormon* and the restoration of the Gospel, other men and women, couples, and families could be spared the terrible end my first marriage suffered. I wanted to share my *knowledge* that the Savior's *living* reality and power was enough to sustain us and save us, even from these terrible developments of the last days.

I began to think of the Twelve Step workbooks mentioned earlier. What if a book similar to those could be composed, with suggested readings and thought provoking questions to guide the readers reflections. Using outlines of discussions I had led on each of the "twelve true principles" in the Steps as reflected in the teachings of the Restored Gospel, I was able to finish the original draft of *He Did Deliver Me from Bondage* in a matter of weeks. For the next year or so, I spent a lot of time at the local copy shop reproducing the manuscript in 10's, 20's, and then 50's. Then, in 1991, a wonderful benefactor offered to pay the cost of actual publication of the book. From that point its readership has continued to grow exponentially with virtually no "marketing." It has definitely been a pathway of "attraction," not "promotion."

I have received a constant flow of letters and phone calls filled with deeply moving endorsement of the book's positive effect in the lives of LDS members struggling with addiction in their own lives or in the lives of loved ones. I watched in awe as my prayers to the Father were answered. Others were being helped to understand addiction's subtle and spiritually deadly grip. They were being taught a practical application of true principles that were proving to be addiction's antidote. Still, I didn't know the extent Heavenly Father intended to answer my plea.

In the fall of 1995 I received a phone call from what was then known as LDS Social Services. They had been introduced to *He Did Deliver Me from Bondage* and felt it might be an asset to the newly formed substance abuse recovery group pilot program. Would I be willing to allow it to be used in that setting? I was in tears as I beheld in awe how far the Lord intended to take His answer to my prayers.

Since 1995, LDS Social Services has become LDS Family Services, and the pilot program has become the Substance Abuse Recovery Services (SARS) program and has been approved for use throughout the Church. I have to admit I feel like the inspired Twelve Step recovery model has now found a most appropriate home in the LDS community. It is my constant prayer that whoever receives a copy of this study guide will let it lead him or her to the truth that Heavenly Father and the Savior are very real and very interested in each of us personally. With Their living reality in our minds and hearts—in our *lives*—we can be led out of the bondage of addiction and blessed to survive the terrible sorrow of these last days. I bear testimony that if we truly desire to repent, there is no sin so great—whether it be committed by ourselves or has been committed against us—that the Savior Jesus Christ, through power from His Father, cannot heal. I testify of this humbly and in the Name of Jesus Christ, Amen.

— *Colleen H.*

January 2002

But behold, he did deliver them because they did humble themselves before him; and because they cried mightily unto him he did deliver them out of bondage; and thus doth the Lord work with his power in all cases among the children of men, extending the arm of mercy towards them that put their trust in him.

—Mosiah 29:20

I TEACH THEM CORRECT PRINCIPLES

An Introductory Discussion

INTRODUCTION

The Prophet Joseph Smith was once asked how he had been able to inspire and govern a people who appeared to be as productive and *happy* as the Latter-day Saints. His answer was short and to the point: "I teach them correct principles and they govern themselves." As with many prophetic utterances, this statement cuts deep, to the very *heart* of the matter of self-governance, an issue of central importance to addicted people.

Addicts are people with a problem—a problem they can't solve on their own, a problem they can't find enough willpower or "intestinal fortitude" to conquer on their own. Sometimes they feel unique in their weakness, that they are the worst of humanity. Sometimes the rest of humanity agrees. Little does the addict, or any of their critics, realize that when any of us face a problem of insurmountable proportions, we are actually facing the greatest truth we can ever know in mortality—the nature of our true relationship to God, that of ourselves we are "nothing," while in God all wisdom and power reside.

It is very humiliating to admit such complete personal powerlessness and neediness, but addicts must admit it or die. The stark and startling truth, however, is all of us, *without exception,* come short of the power to save ourselves. No matter how minimal we've been able to keep our list of sins and shortcomings, no matter how much willpower and self-discipline we've been able to muster, we still fall short of His glory. Thus, the message of the Twelve Steps, especially when coordinated with the power and precepts of the *Book of*

Mormon, is a message for *all* who are trying to survive these last days. It is more than appropriate for each of us to examine our lives, not just for alcohol or drug addiction, but for any challenge which leaves us devastated and demoralized, bankrupt of any will or desire to believe in ourselves, in life…and maybe even in God. The Twelve Steps were designed to bring us to a knowledge of God which is more honest, more personal, and more real than most of us have ever thought possible. And so I ask:

Do you have a problem? An insurmountable problem of any nature? Is there some aspect of your life in which you are out of control, unable to "govern" yourself or your life? Is it alcohol or some other drug, legal or illegal? Is it a compulsive sexual behavior pattern? Is it your weight or a disordered behavior towards food and eating? Is it compulsive use of money? Or excessive work commitments that consume you and your family's lives? Or is your downfall a desperate obsession with trying to help and control and fix other people and their mistakes or die trying? All these problems and literally *any other* can be overcome by the application of true principles especially if applied in a certain order as set forth in this study guide.

I can take no credit for discovering these principles. Nor did I discover this formula for their successful application. The principles are of God, and as we will see, they are totally revealed and supported in the scriptures and teachings of the prophets. The successful formula or order for their application came from, of all seemingly unlikely sources, the program of Alcoholics Anonymous. These are the principles behind A.A.'s powerful Twelve Steps. To those of you who may be puzzled, thinking Alcoholics Anonymous a very unlikely source of guidance for those who already have the fullness of the Restored Gospel, I recommend a prayerful pondering of the following description of the prophet Mormon's mind and the result of having such a mind:

...and being somewhat of a *sober mind,* therefore I was visited of the Lord, and tasted and knew of the goodness of Jesus. (Mormon 1:15; emphasis added)

If, as Mormon implies, being "sober" is conducive to and eventually the equivalent of *knowing* Christ, it would seem to me that all of us could stand to pursue a course that has proven able to get more people sober than any other, and that we should certainly *not* fear it. According to the first two prophets of this dispensation, we of all people should be open-minded and willing to embrace truth no matter where we find it.

[Latter-day Saints] must gather all the good and true principles in the world and treasure them up. (Joseph Smith, Teachings of the Prophet Joseph Smith, p. 316)

I want to say to my friends that we believe in all good. If you can find a truth in heaven, earth or hell, it belongs to our doctrine. We believe it; it is ours; we claim it. (Brigham Young, *Journal of Discourses,* 13:335)

QUALIFICATIONS

What is my motive in sharing this material with you? It is only to share the absolute witness I have found that there is power in the principles of the gospel of Jesus Christ:

...to bind up the brokenhearted, to proclaim liberty to the captives, and the opening of the prison to them that are bound. (Isaiah 61:1)

And how do I presume to be able to do this? What are my qualifications or credentials? They are stated perfectly in Mosiah:

My soul hath been redeemed from the gall of bitterness and the bonds of iniquity. I was in the darkest abyss; but now I behold the marvelous light of God. My soul was racked with eternal torment; but I am snatched, and my soul is pained no more. (Mosiah 27:29)

In the years since I was led into a Twelve Step program, I have continually subjected the Twelve Step model to a gospel interrogation, testing it by the words of the prophets, both ancient and modern. In nothing have I found it lacking. Continually, it proves itself, when correlated with the teachings of the prophets to be "good"—as in, God-given.

> **"And whatsoever thing persuadeth men to do good is of me; for good cometh of none save it be of me. I am the same that leadeth men to all good." (Ether 4:12)**

In fact, not only have I not found it wanting, I have found it to be one of the simplest, most straightforward tools for connecting my confused and rebellious heart to the heart, mind and will of the Lord. In the process of coming down into the "depths of humility" (not just skimming its surface), and "becoming a fool before God" (losing every single 'trapping' of the traditional Mormon woman—my marriage and "happy" home), my heart has been purified, freed from idolatry, reliance on fragile, earthly sources of well-being and validation. Gradually, in a very human, very imperfect, ebbing and flowing process, I have watched my heart transform. Though I have not crossed hundreds of miles of earthly wilderness in my personal trek, I have crossed light-years of mental, emotional and spiritual wilderness. And through the power of Christ, in the course of my scripture-based, Twelve Step directed recovery, found a change of heart I can only identify as Zion.

As I struggled through this journey of recovery, I kept extensive journals—and continue to do so. They are my confidante and sounding board as I record thoughts, feelings and even prayers. My journals are my liahona as I record thoughts and impressions from the Lord as conveyed to my heart and mind through the witness of the Holy Spirit.

As other people have asked me to share these things, I have done so with only one reservation. I have expressed this concern to the Lord in these terms, "Please don't let them rely for long on me or anyone else for inspiration and personal witness. Please let my testimony to them be a taste of the truth and reality of finding their own way through these Steps to a living, working, loving, honest relationship with Thee, dear Lord." You see, while it is true we can *begin* our journey of recovery leaning on others, borrowing light, eventually we each come to a place where we must walk by our own personal revelation. As President James E. Faust testified:

> **Some time ago in South America, a seasoned group of outstanding missionaries was asked, "What is the greatest need in the world?" One wisely responded, "Is not the greatest need in all of the world for every person to have a personal, ongoing, daily, continuing relationship with Deity?" Having such a relationship can unchain the divinity within us, and nothing can make a greater difference in our lives as we come to know and understand our divine relationship with God and His Beloved Son, our Master. (James E. Faust, "That We Might Know Thee," *Ensign*, Jan. 1999, 2)**

It is my testimony, because I have lived it through this recovery process in the Twelve Steps, that as we study and liken the scriptures and these true principles to our own lives, we can all come to know the voice of the Lord as it comes into our minds, even as Enos **(Enos 1:5, 10)**. And we can perceive Him testify to us, as Enos did, that our sins are forgiven. This is not the testimony of a therapist, doctor, priesthood leader, parent or friend, but of the Lord Himself, who cannot lie. This is the testimony which breaks the chains of the adversary's lying power over our souls.

Finally, I am very aware of the elements of "priestcraft,"

> **"That men preach and set themselves up for a light unto the world, that they may get gain and praise of the world; but they seek not the welfare of Zion." (2 Nephi 26:29)**

and I have covenanted with God to do three things to avoid it:

1.) Never allow myself or others to forget that there is only one name given whereby salvation cometh—Jesus Christ. He is Alpha and Omega, the beginning and the end of our mortal experience **(3 Nephi 9:18)**. I can teach, but I cannot transform. We must all rely **"wholly upon** [His] **merits." (2 Nephi 31:19)**

2.) To self-publish these attempts to carry the message of recovery and hope in Christ, so that they can be sold as close to cost as possible and the profit can be channeled back into the production of similar materials.

3.) To labor always for the building up of the kingdom of God and the establishment of Zion (the purifying of hearts) in all the earth.

> **"But the laborer in Zion shall labor for Zion; for if they labor for money they shall perish." (2 Nephi 26:31)**

Back to our basic question: *Do you have a problem? Do you deal with something that you've tried everything you can think of to solve, and yet it continues and even gets worse?*

If you have a problem that fits this description, then this course is for you. If you don't, then you're probably not ready—yet. That's the only requirement for being part of this course—that you have a problem that you can't whip, and you're ready to admit it.

THERE IS A SOLUTION

Don't be afraid to admit that you can't beat this problem on your own. That is the first step to overcoming it. There is a solution, I promise you. And this solution will not solve just the original problem that brought you here but *all* problems you apply it to.

I guess I sound a bit like one of those door-to-door people who sell a liquid cleaner that cleans *everything*. You know, now that I think about it, those peddlers have the advantage over me. Their solution is visible, and the very first thing they tell you to do with it is pour it directly on the problem spot and scrub on it. At least that makes sense.

As illogical as it may sound, what I'm going to do is ask you to stop focusing on the problem you're in a life and death struggle with, and turn your full attention instead in a direction that to the agnostic mind seems totally unrelated.

Wait, before we go on let's deal with my use of this phrase "the agnostic mind." Do you balk at the use of that phrase? Whether active LDS or not, whether self-destructing on work, food, sex or booze, do you still consider yourself a believer in God? Let me tell you, so did I. When I first read *Alcoholics Anonymous*, I totally skipped "Chapter Four: To the Agnostic." Not me, I thought. I'm not an agnostic.

But, then, in my second recovery effort, the one where I reopened the basic A.A. texts after three years of relapse, I read the Fourth Chapter and wept as I realized that while I had been so very active in the Church, like the "good son" in the parable of the prodigal son, I had not come to know the Father or His Son, Jesus Christ. I began to realize the term "agnostic"—which applies to someone who only *hopes* God exists, but doesn't feel they can say they *know*—was actually true of *me*. I had to stop denying the fact that I had serious doubts about God's capacity to love and help someone as "messed up" as I was. I had to admit I turned to all kinds of other things for comfort and solace and strength to get through my days—things like food, money and compulsive working (cleaning, canning, cooking, controlling others, trying to be the perfect mother). I had to admit that, just like my alcohol-addicted mother, I was trying to drown my doubts and fears and guilt in my own forms of addiction.

I strongly suspect many of you, if you looked honestly and deeply enough, would have to admit you've shied away from seeking a spiritual answer to your struggle with addiction. I suspect that like me, whether you're active in the church or not, you're going to be very challenged to think a spiritual solution could eliminate addiction from your life when the best of science, psychological, medical and social efforts have failed. The solution is going to be predominantly spiritual, invisible and totally paradoxical. But I can promise you, the results will be very observable with the human eye and very measurable. Days of sobriety from alcohol, drugs, and/or sex will begin to accumulate, with fewer and milder slips or temptations to slip. Weight will be lost, your checking account will balance consistently, confidence will increase, relationships with loved ones will adjust to healthier levels of honesty and respect.

And how can I promise you these results? Because it really is true: we were (and still are) spiritual entities, first and foremost. All things, including us, were and must always be created spiritually before they can be created physically.

> **For by the *power of my Spirit* created I them; yea, all things both spiritual *and* temporal. (D&C 29:31; emphasis added)**

In this verse we hear God explain to us plainly that *all* that He does is accomplished by *spiritual* power. Any efforts on our part to create or to change something will be unsuccessful if we focus on the physical plane only. We might experience temporary success, but always the outward reality will go back to match the inner reality. *Permanent* change must begin from within. Our primary emphasis must be on the *spiritual*.

> *First spiritual, secondly temporal,* **which is the beginning of my work. (D&C 29:32; emphasis added)**

> **The Lord works from the inside out. The world works from the outside in. The world would take people out of the slums. CHRIST [first] takes the slums out of people— and then they [have the vision and power to] take themselves out of the slums. (Ezra T. Benson, *Ensign*, July 1989, p. 4)**

What I lacked all those years that kept me from making President Benson's promise a reality was belief in, and focus on, the "inside-out" approach to problem solving. This program of twelve true principles has been called a "program of recovery." That is an appropriate description because if we will take the suggested action the program outlines, we will find ourselves recovering our spiritual selves as we are restored to the closeness we once had with God. With that recovered relationship will come the vision of who we are and the power to transform the physical circumstances of our lives to reflect the new inner serenity—*and it will happen automatically.*

As I said earlier, I know I sound like one of those door-to-door miracle workers again, telling you that you won't even have to scrub on those problem spots in your life. That's okay, because I know I'm in good company. Not with them necessarily, but with Him who also knocked on doors wanting to come in and share a seemingly impractical answer **(Revelations 3:20).**

You see, the truth is that He, too, offered a solution that didn't seem to relate, a way that seemed totally irrelevant to the problem at hand. As far back as when He was dealing with Moses and the Children of Israel in the wilderness, He challenged His people to see through logic to spiritual power. Remember the story of the brass serpent which God told Moses to make and raise up, promising that simply *looking upon* it would heal the people. How much sense did that make? I can just hear the people now: "This guy's got to be crazy. Surely we have to do something more than that! Let's see, first we'll use a knife to make little cuts over the puncture wounds. Then we'll..."

Heart-deep, soul-deep healing doesn't happen by the efforts or power of man, no matter how logical or wise. Putting the emphasis on the spiritual reality and turning to God must come *first.*

> **When we put God** [and the spiritual life] **first, all other things fall into their proper place or drop out of our lives. Our love of the Lord** [must] **govern the claims for our affection, the demands on our time, the interests we pursue, and the order of our priorities. (Ezra T. Benson,** *Ensign,* **May 1988, p. 4)**

Convinced? I hope so, because it's time to get on with getting on.

EXPERIMENT UPON MY WORDS

So what are these correct principles? That's a good question, and that's what this course of study is all about.

Notice the words "course of study." This isn't a book you just read or a series of lectures you just listen to. This is a course, a journey, a program. It will take willingness to act upon it, willingness to get involved. Remember Alma's words:

But behold, if ye will awake and arouse your faculties, even to an experiment upon my words... (Alma 32:27)

That's all I'm asking of you. You must be willing to "experiment" upon these words, to *act* upon these correct principles. This is a *spiritual* program of *action*. What you are going to learn herein is the process of weaving spiritual power into physical actions.

Now, as you begin, you will need to realize that to whatever extent you have been trying to fix your life from the outside in and neglecting the inner person, you will find that inner self an undernourished and out-of-shape spiritual being. You will be tempted to think this malnourished, unexercised spiritual self is all there really is of you spiritually, that somehow you must have stowed away in the transport area when all the really valiant spirits were coming in the last days. I want to encourage you to withhold judgement until the end of this course of study. You see, the truth is, our spiritual self adapts to and is shaped by our beliefs and choices, and these beliefs and choices are either nourishing or starving our spiritual selves.

That's the good news of the Gospel and the good news of this course of study. We don't have to be discouraged by the neglected, undernourished/underexercised condition we find our spiritual selves in. We need only begin to spend the kind of time and attention in nourishing and exercising ourselves *spiritually/emotionally* as we *thought* we had to physically, and with miraculous quickness that spiritual self will begin to recover.

SUMMARY

Though the promised results of this program will ultimately affect your physical/mortal circumstances and self, the program itself is a spiritual one. It will lead us through the study and application of twelve true principles. The study part we can help each other with. The application part, though, is totally individual. Each of you must take the action that is asked of you on your own. This is when it becomes a *totally* individualized program, reflecting completely your own sincerity and diligence. I'm familiar with a saying: *When the pain of the problem gets worse than the pain of the solution, we'll be ready to change.* (If you are puzzled over the meaning of that statement and need an example of what it means, just think how desperately ready to face labor and delivery the ninth month of pregnancy makes most women.)

In other words, if you find yourself not really willing to put forth the effort to work this program of spiritual focus, don't worry. Life will eventually bring you to a place of readiness to accept the truth that God and His ways (which are manifest *first* in spiritual powers) are the only solution that works. You see, that's what this life is all about—not to teach us self-reliance and self-sufficiency—but to bring us to a place of complete humility, to consider ourselves fools before (and without) God **(2 Nephi 9:42)**. But then that brings us to the first principle of our journey of recovery. We'll study and discuss that next week.

ASSIGNMENT FOR THIS WEEK:

Many people have asked me, "It's great to read President Benson's counsel to put God first in your life, but how do you do that?" The answer is so easy and simple that many won't believe it: I put God first in my life by putting Him first in my days—one day at a time.

Before our hearts and lives can change, we must be willing to change our level of effort—we must become willing to go to any length. If we're not willing, there is nothing God can do for us, for as the hymn says, "God can force no man to heaven" or even change a man (or woman) for the better.

In return for my efforts to get up early and put Him first, I have had this promise from Him literally fulfilled:

> **He that seeketh me early shall find me, and shall not be forsaken. (D&C 88:83)**

1. So get yourself a notebook or use your permanent journal (these things will be precious to you, I promise) and do three things:

    PRAY

    READ

    WRITE

2. Read "What Is Capturing?" (page A–3) in the appendix at the end of this workbook.

3. Come prepared to share next week from your writing—that is, if you feel like it. See you next week.

PREPARATION FOR DISCUSSION OF PRINCIPLE ONE: "O HOW GREAT IS THE NOTHINGNESS OF THE CHILDREN OF MEN" (HELAMAN 12:7)

Step 1: Admitted that we of ourselves are powerless, nothing without God. (Mosiah 4:5; Alma 26:12)

The following scriptures are provided to enable you to practice using the tools of scripture study, prayer and capturing, and to introduce you to the principle we will study in the next chapter. There are seven references listed—one for each day of the week. Take one reference each day and spend at least ten minutes prayerfully pondering and writing your thoughts about these references. *Although it may be tempting, please do not pass over these exercises.* Remember, this book is not meant to be a "quick-fix" or an end in itself. It is a means to the end we all hope to reach some day—a living testimony of our Heavenly Father and our Lord, Jesus Christ.

This end is well described by President Gordon B. Hinckley, encouraging us to:

> **constantly nourish the testimony of our people concerning the Savior...** [and to instill] **a true witness in** [each] **heart of the living reality of the Lord Jesus Christ,** [in order that in each of our lives] **all else will come together as it should...** (*Ensign,* **August, 1997, p.3, emphasis added.**)

Day 1: **2 Nephi 9:39**—We often think of the word *carnal* as applying only to those people who appear to be very wicked. Look up the word *carnal* in the dictionary. Think of its definition as it applies to our efforts to solve our problems. Write about an area in your own life in which you are guilty of being "carnally minded" in regard to seeking solutions.

Day 2: **2 Nephi 12:11**—Because we usually try to overcome our weaknesses alone, we fail time after time. How can this help in the process of humbling us? Write about a problem you have sought to solve yourself and how peaceful or permanent your efforts have been. What do you suppose it means that **"the Lord *alone* shall be exalted in that day"**—the day when our "lofty looks" shall be humbled and *all* truth shall be known?

Day 3: **2 Nephi 31:19**—**"for ye have not come thus far save it were by the _____ with _____ relying _____ upon the _____ of _____ who is mighty to _____."** Copy the above scripture into your journal, filling in the blanks. Have you ever been told or have you thought that a lack of self-esteem was the reason you were having problems? What does this scripture say to you in regard to this modern "god" of self? Who has power enough to save you? Who should you esteem? How much? Is it yourself?

Day 4: **Mosiah 2:21**—In this scripture we are taught that we can never, even if we try with *all* our energy, return more to the Lord than we are receiving. How does this scripture translate into your everyday life? Does it bring you despair or relief? Write to Him about your feelings.

Day 5: **Alma 26:12**—We are bombarded with philosophies, programs, planners, commercials, products, and medications that promise personal power. Think back over your life and admit in writing some of these things that have lured you. Did they solve your problem? Did they improve your relationship with the Lord? The principles in this course can introduce you to the true Source of power so that you can say as Ammon did, **"I will not boast of myself, but I will boast of my God, for in HIS strength I can do all things."**

Day 6: **Helaman 12:7**—**"O how great is the nothingness of the children of men."** This is a pretty plain statement. Notice the phrase "the children of men." That expression is used repeatedly through the scriptures, applied to those who have not yet been born of God and become His sons and daughters (see **Mosiah 27:25**). Write about this verse. (Look back to the previous verse [6] for some clues as to why we are nothing when we are the "children of men.")

Day 7: **Moses 1:10**—After being in the presence of God for many hours, Moses witnesses to us the tremendous contrast in power, glory and strength between God and man, using the same word that is used in Helaman, that man is "nothing." Why do you suppose we resist relying on God's power and choose to lean, instead, on self and the answers the world provides?

O HOW GREAT IS THE NOTHINGNESS
OF THE CHILDREN OF MEN
(Helaman 12:7)

Step One: Admitted that we of ourselves are powerless,
nothing without God. (Mosiah 4:5; Alma 26:12)

Principle One: I of myself am powerless—
nothing without God.

In October 1986, President Ezra T. Benson addressed the assembled body of the Church, making a solemn pronouncement concerning the importance of the *Book of Mormon. Reading* this great book was not enough; we were also admonished to *live* by its precepts. Citing **D&C 84:54-58**, he applied those words directly to us in our day, calling upon us to examine our own attitude towards this book which would bring us closer to God than any other book. (See Introduction to the *Book of Mormon* for the full statement from the Prophet Joseph Smith.) President Benson all but openly charged us with treating this sacred record lightly. He reminded us that such **"vanity and unbelief have brought the whole church under condemnation" (D&C 84:55).**

I was deeply affected by President Benson's words that day. It felt like a prophetic warning, if not an outright reprimand. The word "condemnation" held the same chilling connotation to me as the word "bondage." I was riveted by the similarity. I sensed there was a connection between this "vanity and unbelief" and the state of heart and mind which lures people into addiction.

But what form of "vanity and unbelief" was President Benson referring to? I had to admit I knew a lot of church members, myself included, who would be delighted to have a bigger house, newer car, more clothes. Was that what this indictment of vanity meant? Somehow, the inclusion of the word "unbelief" with vanity seemed to imply something deeper than mere material wealth or appearances. How would the Prophet of the Lord—and the Lord through His Prophet—apply the concept of unbelief to the church as a whole, active members included? After all, there we all were, within reach of his spoken or written declaration, dutifully paying attention. I puzzled and pondered these things as I continued to search the *Book of Mormon* for validation of the principles of Twelve Step recovery.

THE DANGER IN EMPHASIZING SELF-RELIANCE OVER RELIANCE ON GOD

As I studied, the witness grew brighter and brighter to my mind and heart that this book—this amazing, wonderful *Book of Mormon*—was a clear and resolute testimony that there is no power in any of us—even the most righteous of us—that is not a gift of empowerment given through the grace and goodness of God, even the Lamb of God, Jesus Christ. We are mistaken to think anything more of ourselves—to think our success or salvation in any area of life was coming because of our own "industry"(**Alma 4:6**), management, or genius (**Alma 30:17**).

Of course! This was it! This was the "vanity" and the "unbelief" that brings us into "condemnation" or bondage. It was the vanity of placing emphasis on *self*-reliance, *self*-sufficiency, *self*-anything *above* and *before* emphasis on the reality of seeking salvation in and through the Savior. One of the most damning fallacies Satan had so subtly twisted in my mind during all the years I had listened to church leaders stress self-reliance in temporal concerns, was that I also had to be self-reliant in my own salvation.

As I continued to study the *Book of Mormon*, I found no support for any of the ideas of self-reliance, self-mastery, or self-sufficiency. Instead, I found testimony everywhere that all my efforts at goal-setting, life planning or life-management were manifestations of vanity and unbelief, if they were not first based on prayerful counsel with the Lord **(Alma 37:37)** and then empowered by His grace (power to carry them out).

Insisting that all it takes to be successful in life is careful management sounds too similar to Korihor, one of the most adamant anti-Christ's in history.

And many more such things did he say unto them [deemphasizing God's power in their life], **telling them...every man fared in this life according to the management of the creature.** (Alma 30:17)

And not only did Korihor insist that management was a sure source of salvation and success, he echoed our modern tendency to almost revere intellectual giftedness, advanced degrees and certain professions as a sign of the Lord's extraordinary favor.

Therefore every man prospered according to his genius. (Alma 30:17)

I was astounded as I honestly admitted how much like this *anti-Christ* my thinking had become. I had focused my attention and energy on management and genius as the "ways and means" to save myself. I shuddered to think how easily I was kept trying one "half-measure" after another—all to no avail. I had to confess I had kept myself distracted and busy looking "beyond the mark." I began to inventory and assess myself. Had I been drawing near to Him with my lips, and even my actions, but doing so half-heartedly? Keeping my heart from Him? Was I professing Christ and then living as if He didn't really matter in my life, all in the name of self-sufficiency, self-reliance and self-mastery?

Awakened by my Twelve Step study of the *Book of Mormon*, I finally realized, as I had once heard it said: *True self-mastery comes from turning our "self" over to the Master.* In the same spirit, I began to see that true reliance is reliance on the Master **(D&C 3:20)** and true sufficiency is found in turning to Him only who is sufficient **(Moroni 10:32)**. I felt like I was seeing all these principles with new eyes— awakened eyes, and awakened ears and heart.

Church leaders were not promoting self-reliance *before* "God-reliance." They were talking about the kind of sufficiency that comes from relying on the Lord *above* and *beyond* anyone or anything else.

> **If we increase our dependence on anything or anyone except the Lord, we will find an immediate decrease in our freedom to act. (L. Tom Perry, *Ensign*, Nov. 1991, p. 65)**

> **We should put God ahead of *everyone else* in our lives. (Ezra T. Benson, Ensign, May 1988, p. 4; original emphasis)**

> **Yet no matter what the source of difficulty and no matter how you begin to obtain relief—through a qualified professional therapist, doctor, priesthood leader, friend, concerned parent, or loved one—no matter how you begin, those solutions will never provide a complete answer. The final healing comes through faith in Jesus Christ and His teachings, with a broken heart and a contrite spirit and obedience to His commandments. (Richard G. Scott, Ensign, May, 1994, p.7)**

Instead, we as a people have turned to "self" *first*, putting the greatest emphasis on our own "industry," bringing ourselves dangerously in line with the "people of the church" in Alma's day:

> **And it came to pass... that the people of the church began to wax proud** [of their appearance, possessions, and position],**...which they had obtained** [according to their definition] **by their industry. (Alma 4:6)**

THERE IS ONLY ONE WHO HAS ALL POWER

In my search of the *Book of Mormon*, I found a totally different perspective. I found testimony of the Savior's preeminence as the only source of salvation. I also found some pretty strong statements concerning the state of my "self" when not surrendered to the mind and will of the Lord.

Wherefore, all mankind were in a lost and in a fallen state, and ever would be save they should rely on this Redeemer. (1 Nephi 10:6)

Here was all the "plainness" and truth that Nephi gloried in: *All* mankind must rely on the Savior, even those who chart and goal-set their way through life. None are exempt, and nothing we do will recover us from the mortal weaknesses and character defects we have developed in our "lost and fallen state"—unless it includes coming to Christ in a *very* personal and singular way.

Behold, he offereth himself a sacrifice for sin, to answer the ends of the law, unto all those *who have a broken heart and a contrite spirit;* and unto none else can the ends of the law be answered. (2 Nephi 2:7)

We are here on earth for the very purpose of either breaking or softening our hearts in order that they might be turned to God and godliness. We can either resist the laws of God, in which case our hearts will inevitably be broken, or we can try with all our hearts to live the law and gradually realize that no matter how hard we try, we can't do it perfectly. Only after truly internalizing the fact of my own nothingness and powerlessness without God, can I hope to be endowed with the power of God. Meanwhile, whether we come to a broken heart by sinning, being sinned against or struggling futilely to perfect ourselves, we must all come to a place where we are humble enough to acknowledge that without Him we are nothing and can never answer the "ends of the law" ourselves. Jacob also testified of the need for total humility before God—even if it means looking like a fool:

And save they shall cast these things away, and consider themselves fools before God, and come down in the

depths of humility, he will not open unto them. (2 Nephi 9:42)

What things must we cast away? Any pride we connect to what we think are our own accomplishments due to our own wisdom, learning, and smart management.

We must come to realize that no matter how rich or educated or talented we become in ways that impress other people, we are still *totally* upheld by the power of God, and God alone.

Brigham Young made it clear just where all accomplishments begin:

> Men know how to construct railroads and all manner of machinery; they understand cunning workmanship, etc; *but all that is revealed to them by the Spirit of the Lord though they know it not.* (Brigham Young, *Journal of Discourses*, 5:124 p. 125; emphasis added)

Quoting Isaiah, Jacob also teaches us the following:

> And it shall come to pass that the lofty looks of man shall be humbled, and the haughtiness of men shall be bowed down, and the Lord alone shall be exalted in that day. (2 Nephi 12:11)

In what day shall the Lord alone be exalted? Generally, in the day of His glorious second coming. But this scripture applies in a far more personal way.

All of us must someday receive His coming into our own lives. We can either wait for that day when all will come to know His reality as He appears in the skies surrounded by legions of angels, *or* we can believe and study, search and hunger for a *personal* spiritual experience that would endow us with a sure knowledge of His living reality long before He comes to the world as a whole. The Prophet Joseph Smith stated it this way:

> For the day must come when no man need say to his neighbor know ye the Lord for all shall know him [who

remain] from the least to the greatest. (Andrew Ehat and Lyndon Cook, eds. *The Words of Joseph Smith*, p. 4)

Not only can the reality of Christ be personally revealed to us, but *all* that the greatest prophet in the world knew is waiting to be unveiled to us as soon as we are ready. Joseph Smith himself promised this:

> God hath not revealed any thing to Joseph, but what he will make known unto the Twelve and even the least Saint may know all things *as fast as he is able to bear them*. (Ehat and Cook, ed. *The Words of Joseph Smith*, p. 4; emphasis added)

More recently Elder Bruce R. McConkie encouraged all members of the Church to seek this personal degree of revelation:

> I say that every member of the Church, independent and irrespective of any position that he may hold, is entitled to get revelation from the Holy Ghost; he is entitled to entertain angels; he is entitled to view the visions of eternity; and if we would like to go the full measure, he is entitled to see God the same way that any prophet in literal and actual reality has seen the face of Deity. (Bruce R. McConkie, "How to Get Personal Revelation," *New Era*, June 1980, 46)

However, before He can extend this degree of knowledge to us, He must be sure we are thoroughly convinced of our own powerlessness without Him. Thus we all must follow a path into the depths of humility.

GOD IS NO RESPECTER OF PERSONS—ONLY OF HUMILITY AND DESIRE

> And my soul hungered; and I kneeled down before my Maker, and I cried unto him in mighty prayer and supplication for mine own soul. (Enos 1:4)

Enos is an example for those of us who have been active members of the Church all our lives and are still feeling empty and not really connected with God. Thus was Enos also. One day, as he was hunting, he began to recall the words his father had spoken concerning the joy of the Saints and eternal life. (If we've been raised by active parents who didn't, despite all their church work, ever convey to us that being a member of the Church was joyful, and that eternal life was an attainable hope, we might have difficulty relating to Enos and to his being motivated by his father's words.)

The point is still the same: Whether we come to this place of *hunger*, of intense need, of being at the end of our ability to go on as a result of rebelling against the law or being fervently obedient to the law, we *all* come to it eventually, without exception.

> **I say unto you that if ye should serve him who has created you from the beginning, and is preserving you from day to day, by lending you breath, that ye may live and move and do according to your own will, and even supporting you one moment to another—I say, if ye should serve him with all your whole souls yet ye would be unprofitable servants. (Mosiah 2:21)**

There it is, in black and white—the *truth* that we cannot *work* our way to worthiness; the *fact* that the busiest Relief Society president must be just as reliant on the mercy and grace of Christ as the most inactive and skeptical "lost sheep."

Facing this thought, some of you might ask, "Then why have I been doing all of this? If that's true then why should I do any of this striving to be active in the Church?"

The answer to this question is actually pretty simple: *love*. This is another one of those places where we are looking past the mark **(Jacob 4:14)**. Love is the only *valid* reason for all our work and devotion to the Church. However, love of others isn't always suffi-cient to motivate us to good works. Often, it is only our love for the Savior which moves us to act when we are feeling less than charitable towards others **(Alma 37:36)**. Sometimes we act out of duty, but duty is a poor substitute for genuine compassion and love. Duty can often deteriorate into a feeling of grudging participation. Such service may still bless those we serve, but according to the prophets, it will do the one giving it no good **(Moroni 7:8)**.

As these concepts began to settle into my heart and mind, I began to realize how often I had given grudging gifts because of my focus on others and their weaknesses. Even after I began to understand the need to be motivated by love, I couldn't make my heart change. Even as King Benjamin had solemnly pronounced, I could not keep up with all the ways that I, as a mortal in a fallen state of existence, could be enticed into sin.

> **And finally, I cannot tell you all the things whereby ye may commit sin; for there are divers ways and means, even so many that I cannot number them. (Mosiah 4:29)**

The truth is that even **"after all that [I] could do"** (2 Nephi 25:23), I would always fall short of being worthy to enter into His glory. I must have His grace, or in other words, His enabling power, or I was lost. (See "Grace" in the Bible Dictionary.) As the scriptures testify, we can answer the *beginnings* of the law, but we cannot answer the *"ends* of the law." We have the power to choose to begin the journey Homeward by desiring it more than anything in this world and by being willing to set our feet on the path, but only He has the power to enable us to finish that process or journey. *Without Him we are powerless to maintain any good work.*

> **And now I ask, can ye say aught of yourselves? I answer you, Nay, Ye cannot say that ye are even as much as the dust of the earth; yet ye were created of the dust of the earth; but behold, it belongeth to him who created you. (Mosiah 2:25)**

And now I ask, Can you or I say anything different of ourselves? No, we cannot.

TOTAL BANKRUPTCY

For the natural man is an enemy to God [lives in ways that separate himself from God and His true principles], **and has been from the fall of Adam, and will be, forever and ever.** (Mosiah 3:19)

Here's another one of those scriptures that we avoid likening to ourselves *personally* by applying it *generally* to all of humanity. It's too bad when we use this kind of generalization. This scripture, like all others, does not have power to change our personal lives until we read it for ourselves, applying it to ourselves individually. (For I, _____ [insert your name here], when I am turning away from God, living on my own resources, thinking I have some power outside of what He gives me, am choosing to behave like a "natural man" type of person. I have had the potential and freedom to choose that way from the time of my own personal fall when I left heaven and came to earth. Now, as a mortal, I am powerless to restore my former oneness with Him and with my eternal family in heaven. And besides that, I can't even quit using my addiction without His grace and power.)

Therefore they have drunk *damnation* to their own souls. (Mosiah 3:25; emphasis added)

Therefore, I had drunk (or in my case, eaten) damnation to my own soul—behaving in a way that blocked my spiritual growth. This damnation, or bondage, is the inevitable result of a life run on self-will and self-reliance.

And they had viewed themselves in their own carnal state, even less than the dust of the earth. (Mosiah 4:2)

The day had to finally come for me when I was willing to admit I was in that completely powerless situation of nothingness.

Even so I would that ye should remember, and always retain in remembrance, the greatness of God, and your own nothingness... and humble yourselves even in the depths of humility. (Mosiah 4:11)

For behold, are we not all beggars? (Mosiah 4:19)

It's tempting to consider it some kind of cruel fate that God would require us to come unto Him—and when we do, to have our own nothingness "rubbed in our face." With that to look forward to, why even go? Who wants such a helping of humble pie? Practically no one. Little do we realize that while we resist this admittance of total bankruptcy, the Lord Jesus Christ has enough mercy and grace to make up for all our shortcomings. He only awaits our thorough and fearless admittance of need. Hear His tender affirmation of this:

And if men come unto me I will show unto them their weakness... For if they will humble themselves before me, and have faith in me, then will I make weak things become strong unto them. (Ether 12:27)

Speaking of those who would inherit the promised land, the Lord said:

And except they repent and turn to the Lord their God, behold, I will deliver them into the hands of their enemies; yea, and they shall be brought into bondage; and they shall be afflicted by the hand of their enemies. (Mosiah 11:21)

Until the fateful day of September 11, 2001, we who have been born and grown to adulthood in the United States of America had no idea there were vicious and merciless enemies in our midst. The closest most of us have come is the little girl in sixth grade who enjoyed hating us as much as we did her; or maybe the neighbor who didn't keep a confidence we once shared. Under these circumstances we have been lulled into a slumber of complacency.

Most of us are just as ignorant or complacent towards the "enemies" of our spiritual life—our fears, resentments, guilt and sorrows—as we were of our physical enemies. We choose to hide in various compulsive or addictive behaviors rather than confront them. These retreats from the battle line of reality eat away at our sanity and our security and make us our own—and our loved ones—worst enemy. Just as in the time of Captain Moroni, the enemies within our hearts are our greatest threat.

While we here in the United States were spared for over two hundred years from the attacks of outside enemies, we were free to become a people who could pay attention to the deadly enemies of the human spirit—our fears, resentments, guilt, and bitterness of heart. Instead, far too many of us spent most of our discretionary time and money on the "things of this world." It is my prayer that it is not too late for us to repent (turn again) to the Lord God of this land, even Jesus Christ **(Ether 2:12)**.

CONCLUSION:100% POWERLESS WITHOUT GOD

And there was no way that they could deliver themselves out of their hands. (Mosiah 21:5)

For I am unworthy to glory of myself. (Mosiah 23:11)

And were it not for the interposition of their all-wise Creator,...they must *unavoidably* remain in bondage until now. (Mosiah 29:19; emphasis added)

Here are three more scriptures to "liken unto ourselves" if we want them to really speak to us. Blending them together, we might hear them say: There is no way, child, that you can deliver yourself from your enemies—your fear, your anger, and your guilt—that you are attempting to avoid by using your addiction. *Avoidance is not deliverance.* Of yourself you are unworthy and have no glory or power. Until you realize that it is the power of Christ and His atonement and grace that is "sufficient for you" **(Moroni 10:32)**, you will remain in bondage, having no power of yourself to free yourself.

We must all come to a place where we realize the following as Ammon did:

Yea, I know that I am nothing; as to my own strength I am weak; therefore I will not boast of myself. (Alma 26:12)

> I behold that ye are *lowly in heart;* and if so, blessed are
> ye. (Alma 32:8; emphasis added)

> And now, because ye are compelled to be humble
> blessed are ye; for a man sometimes, if he is compelled to
> be humble, seeketh repentance; and now surely, whoso-
> ever repenteth shall find mercy. (Alma 32:13)

In this last verse God reveals to us plainly His motive in allowing
us to be afflicted by our own sins or the sins of another: He is trying
to bring us to a place where we are so "bottomed out" in the depths
of humility that we will finally give up hope on any other sources
except Him, and turn from reliance on "the arm of flesh," whether
it's our own or someone else's. He can't give us all that He has unless
we repent (which means simply to *turn again* to Him). He can't cross
our agency and just make us be humble, so the only resort He has is
to allow us to be buffeted and to suffer until we are ready to turn to
Him.

> For he beheld that their afflictions had truly humbled
> them, and that they were in a preparation to hear the
> word. (Alma 32:6)

We face two kinds of afflictions in this world: those that come
upon us seemingly without our choice or foreknowledge, and those
we bring upon ourselves by our own choices. One way or the other,
all afflictions are for only one purpose: to bring us to Christ, for He
is "the word," and the *only* name whereby salvation cometh.

> Thus we may see that the Lord is merciful unto all who
> will, *in the sincerity of their hearts,* call upon his holy
> name. (Helaman 3:27; emphasis added)

The key phrase here is "sincerity of their hearts." If we are rigorously honest with ourselves, we have to admit that we have really
prayed "in the sincerity of our hearts" (with real heartfelt emotion)
only when something so big and so traumatic was happening—a
loved one was dying, for instance—that we knew we had *no other
resort* except God. On those occasions we prayed as if every word,

every emotion, was being ripped straight out of our deepest, most central inner place—our hearts.

Only when we can get up every day of our lives and admit our own powerlessness in the same manner we do in the face of death will we have come to realize the truth as these scriptures have been trying to convey it to us.

ASSIGNMENT FOR THIS WEEK:

1. Think and pray about being willing to attend a Twelve Step meeting if it's possible to do so, and take part in the sharing time. It is the tradition in Twelve Step meetings that each person who so desires may have a turn to share his or her thoughts, feelings, and insights without interruption or comment from others. A great deal of learning goes on, in the same spirit described in the following quote from the Prophet Joseph Smith, found in Truman Madsen's book *Joseph Smith the Prophet* (p. 84):

    First, they were not simply to listen to one speaker. A teacher was to be appointed, said the revelation, and **"let not all be spokesmen at once; but let one speak at a time, and let all listen to his sayings, that when all have spoken that all may be edified of all, and that every man may have an equal privilege."**

    A beautiful teaching principle: the need for each person present to participate, contributing his or her insight and experience on a given theme.

2. Call another member of the Twelve Step program you have chosen to attend (or a good friend) and share something you've thought or felt as you've done your reading, scripture study, and capturing. These "reach out" calls are some of the most powerful services we can give in a Twelve Step program.

3. Be willing to teach your spouse, child, parent, or close friend some of these ideas if the comfortable opportunity presents

itself. As you teach by the Spirit, you will find that *you* learn more every time you rehearse the material.

PREPARATION FOR DISCUSSION OF PRINCIPLE TWO: "I GLORY IN MY JESUS" (2 NEPHI 33:6)

Step 2: Came to believe that God has all power and all wisdom and that in His strength we can do all things. (Mosiah 4:9; Alma 26:12)

Day 1: **2 Nephi 2:2**—One element of the greatness of God is His ability and desire to consecrate our afflictions for our gain. Look up the meaning of the word *consecrate* in the dictionary. Write the definition in your journal. Write about the afflictions that have come into your life. Keep in mind that afflictions can be trials, heartaches, or illnesses, anything that causes you pain and distress, including your own mistakes. How have you seen the consecrating power of God applied to these afflictions?

Day 2: **2 Nephi 4:19**—Nephi, a prophet of God, humbly admits to God that he is harassed by temptation and sin. Why do you think God wanted him to record this and then allowed it to be preserved and handed down to us? Who is it that has strengthened Nephi? Who has he learned to trust? What do you think it is that he trusts the Lord can do for him? Can you trust that the Lord has enough mercy and power to redeem even you? Why?

Day 3: **2 Nephi 33:6**—I glory in _____, I glory in _____, I glory in *my* _____, for he hath redeemed my soul from _____. Copy this scripture into your journal, filling in the blanks. Hell is a state of being "dead" or "damned." Addictions put us in hell on earth. Our spirits feel dead or stopped from growth. Write about a behavior that you keep repeating that keeps you from growing and being a progressively better you. Who is it that Nephi assures us has power to get us out of our personal hell?

Day 4: **Mosiah 4:6**—I often say that I believe in the goodness of God, but when it comes right down to believing that this goodness is extended to *me* by *my* Savior I lose my faith. I would ask you in the words of King Benjamin **"if you have come to a knowledge of the _____ of God, and his matchless _____, and his _____ and his _____ and his _____ towards [you]"?** Has this happened to you? Describe how this belief (or lack of it) impacts your life and influences your compulsive/addictive behaviors.

Day 5: **Mosiah 4:8**—Salvation means to save or preserve something precious. Christ's atonement is His testimony to us of how precious we are to Him and to the Father. Keep track today of some of the little ways, the positive coincidences, the tiny blessings that demonstrate your preciousness. At the end of the day, record a few in your journal. If you do not honestly feel precious before Him, speak to Him, in writing, of your honest feelings.

Day 6: **Mosiah 11:23**—When we are under the influence of any addiction, one way to describe our situation is to say that we are in _____. Is our addiction really the primary sin we need to repent of, or is it just a symptom? According to Abinadi, what is the true root of sin?

Day 7: **Alma 24:10**—Capture this scripture for yourself. What does it teach you personally? Freedom from the bondage of addiction is a gift from God. Here Alma thanks God for three great gifts. What are they? Write about them in your own words.

I GLORY IN MY JESUS
(2 Nephi 33:6)

Step Two: Came to believe that God has all
power and wisdom and that in His strength
we can do all things. (Mosiah 4:9; Alma 26:12)

Principle Two: All power of redemption and atonement
is vested in the Lord Jesus Christ and can only be
effective in my life as I am willing to have a
personal relationship with Him.

"Came to believe that a Power greater than myself..." These words in the original Step Two of Alcoholics Anonymous really tripped me up when I first heard the Twelve Steps. Of course I believed in a "Power greater than myself"—with a capital "P"! While it was true there had been seasons when I had deliberately turned away from God and just used my addictive behavior with complete despair, there were many times when I sobered up enough to sincerely long for deliverance from my slavery. Surely I had tried the equivalent of this step. Surely Step Two was one I could shortcut. But then I had to honestly ask myself, "If I really believe in God, why haven't I been able to find salvation and the power to stop my self-defeating, self-destructive behaviors (addictions) in that belief? "

Once again, it was a desperately humble personal study of the precepts of the *Book of Mormon* (compelled by my life-or-death need for sobriety), followed immediately with a willingness to liken them to myself, that gave me the answer to my question. It began when I finally heard with my heart just one little word—Nephi's use of the word "my"—in describing the Holy Messiah, the Savior of the world.

A SPIRITUAL AWAKENING

> **I glory in plainness;** *I glory in truth; I glory in my Jesus,* *for he hath redeemed my soul from hell.* **(2 Nephi 33:6; emphasis added)**

I felt as if I had never read these words before, though I'm sure I had. There had been seminary, Institute, Sunday School, family scripture study, Relief Society contests—all excuses to read the *Book of Mormon* cover to cover. But, then, none of those occasions had been a matter of life or death to my soul. This time I prayed constantly as I read, holding my heart and mind open, thirsting for relief from my addiction.

This time, as I read these words my breath caught in my throat. I felt as if someone had thrown cold water in my face or slapped me to bring me to my senses. I looked down at the words in front of me, reading them over again and *again*. Could they possibly have said what I felt them saying?

Shades of tent revivals and crowds shouting as "with one voice" **(Mosiah 5:2)** went through my conservative Mormon mind. I read the words again. After all, maybe I had just read too much into them. *"I glory in plainness; I glory in truth; I glory in MY Jesus, for he hath redeemed my soul from hell."* No. Even reading it in as subdued a voice as I could, there was no way to avoid the possessive, *intimate knowing* of the Savior, the Lord Jesus Christ, conveyed in the use of that single word "my."

"I glory in my Jesus…" My Jesus… My…Mine! I could not get past the personal intimacy of Nephi's statement. Tears welled up, spilling down my face. I burned through and through as with a fire, a

passionate and yet childlike love for God. I felt as if someone had just given me permission to approach the Lord, to actually embrace Him, at least in spirit. I felt such a burning, such a passionate and yet childlike adoration for the Lord. It felt as if I had suddenly awakened to Nephi's example of approaching the Lord and coming to know Him as my dearest friend, as *my* Jesus.

I wept in gratitude to the humble, tender Nephi who had preserved this saving truth of Christ's availability. His personal administration in our lives can be ours, as soon as we are ready to believe and receive it from Him. I mounted up in my imagination as on eagle's wings **(D&C 124:99)**, carried by the power of the love I felt for Him and from Him. I had never before comprehended how close the Savior is willing—and even desires—to be to us.

How can I possibly convey the spiritual awakening, the change, that began to dawn in my heart from that hour? As I continued to read the *Book of Mormon,* I found one witness after another that there did not have to be any distance between the Lord and me; that His love and power to redeem were enough to save even me. His arm was strong enough to encircle me and give me safety from my weaknesses. A few pages later I read Jacob's words:

> **Wherefore, my beloved brethren, I beseech of you in words of soberness that ye would repent, and come with full purpose of heart, and** *cleave unto God as he cleaveth unto you.* **And while his arm of mercy is extended towards you in the light of day, harden not your hearts. (Jacob 6:5; emphasis added)**

I knew it was true. I knew by my own experience that He lives and that He lives for me. Something had changed. I had lived this reality with the Savior. He was my friend, *my* Jesus.

A SONG OF REDEEMING LOVE

With an even greater hunger, I plunged into the *Book of Mormon.* This was not the hunger of a starving person looking for sustenance.

This was the hunger of a person who had partaken of the fruit that is sweet above anything I had ever tasted. I had lived (not just read or heard about) the pure love of Christ for me—His charity for me. I wanted more. I could not be restrained from seeking more in the precious words of the *Book of Mormon*.

And there, like voices rising from the dust just as the prophets foresaw, was testimony after testimony of the new life and love I had entered into.

> And we talk of Christ, we rejoice in Christ, we preach of Christ, we prophesy of Christ, and we write according to our prophecies, that our children may know to what source they may look for a remission of their sins. (2 Nephi 25:26)

> And never, until I did cry out unto the Lord Jesus Christ for mercy, did I receive a remission of my sins. But behold, *I did cry unto him* and I did find peace to my soul. (Alma 38:8; emphasis added)

> And now, I would commend you to seek this same Jesus of whom the prophets and apostles have written, that the grace of God the Father, and also the Lord Jesus Christ, and the Holy Ghost, which beareth record of them, may be and abide in you forever. Amen. (Ether 12:41)

> Yea, come unto Christ;…then is his grace sufficient for you. (Moroni 10:32)

> Therefore, let us glory, yea, we will glory in the Lord; yea, we will rejoice, for our joy is full; yea, we will praise our God forever. Behold, who can glory too much in the Lord? Yea, who can say too much of his great power, and of his mercy, and of his long-suffering towards the children of men? Behold, I say unto you, *I cannot say the smallest part which I feel.* (Alma 26:16; emphasis added)

By the time I read and truly heard the harmony in all these statements, I could not say the smallest part of how I felt either. As I kept reading, something began to stir in my inner soul—a feeling whose name I had nearly forgotten. It was *hope*. I was beginning to have hope for myself again, but not hope based on my own wavering and feeble efforts. Having hope in even my very best efforts had never supplied me with enough power to overcome my weaknesses. In fact, focusing on my efforts had always led to an experience similar to the people in Helaman:

> **And because of...their boastings in their own strength, they were left in their own strength; therefore they did not prosper. (Helaman 4:13)**

No. This hope I now possessed was not about me or any other power. It was a hope borne of His friendship, His mercy and His grace! It was a perfect brightness of hope in Christ! **(2 Nephi 31:20)**. My emotions were almost more than I could keep calm or quiet about. *I felt consumed with love for Jesus, as intense and total as I finally knew He had always felt for me!*

IT MUST BE AN INDIVIDUAL ATONEMENT

But as always in this mortal world, fears were waiting to tempt me. Maybe I was loving Him too much. After all, I noticed as my joy in Him increased, some "active" members of my ward seemed to be somewhat "put off" or bothered by the new me. I had a hard time sitting on my hands in church classes. It just seemed as if thoughts were always coming to me—excited thoughts, enlightened thoughts, joyful thoughts about Him and His gospel. I didn't have as much inclination to talk of negative things; complaining and gossiping fell away and eventually, so did some long-standing and "exemplary" friends. I had to learn some quick lessons about what it meant to care more for the love of God than the love of my fellow mortals.

As I turned to Heavenly Father in prayer, I felt His counsel to me through His Son. I began to understand that Christ doesn't atone for all of us at once, *en masse*. He atones for us one person at a time; He cleanses us one heart at a time, and He loves us one at a time as choice and unique individuals. I had to realize that while I had awakened unto God's love and tender mercy, and my soul had been illuminated by the truth about Christ's tenderness and nearness, others were still struggling with fear and doubt concerning Him. Even so, I still have a continuous struggle to not break into a rousing and unique version of Handel's "Messiah" or song of redeeming love. It's always there, humming in my heart:

> For unto [*me*] a child is born, unto [*me*] a son is given; and the government [of my life] shall be upon his shoulder; and his name shall be called Wonderful, *Counselor*, The *Mighty* God, The Everlasting Father, The Prince of *Peace*. (2 Nephi 19:6; emphasis added)

ANOTHER TESTAMENT OF JESUS CHRIST

Today I pay close attention to the first five words immediately following the title of the *Book of Mormon*—"Another testament of Jesus Christ." It is so important to remember that the *Book of Mormon* was written for our day—not just to convert the nonmember to the Church, *but also to convert the Church to Christ.* On the day we each become His individual convert (His "prisoner," as Paul terms it in **Ephesians 4:1**), we will know His peace, and be no longer His servants, but His friends.

> And it shall come to pass in that day that the Lord shall give thee rest, from thy sorrow, and from thy fear, and from the hard bondage wherein thou wast made to serve. (2 Nephi 24:3)

If you are like I have been—so lost in the effects of sin—you may still fear and tremble. After all, you've worked for years on your weaknesses, your negative traits and behaviors, you've spent a lifetime in battle against them and have thought that you had only two choices—to go down for the count, or just endure to the dreaded end. How could reaching out to Christ, no matter how sincerely, be enough to affect such a complete change? It all sounds too easy and simple. Didn't *I* still have to figure my way out of my problems? Again the *Book of Mormon* held my answers:

And the labor which they had to perform was to look; and because of the simpleness of the way, or the easiness of it, there were many who perished. (1 Nephi 17:41)

And now, if the Lord has such great power, and has wrought so many miracles among the children of men, how is it that he cannot instruct me, that I should build a ship? [solve my problems] (1 Nephi 17:51)

For I know that the Lord giveth no commandments unto the children of men, *save he shall prepare a way* for them that they may accomplish the thing which he commandeth them. (1 Nephi 3:7; emphasis added)

Yea, and how is it that ye have forgotten that *the Lord is able to do all things* according to his will, for the children of men, if it so be that they exercise faith in him? Wherefore, let us be faithful to *him.* (1 Nephi 7:12; emphasis added)

CHRIST IS THE LORD, THE GOD OF THE BOOK OF MORMON

Behold, God is my salvation; I will trust, and not be afraid; for the Lord JEHOVAH is my strength and my song; he also has become my salvation. (2 Nephi 22:2)

Jehovah of the Old Testament, Christ of the New Testament, and the Lord of the *Book of Mormon* are the same individual **(Helaman 14:12, 3 Nephi 15:5)**. Nephi, Jacob, Enos, Benjamin, and later Alma, the brother of Jared, Mormon and Moroni—all these men, even like Adam, Abraham, Moses, Peter, James and John, had a "working, walking," intimately personal relationship with Him, even the Lord Jesus Christ. While they kept the supremacy of the Father always in perspective, they cried out to the Lord, counseling with Him and praising Him continually in their hearts and minds **(Enos 1:2, 4, and 10; Mosiah 2:19; Alma 36:18)**.

Each discovered in turn (even as we must) that the Son is *the* member of the Godhead sent by the Father to represent Him in full authority and power, as the **"mediator of the new covenant" (D&C 107:18–19)**, and that it is the *Son* whose words are conveyed to us by the Holy Ghost **(Moses 5:9)** and will lead us along in *all* things whatsoever we should do **(2 Nephi 32:3)**.

For us to seek the Son's counsel, to talk to Him, visualize Him, walk with Him, labor with Him and love Him with all our heart, might, mind and strength, *delights* the Father **(Colossians 1:19)**. He knows full well that the Beloved Son will attribute all glory, honor and power to the Father **(Matthew 6:13)** and will always teach us to pray unto the Father in His own name. There is no jealousy between them. They are, along with the Holy Spirit who administers for both of them, even as one **(John 10:30)**. They think as one, work as one, and rejoice as one when we become **"born of God" (Mosiah 27:28)** and become one with Christ **(D&C 50:43)**.

> And now, my sons, remember, remember that it is upon the rock of our Redeemer, who is Christ, the Son of God, that ye must build your foundation; that when the devil shall send forth his mighty winds, yea, his shafts in the whirlwind, yea, when all his hail and his mighty storm shall beat upon you, it shall have no power over you to drag you down to the gulf of misery and endless wo, because of the rock upon which ye are built, which is a sure foundation, a foundation whereon if men build they cannot fall. (Helaman 5:12)

If we would escape our afflictions, and break the cords of the destructive things we feel and do, we must heed Alma's words:

> And Alma cried, saying: How long shall we suffer these great afflictions, O Lord? O Lord, give us strength according to our faith which is in Christ, even unto deliverance. And they broke the cords with which they were bound. (Alma 14:26)

We must never forget:

> **And this is the means whereby salvation cometh. And there is none other salvation save this...Believe in God; believe that he is, and that he created all things, both in heaven and in earth; believe that he has all wisdom, and all power, both in heaven and in earth; believe that man doth not comprehend all the things which the Lord can comprehend. (Mosiah 4:8–9)**

And believe that He loves us—each of us, without exception and beyond our ability to comprehend or imagine.

CONCLUSION: COME UNTO CHRIST

Today my whole heart is consumed by a desire to share with others what God has shared with me—that Jesus is the Christ, *my* Christ and *yours*. And He waits to receive and embrace each of us. But we must each come unto him individually, even as Alma. When the day comes, as it did for Alma, when we can no longer go on the way we're going, when we are harrowed up by the memory of our many sins, and when we are racked with torment, we will each begin to think of "one Jesus Christ, a Son of God." On that day we too will have no formal protocol on our mind. In the deepest anguish of spirit we will finally cry out, as did Alma:

> **O Jesus, thou Son of God, have mercy on me, who am in the gall of bitterness, and am encircled about by the everlasting chains of death. (Alma 36:18)**

We are all very aware that our leaders have cautioned us against addressing anyone except the Father in our public prayers. This is absolutely as it should be and in perfect harmony with the teachings of the Savior in **Matthew 6:9**. After all and above and beyond all, our Father in Heaven is the One who oversees all, including the administration of the First and Second Comforter. He is the Most High, the Holy One, Man of Righteousness, the Father of Lights, the Great Elohim. Without Him and His faithfulness in all of us—including

His only begotten Son in the flesh, even Jesus Christ—none of this glorious mortal experience would happen. It was the Father's great plan of salvation, complete with the opportunity to fall, to experience the sorrow of sin, and to be atoned for and redeemed, that the Son volunteered to carry forth—and in so doing, has qualified Himself to be addressed as Father also **(Mosiah 3:8; Helaman14:12;** and His own words in **Ether 3:14).**

And so, in our formal prayers, in public and in private, morning and evening and as often in between as we feel our Savior's testimony to do so, it is our Father in Heaven we should always address—even as our Lord taught us **(Matthew 6:9; 2 Nephi 25:16; Jacob 4:5; 3 Nephi 20:31).**

Nevertheless, that great truth does not cancel out, but rather complements and supports the witness of the *Book of Mormon* that it is acceptable, and even commendable by our Father in Heaven, for us to counsel with His Son, to cry out unto Him in our need for redemption, to become as honest and self-disclosing as best, first-name, friends would be **(2 Nephi 33:6).** After all, in several sacred interventions of the Father in the history of mankind, His constant entreaty to us all, speaking of His Beloved Son Jesus, was "hear Him."

The goal of the Father is to have each of us give ourselves without reservation to His Beloved Son. The goal of the Son is to bring us Home to our Father. The only question or diversion from this oneness of purpose is our own desire (goal). Is our desire to seek the Holy Ghost and allow Him to quicken and empower us with a sufficient portion of celestial glory, even while in this life, so that we may inherit a fullness in the resurrection **(D&C 88:29)?** Or will we keep running away and hiding in the things of this world—in our excuses and addictions?

Can we muster enough faith in Christ, even in the face of our mortal sins and failings? Can we look to Him and receive Him—His Spirit, His counsel, His comfort, His will—and become perfect in Him, as we allow Him to find place in our minds and hearts and lives? I have found that as paradoxical as it may seem at first consideration, one of the times and places that many of us find the Savior is when we are in the midst of what could be termed "the pit" or "the darkest abyss" (or as it is sometimes spoken of in addiction recovery groups, at "a bottom"). Like Paul, we are blinded by the incorrect traditions of our parents, or like Alma the Younger, blinded by our own immaturity and foolish willfulness.

Many of us find the living reality of Christ in our darkest, and sometimes most sinful, hour. In that moment of crisis, if our prayer is sincere, filled with real intent and a desire to believe in Christ, He will apply His atoning blood.

This kind of moment is seldom polite. It is always passionate, filled with emotion so powerful that only He can comprehend it. Why? Because He felt it in His act of Atonement for us. At this point we are in "hard labor" and the soul that is being born is our own. At this point there is no heart in us to be polite and "legalistic" and "letter-of-the-law" about our expression of our need for God—specifically for the atonement of Christ. And if, like Alma, we cry out unto Him who the Father sent to save us, the heavens weep with joy over us. We cry out unto Him with all our hearts, might, mind and strength—holding nothing back—willing to give away all our sins that we might finally come to Him and come to know Him. He employees no servant there.

And when we do come to Him, we will find joy as exceeding as was our pain and fear before we turned to Him.

And oh, what joy, and what marvelous light I [do] behold[!] ...yea, [my] joy [is] as exceeding as was my pain! (Alma 36:20)

We *must* each come unto Christ, and in the same manner and spirit as did Alma. This is one time when we cannot slip through on someone else's coattails or apron strings. It is only when we repent of turning to any other source for strength or salvation and place our faith *on the Lord Jesus Christ* that we are able to withstand the temptations of him who would rejoice at our misery and destruction.

I have found that it helps to keep me in remembrance of my absolute need for His power if I take every opportunity to do as **Alma 37:33** entreats us:

> **Preach unto them repentance, and faith on the Lord Jesus Christ; teach them to humble themselves and to be meek and lowly in heart; teach them to withstand every temptation of the devil, with their faith on the Lord Jesus Christ.**

Let us never forget the witness of the *Book of Mormon*, and remember that every day we must counsel with the Lord in all our doings, and let the affection of our hearts be placed upon Him forever, for we can be sure His is placed on us forever **(Alma 37:36–37)**. We must never again forget that salvation cometh only by **"relying wholly upon the merits of him who is mighty to save" (2 Nephi 31:19)**.

ASSIGNMENT FOR THIS WEEK:

1. Write about how thinking of Christ as "my Jesus" could affect your feelings for Him. Does this expression feel comfortable to you? Why or why not?

2. Read "Born of God" by President Ezra Taft Benson, *Ensign*, July 1989. Capture some thoughts from it.

3. Call someone and share your thoughts and feelings about what you've read.

PREPARATION FOR DISCUSSION OF PRINCIPLE THREE: "I KNOW IN WHOM I HAVE TRUSTED" (2 NEPHI 4:19)

Step 3: Made the decision to reconcile ourselves to the will of God, offer our whole souls as an offering unto Him, and trust Him in all things forever. (2 Nephi 10:24; Omni 1:26; Mosiah 3:19; 2 Nephi 4:34)

Day 1: **1 Nephi 18:11**—Write about why, according to this verse, the Lord "suffers," or in other words "allows," us to be in bondage at times. (See also **John 9:1–3** for further insight into why God allows forms of bondage such as physical handicaps.)

Day 2: **2 Nephi 10:24**—Nephi asks us to conform, to adapt our will to the will of God. When we act on our compulsive/addictive behavior, it is because we want something we can't have. Our will is at odds with the will of God. We have surrendered it instead to the will of the flesh or the devil (two different phenomena, by the way). Write about the struggle you'd like to be saved from, and whose power it is that can save you. What is that power called?

Day 3: **Jacob 4:10**—To counsel means to give advice. Often when we pray we seek more to advise the Lord in what *we* think He should do for us or others ("Dear Lord, please bless so-and-so that such-and-such will happen"), than to listen for His counsel or advice. Write in the form of a question something that has been troubling you, addressing it to the Lord. Then listen and record the answer you receive.

Day 4: **Mosiah 3:19**—How old do you picture the "little child" mentioned in this scripture? A tiny infant? A two-year-old? Remember that two-year-olds aren't too good at "yielding" or "submitting." Write about how young a child you are willing to become to your Heavenly Father and just how far you are willing to submit in all things that He might see fit to "inflict" upon you.

Day 5: **Mosiah 7:33**—Often, being released from the bondage of a compulsive/addictive behavior is a process rather than a singular event. Write about your willingness or lack of willingness to submit to the Lord's will and "pleasure" (remembering that His pleasure is to bring to pass your immortality and eternal life through your experiences of this life—both good and "bad").

Day 6: **Mosiah 24:14–15**—What happened to the burdens these people struggled with when they put their trust in God to deliver them? Write about whether you could be satisfied to have God *lighten* your burdens instead of removing them. Can you be long-suffering and patient with Him and with yourself? (There's a saying in Twelve Step programs: "You've got to love the process.")

Day 7: **Alma 5:13**—In this verse the mighty change of heart is equated with humbling yourself and putting your trust in "the *true* and *living* God." Write about what the words *"true and living,"* as applied to God, mean to you. How is He "true" and "living" as compared to the "god" (source of strength and comfort) you've made of your compulsion?

P.S. May I encourage you again to take the phone number of someone else in the Twelve Step group you are attending and call and share with them what you're learning. We never learn better than by teaching someone else. Teach someone else something you've learned from this lesson.

I KNOW IN WHOM I HAVE TRUSTED
(2 Nephi 4:19)

Step Three: Made the decision to reconcile ourselves
to the will of God, offer our whole souls as an
offering unto Him, and trust Him in all things forever.
(2 Nephi 10:24; Omni 1:26; Mosiah 3:19; 2 Nephi 4:34)

Principle Three: Trusting God in all things is the
highest form of worship I can extend to Him.

There are many ways of worshiping God. I used to think the only valid form of worship I could show was to be feverishly active, working harder and harder, using more and more of my addiction to cope with the stress and the emptiness I felt as a result of trying so hard on my own to be perfect.

As the message of Step Three settled in my heart and mind, a whole new depth of worship became clear to me. As I admitted powerlessness in Step One, and recognized the reality of Christ's continual love and guidance to my heart and mind in Step Two, I began to realize that trusting Him in all things—letting Him be in charge of my life (and the lives of everyone else, as well as the entire universe)—was the highest form of worship I could offer to Him and to Heavenly Father. I became willing to trust Him in all things forever—especially in the things I didn't understand.

True worship is *not* something you only do once a week, or even twice a day in prayer. Complete dedication to and trust in God's will is the highest form of worship we can show Him—something we must practice daily and sometimes even hourly.

> **The *constant* and *recurring* question in our minds, touching *every* thought and deed of our lives should be, "*Lord, what wilt thou have me to do.*" (Ezra T. Benson, Dec. 1988 *Ensign;* emphasis added)**

To **"love the Lord thy God with all thy heart, with all thy might, mind and strength" (D&C 59:5)** means to trust the Lord with every fiber of your being—or at least to be willing to *practice* doing so, having charity for yourself when you fall short.

ALL THAT WE HAVE, ALL THAT WE ARE

God doesn't want a *part* of our hearts and souls. He wants *all* of us. For instance, those of us who bring our bodies to church while our minds are at home tending to other affairs—or hunting or golfing—are *not* satisfactory to Him, although His patience and long-suffering, His mercy and grace, give us a lot of leeway. Those of us who have minds filled with scriptures and quotes but whose *hearts* are far from Him probably cause Him even more sorrow.

The following quotes from church leaders, both ancient and modern, may help to give us some feeling for how much of our "self"—our loyalty and trust—the Lord desires of us.

> **And now, my beloved brethren, I would that ye should come unto Christ, who is the Holy One of Israel, and partake of his salvation, and the power of his redemption. Yea, come unto him, and offer your whole souls as an offering unto him. (Omni 1:26)**

> **Christ says, "Give me All. I don't want so much of your time and so much of your money and so much of your work: I want You. I have not come to torment your natural self, but to kill it. No half-measures are any good.**

I don't want to cut off a branch here and a branch there, I want to have the whole tree down...Hand over the whole natural self, all the desires which you think innocent as well as the ones you think wicked—the whole outfit. I will give you a new self instead. In fact, I will give you Myself: my will shall become yours." (Elder Robert L. Backman, quoting C. S. Lewis, *Ensign*, Nov. 1991, p. 8)

Every intelligent being on the earth is tempered for glory, beauty, excellency and knowledge here, and for immortality and eternal lives in the world to come. But every being who attains to this must be sanctified before God and *be completely under the control of His Spirit.* (Brigham Young, *Journal of Discourses*, 13:273, emphasis added)

Our business is then to find out what the Lord's will is, to guide us in our everyday life, not only to make us feel good, to exalt our spiritual nature, our emotions, our sentiments, our thoughts...but to guide us in our daily lives, so that all our acts may be squared according to the rule of right, that we may do that which is pleasing to our Heavenly Father...*to do the will of Him that has sent us here on the earth.* (Charles W. Penrose, *Journal of Discourses*, 25:46-47; emphasis added)

You can change human nature, *your own,* if you surrender it to Christ. (Beverly Nichols, as quoted by David O. McKay, *Stepping Stones to an Abundant Life*, p. 23; emphasis added)

The new birth takes place only for those who actually enjoy the gift or companionship of the Holy Ghost, only for those who are *fully* converted, who have given themselves *without restraint* to the Lord. (Bruce R. McConkie, *Mormon Doctrine*, 2nd ed., p. 101; emphasis added)

To love God with all your heart, soul, mind and strength is all-consuming and all-encompassing. It is no lukewarm endeavor. It is total commitment of our very being—physically, mentally, emotionally, and spiritually—to love the Lord. (Ezra T. Benson, *Ensign*, May 1988, p. 4)

IN ALL THINGS—NOT JUST ALL GOOD THINGS

One of the most challenging concepts in coming to an absolute trust of God is to stand back far enough and recognize that evil is part of God's plan. It is here because He allows it to be, so that each of us might have the opportunity to learn *by our own experience* the good from the evil.

Part of the process of coming unto Christ and truly applying His atonement to our own lives and the lives of others is to lose our fear that there is some power or effect of evil the Savior can't overcome (D&C 19:3). Coming to *know* the perfect love of God, that all is happening for a benevolent and loving reason (no matter how terrible it looks from our present perspective), is essential to developing unwavering trust.

> We would subject ourselves to the yoke of bondage if it were requisite with the justice of God, or if he should command us so to do. But behold he doth not command us that we shall subject ourselves to our enemies, but that we should put our trust in him, and he will deliver us [in His own due time]. (Alma 61:12–13)

> But if ye will turn to the Lord with full purpose of heart, and put your trust in him,…he will, according to his own will and pleasure, deliver you out of bondage. (Mosiah 7:33)

We need to remember that his "will and pleasure," or in other words "work and glory," is to bring to pass **"the immortality and eternal life"** of each of us **(Moses 1:39)**. That is to say, we need to realize His whole purpose is to help us come to where He is and inherit all that He has.

> Yea, and how is it that ye have forgotten that the Lord is able to do all things according to his will, for the children of men, if it so be that they exercise faith in him? Wherefore, let us be faithful to him. (1 Nephi 7:12)

The following scripture reveals to us that sometimes our suffering is the result of God *having* to allow other people to have their freedom, even if they choose evil. No one could choose evil if there were not others willing to risk being their victims. We need to realize there is a great orchestration going on here in this life, beginning in the premortal realm, with its results still to be seen in the stage of life following mortality.

In the Old Testament, we find one of the most powerful testimonies that God is working in all things, even in uninspired, rebellious, outright wicked things that are done in this world:

> Now therefore be not grieved, nor angry with yourselves, that ye sold me hither: *for God did send me before you* to preserve life... *And God sent me before you* to preserve you a posterity on earth, and to save your lives by a great deliverance. *So now it was not you that sent me hither, but God...* (Genesis 45:5–8; emphasis added)

As we come to know the goodness and mercy of the Lord, we begin to awaken to the truth—paradoxical as it may seem to us—that the seeming triumph of evil here in this telestial world is only temporary; its complete defeat can be found even now on a personal level by surrendering our lives totally to Christ and to the Father who sent Him. It is that kind of trusting relationship that will give us, as Nephi, the knowledge of the truth—that evil has a purpose and a very short "shelf life."

> And it came to pass that...they did treat me with much harshness; nevertheless, the Lord did suffer it that he

> might show forth his power, unto the fulfilling of his
> word which he had spoken concerning the wicked.
> Nevertheless, I did look unto my God, and I did praise
> him all the day long; and I did not murmur against the
> Lord because of my afflictions. (1 Nephi 18:11, 16)

> And they did submit cheerfully and with patience to all
> the will of the Lord. (Mosiah 24:15)

> Be humble...submissive and gentle; easy to be entreated;
> full of patience and long-suffering; being temperate in
> all things...always returning thanks unto God for what-
> soever ye do receive. (Alma 7:23)

Possessing this *ultimate* trust for God allows us not only to bow
stoically beneath "the lash" of this life's trials and mistakes, but to
actually feel grateful for the lessons learned. By learning the lessons
that our trials and mistakes have to teach us, these sad experiences
are actually converted to our good (**D&C 122:7**).

TRUST, FAITH, TOTAL HUMILITY

Trust, faith and total humility—these words are synonymous.
There are a lot of scriptures on trusting God. When you also consider
those pertaining to faith and humility (look in your "Topical
Guide"), you can begin to feel how earnestly the Lord's prophets
have pled with us to take this essential step toward becoming one
with the mind and will of God.

> And according to his faith there was a mighty change
> wrought in his heart. And they humbled themselves and
> put their trust in the true and living God. (Alma 5:12–13)

> And becometh as a child, submissive, meek, humble,
> patient, full of love, willing to submit to all things which
> the Lord seeth fit to inflict upon him; even as a child doth
> submit to his father. (Mosiah 3:19)

Wherefore, brethren, seek not to counsel the Lord, but to take counsel from his hand. For behold, ye yourselves know that he counseleth in wisdom, and in justice, and in great mercy, over all his works. (Jacob 4:10)

O Lord, I have trusted in thee, and I will trust in thee forever. I will not put my trust in the arm of flesh. (2 Nephi 4:34)

RESULTS WE CAN TRUST

As I kept coming back to these principles and to my Twelve Step support group, I very gradually began to realize that the results of turning to God are results we can trust. His promises are sure. It is true He is the same yesterday, today, and forever. It is true He is merciful to the repentant sinner and will pour out His blessings upon the returning prodigal. Here is a partial list of the promises He has made and kept in my life, according to my desire to receive them.

1. He will give us His own words to share when we need them, but often not until the very hour or moment we need them (D&C 100:5–6).

   And I have put my words in thy mouth, and have covered thee in the shadow of mine hand. (2 Nephi 8:16)

   Wherefore I, Jacob, gave unto them these words as I taught them in the temple, having first obtained my errand from the Lord. (Jacob 1:17)

2. We will have the joy and privilege of being His instrument. (And believe me, no one feels the surgeon's closeness more than the scalpel!)

   Yea, and we have been instruments in his hands of doing this great and marvelous work. (Alma 26:15)

3. We will have a peace that passeth understanding (a peace that doesn't make any sense and has nothing to do with our external circumstances).

    Peace, peace be unto you because of your faith in my Well Beloved, who was from the foundation of the world. (Helaman 5:47)

    And it came to pass that there was no contention in the land, because of the love of God which did dwell in the hearts of the people. (4 Nephi 1:15)

4. We will lose our disposition to do evil; evil-doing will automatically ebb out of our lives.

    ...which has wrought a mighty change in us, or in our hearts, that we have no more disposition to do evil, but to do good continually. (Mosiah 5:2)

WHAT STOPS US FROM TRUSTING GOD?

If God will not fail us, then why do we hesitate and resist trusting Him? The following is a list of a few of the ways in which I have watched myself be distracted and discouraged from my willingness to trust God in all things.

1. Looking for answers in the intellect and learning of men. It is a very fine line between being taught of the Lord and being taught by the learning and intellect of mankind. There is so much truth to be found and gleaned and enjoyed through so many sources. The only way we can know we are following the right philosophy, the best path of thought or action, is to counsel with the Lord concerning everything to which we are exposed. We must never forget that the Lord can reveal wisdom *directly* to our minds and hearts.

    Now, I Nephi...did build it after the manner which the Lord had shown unto me; wherefore it was not after the manner of men. (1 Nephi 18:2)

We must always remember that with all our reading, studying and searching out answers, the absolute last word in the construction of our program of recovery from addictive/compulsive behaviors (or from any problem) should be the Lord's.

2. Fear of others' opinions or craving the esteem or approval of others.

Hearken unto me, ye that know righteousness, the people in whose heart I have written my law, fear ye not the reproach of men, neither be ye afraid of their revilings. (2 Nephi 8:7)

Oh, how often I have chosen foolishly, trying to obtain the "love" of others—ignoring my own conscience and the whisperings of the Holy Ghost because I was either afraid of others or seeking their good will. From consenting to premarital sex as a teenager to indulging in compulsive eating as an adult, I was driven by fear of the "revilings" (or just plain reaction) of other people. Through the Savior's grace, we can find the strength and comfort needed to practice respecting His opinion and good will above that of all others.

3. Pride and self-reliance.

I will punish...the stout heart...and the glory of his high looks.
For he saith: By the strength of my hand and by my wisdom I have done these things; for I am prudent.
Shall the axe boast itself against him that heweth therewith? (2 Nephi 20:12–13, 15)

Don't you love the word "prudent?" It's a virtue when blended with and framed by our reliance on the Lord. Thinking we can practice it on our own—without the help of His Spirit—makes it just another form of pride and boasting in our own strength.

4. We don't want what the Lord wants (self-will).

There have been times when I didn't trust that things in my life were being cared for by the Lord—not because I couldn't trust, but because I just plain didn't want things to be happening the way they were. Slowly I am coming to feel more like Alma:

> **I know that which the Lord hath commanded me, and I glory in it. I do not glory of myself, but I glory in that which the Lord hath commanded me. (Alma 29:9)**

> **Behold, they do not desire that the Lord their God, who hath created them, should rule and reign over them; notwithstanding his great goodness and his mercy towards them, they do set at naught his counsels, and they will not that he should be their guide. (Helaman 12:6)**

> **If I were to ask you individually, if you wished to be sanctified throughout, and become as pure and holy as you possibly could live, every person would say yes; yet if the Lord Almighty should give a revelation instructing you *to be given wholly up to Him,* and to His cause, you would shrink, saying, "I am afraid he will take away some of my darlings." That is the difficulty with the majority of this people. (Brigham Young, *Journal of Discourses* 2:134; emphasis added)**

Remember the quote by President Benson:

> **"When we put God first, all other things fall into their proper place or drop out of our lives." (*Ensign,* May 1988, p. 4)**

The hard, cold truth is that sometimes as mortals, blinded by the veil of forgetfulness, we don't want to put God first because we don't want things to fall into their "proper place" *just yet.* Miserable as we like to pretend mortal life makes us, the truth is it feels pretty comfortable the way it is. All our worries and distractions, our compulsions, obsessions, and addictions have become like old friends who seem more familiar than a life entrusted to God.

5.   It's too *hard*.

> **The great *task* of life is to learn the will of the Lord and then do it. (Ezra T. Benson, May 1988 *Ensign*, p. 4; emphasis added)**

I think it's that word *task* that gets us. Coming to a place of total trust and surrender to God's will is just plain hard work. In fact, it's the hardest work we will ever undertake. It is far harder than any other "good work," and it is the one that is absolutely essential **(3 Nephi 14:21)**.

6.   Fear and worry.

Fear and worry have the effect of freezing us up, confusing and disabling us. "Frozen with fear" is a familiar saying, as is "Fear is the opposite of faith." Faith in its highest expression is loving and trusting God in all things. When we choose to trust God that all things are happening for our good and for our instruction, we are not paralyzed by fear.

As Richard L. Evans so beautifully stated,

> **When we worry, we are less efficient; we contribute to the cause and slow down the cure. (*An Open Road*, p. 38)**

THE PROPHETS' EXAMPLES OF ADEQUATE, NOT PERFECT, TRUST

I include here just a few of the many examples of different prophets' efforts to tell us that they too were mortal, and that they too were not able to maintain anything like *perfect* adherence to these principles.

What they did do is repent continually, having a perfect brightness of hope and steadfastness in Christ. Every time they messed up, they kept up instead of giving up. Having come to know Christ personally, they were not guilty of the blasphemy we indulge in when we think we are somehow more powerful to mess up than Christ is to redeem.

I am encompassed about, because of the temptations and the sins that do so easily beset me.

And when I desire to rejoice, my heart groaneth because of my sins; nevertheless, I know in whom I have trusted. (2 Nephi 4:18–19)

And there came a voice unto me, saying; Enos, thy sins are forgiven thee, and thou shalt be blessed.

And I, Enos, knew that God could not lie; wherefore, my guilt was swept away. (Enos 1:5–6)

Or that ye should think that I of myself am more than a mortal man. But I am like as yourselves, subject to all manner of infirmities in body and mind. (Mosiah 2:10–11)

Nevertheless, after wading through much tribulation, repenting nigh unto death, the Lord in mercy hath seen fit to snatch me out of an everlasting burning, and I am born of God [Alma the younger speaking]. (Mosiah 27:28)

And for the space of three hours did the Lord talk with the brother of Jared, and chastened him because he remembered not to call upon the name of the Lord. (Ether 2:14)

For now I had been tempted of the adversary and saught [sic] the Plates to obtain riches and kept not the commandment that I should have a [sic] eye single to the glory of God. (Joseph Smith, *An American Prophet's Record*, p. 7)

CHRIST'S EXAMPLE—CHRIST'S POWER

As in all things, the answer to our lack of ability or power to muster this kind of trust is in God; in this instance, the answer is in the gifts of the Spirit. This is the time and place for us to be honest with ourselves and God and admit we cannot manufacture this kind of absolute surrender to God and His plan for us and others. This surrender is, like faith, hope and charity, a gift from God. If we desire (that's our agency at work) this kind of trust and faith in God, He will supply it to us as a *gift* of the Spirit. All we have to do is ask. Remember, even if you only have a desire to believe, that is a sufficient beginning.

> I have suffered the will of the Father in all things from the beginning. (3 Nephi 11:11)

> I do always those things that please [God]. (John 8:29)

> For I came down from heaven, not to do mine own will, but the will of him that sent me. (John 6:38)

> Even with the great ability he had, Jesus did nothing of himself. His whole effort was to do the Father's will. All that he did, all that he spoke was given of the Father. If Jesus found it necessary to draw his course of action from God, how much more so do we have a need to be dependent upon the Father to determine the course of our lives in every detail! Those who would follow Christ cannot subscribe to the slogan, "I did it my way." (E. Richard Packham, *Born of the Spirit*, p. 37)

CONCLUSION: THERE IS NO OTHER NAME, WAY OR MEANS

> Know ye not that ye are in the hands of God? Know ye not that he hath all power, and at his great command the earth shall be rolled together as a scroll? (Mormon 5:23)

> Wherefore, my beloved brethren, reconcile yourselves to the will of God...and remember, after ye are reconciled unto God, that it is only in and through the grace of God that ye are saved. (2 Nephi 10:24)

> Finally men [and women] who are captained by Christ will be consumed in Christ. Their will is swallowed up in his will. (Ezra T. Benson, July 1989, *Ensign*, p. 5)

What more can be said? I can only share with you my absolute *knowledge* of the goodness and mercy of God. It is the sincerest desire of my heart to bear witness to others that He is good and merciful, long-suffering and patient beyond any mortal comprehension. I pray they may reawaken to a knowledge of His nature and character, and begin to desire to turn again to Him, not because of fear of Him but because of love for and trust in Him.

All too often, we Latter-day Saints live our lives so near to Him (through our ordinances and good works) and yet so far from Him (through our emphasis on "good son" busy work and so many other things outside of Him). At the center or bull's-eye of everything we do should be our relationship with our Heavenly Father and our Savior, Jesus Christ. Unfortunately we are too often firmly entrenched in the circles *just outside* that bull's-eye, those circles marked "church, home, family, spouse." These things are all good and most certainly given of God, but, at the same time, *they are not* God and can never give us the peace and security He can. They can never supply us with the unfailing support and guidance that only He can. We must be very careful not to set these things up as lesser or demigods and think service to them will substitute for coming to know the Lord personally. When we avoid coming to Him directly, we live far below our privilege—to receive His presence, His voice, and, in His own due time, His very face **(D&C 88:62–68)**.

> **There is no doubt, if a person lives according to the revelations given to God's people, he may have the Spirit of the Lord to signify to him his will, and to guide and to direct him in the discharge of his duties, in his temporal as well as his spiritual exercises. I am satisfied, however, that in this respect, we live far beneath our privileges. (Brigham Young, *Discourses of Brigham Young*, p. 32)**

We have the Savior's own words to describe the "privilege" we have been promised and the preparations we must make to receive the fulfillment of the promise:

It is your privilege, and a promise I give unto you that have been ordained unto this ministry, that inasmuch as you strip yourselves from jealousies and fears, and humble yourselves before me, for ye are not sufficiently humble, the veil shall be rent and you shall see me and know that I am—not with the carnal neither natural mind, but with the spiritual. (Doctrine & Covenants 67:10)

When I think of all the years I was so outwardly "active" in the Lord's behalf—attending church, holding positions—*and* at the same time, in the confines of my own inner, private life, so unbelieving of His promises, I am tempted to great sorrow. How long I **"rejected that Jesus, who stood with open arms to receive [me]" (Mormon 6:17)**, thinking myself beneath or beyond His mercy and grace. It was not until my addiction brought me into a Twelve Step process that I saw how I could **"humble [myself] before [God]"** (Steps 1–3) and **"strip [myself] from jealousies and fears"** (Steps 4–10). Taking those steps prepared my heart and mind to be sensitive to spiritual experiences, to personal communication from Him. It can be done! I know because I have lived it. He loves even the most lost of lambs and the sincerely repentant thief **(3 Nephi 8:19)**. I have received His assurance that there is nothing I have ever "stolen" from anyone, or failed to give anyone, for which He will not compensate. He will restore their loss tenfold as soon as they are ready to look to Him for recompense (recovery).

As I watch people choose other forms of comfort and power instead of choosing to be one with Christ, my heart desires to cry out even as Mormon's, **"O ye fair ones, how could ye have departed from the ways of the Lord!** [Not in action, but in heart and trust.] **O ye fair ones, how could ye have rejected that Jesus, who stood with open arms to receive you?" (Mormon 6:17)**.

PREPARATION FOR DISCUSSION OF PRINCIPLE FOUR: "WO UNTO THE UNCIRCUMCISED OF HEART" (2 NEPHI 9:33)

Step 4: Made a searching and fearless written inventory of our past in order to thoroughly examine ourselves as to our pride and other weaknesses with the intent of recognizing our own carnal state and our need for Christ's Atonement. (Alma 15:17; Mosiah 4:2; Jacob 4:6–7; Ether 12:27)

Day 1: **2 Nephi 9:33**—An "uncircumcised heart" is a heart that is still hardened from within with fear, anger, resentment, guilt, and other negative feelings we choose to harbor there. A heart in this condition is unclean and unfeeling, not able to sense and receive the whisperings of the spirit. To "circumcise" our hearts, we must be humble enough to reveal our innermost self. List briefly one memory you have in each of these areas—fear, resentment, and guilt—that has not been totally cleansed from your heart.

Day 2: **2 Nephi 9:34**—**"Wo unto the liar, for he shall be thrust down to hell."** When we read this scripture, we usually think of the final judgment, but I want you to think of it in the context of today. To lie is to be untruthful or, in other words, not filled with the truth. Who is the Spirit of Truth? **(D&C 93:8–9)** Whose counsel do you lose when you don't think, speak and act in truth? Who are you most likely to be untruthful with before anyone else? In my life, I am most likely to be untruthful to God and myself. Do you see this in your life? Write about a time when you were untrue to God and/or yourself. Write about how and why we are thrust down to hell even in the same hour that we separate ourselves from the truth.

Day 3: **Mosiah 4:2**—To view ourselves in our own "carnal" (worldly) state is to look honestly at ourselves, particularly at our weaknesses and sins. How does honestly facing our mistakes and weaknesses help us to actually forsake them? How does pretending and denying or minimizing them serve to prolong them?

Day 4: Mosiah 4:30—This verse teaches us about the three levels at which we can commit sin, or in other words, separate ourselves from God. What are they? Using these three levels as a guide, write an inventory of your sins from yesterday (those things you did that created distance between you and God).

Day 5: Mosiah 23:9—The word "snare" means trap. Write a brief history of one particular weakness that you feel trapped by. List all the attempts you have made over the years to quit doing this destructive thing. Write about how each new failure made you feel.

Day 6: Alma 36:12–13—Remembering our sins, under any circumstances, is a painful experience, but this verse and others throughout the scriptures plainly demonstrate that to be caught in our sins is the most exquisite pain of all. Write about whether you think it would be better to face our sins and weaknesses voluntarily, now, while we yet have time to repent.

Day 7: 3 Nephi 8:1—"Whit" means a tiny or (seemingly) insignificant amount. Some synonyms for it are "particle," "atom," and "speck." Write about how thorough our repentance needs to be to have miracles (like being healed of our addiction) happen in our life.

WO UNTO THE UNCIRCUMCISED OF HEART
(2 Nephi 4:19)

Step Four: Made a searching and fearless written
inventory of our past in order to thoroughly examine
ourselves as to our pride and other weaknesses with
the intent of recognizing our own carnal state and
our need for Christ's Atonement. (Alma 15:17;
Mosiah 4:2; Jacob 4:6–7; Ether 12:27)

Principle Four: My trials and mistakes are potentially
great learning opportunities, not terrible things
I should try to ignore or forget.

I can't tell you how deeply puzzled I was when, as a youth, I
studied the gospel and wondered about God's reasons for choosing
circumcision as a sign of His covenant with ancient Israel. I remember
thinking, "What a *strange* way to get a man's attention."

My consternation continued for another twenty-five years,
during which time I had six sons, all of whom (for modern purposes
of hygiene) were circumcised. At each occasion I would pause to
reflect and ponder again over such a strange sign. After all, this had
to be *the* most *private* part of a man's body. Why didn't God choose
a more obvious sign, one that everyone could see and say, "Oh,
there's a true Israelite?"

Then came the day when this verse of scripture registered on my newly circumcised heart, which had been softened and made tender and sensitive by the removal of my addiction: **"Wo unto the uncircumcised of heart"** [those who won't submit their heart to be revealed and made clean and sensitive] **(2 Nephi 9:33).**

Suddenly everything I knew about the business of circumcision came flooding back to me, *as it related to the heart!*

But wait! How can we circumcise our own heart? The answer is simple—*we* can't. Only God has the skill and patience and steady hand needed to do this kind of delicate heart surgery. All *we* can do is present our *heart* to him, naked and broken, in absolute honesty, and be willing to have Him repair it. We must be willing to face our shame, guilt, and fear at being so totally exposed. We must be willing to look like a fool before God (2 Nephi 9:42). Yet how can we do that, when every natural-man instinct is crying out in pride?

NOT JUST CLEAN HANDS, BUT PURE HEARTS ALSO

We must come to realize that the repentance process required of us in the Church is really only able to cover the outward "appearances" or practices of our lives. For instance, if we have had immorality problems, and have quit; if we haven't been paying our tithing, and then we start; if we haven't been attending church, but then we begin to—all these are outward, external signs of repentance, and while they are all good—they may not be quite good enough. They may not always reveal a changed *heart*. If we have made any or all of these kinds of changes and are still plagued by feelings of unworthiness and emptiness, we probably need to consider a course of action that will cleanse our "hearts" (our inner lives), as well as correct our outer behavior. Step Four is about that kind of inside-out change.

For he truly spake many great things unto them, which were hard to be understood, save a man should inquire of the Lord; and they being hard in their hearts, therefore

they did not look unto the Lord as they ought. (1 Nephi 15:3)

What we need to do is discover those feelings such as fear, guilt, and resentment that harden our hearts and keep us from surrendering our lives to God. These things still defile our hearts, making it so our confidence can't wax strong in the presence of God **(D&C 121:45)**. Thus, we are afraid to come close to Him.

When we don't feel confident or comfortable in the presence of the Lord, we perceive His Spirit, which is the Spirit of Truth **(D&C 93:8–9; D&C 88:66)**, to be uncomfortable. Thus we hide from, avoid, and deny the truth and the Spirit of the Lord, all at the same time. The truth becomes a hard thing unto us.

Wherefore, the guilty taketh the truth to be hard, for it cutteth them to the very center. (1 Nephi 16:1–2)

TO STUFF SOME YOU HAVE TO STUFF ALL

When we feel uncomfortable in the presence of truth, when we think we must "doctor up" the truth, manage it, manipulate it, mangle it—we begin to use a lot of energy doing so. We get into a process some people call "stuffing their feelings," or denial. And that is spiritually disastrous. Why? Because:

Ye are swift to do iniquity but slow to remember the Lord your God ...and he hath spoken unto you in a still small voice, *but ye were past feeling, that you could not feel his words.* **(1 Nephi 17:45; emphasis added)**

Thus we are taught that God speaks to us through our feelings.

Many of us have spent a lifetime "stuffing down," or repressing *negative* feelings. The sad result is that *all* feelings, including positive ones, are muffled and "numbed out." Or sometimes our inner self might take just the opposite stance. We *over*-feel and *over*-react to things. For example, we may become angry completely out of proportion to a spilled glass of milk. Thus, we are swift to do iniquity (that which is out of proportion, not appropriate or *true* to current circumstances) but slow to remember (hear or feel) the promptings of the Spirit of God.

I propose that the vast majority of us do not sin because we deliberately and maliciously desire to, but because we are "numbed out" by distractions and addictions and cannot feel the Holy Spirit's guidance. We cannot "hear" the warning signals and guiding instructions of the "flight tower." We're flying as if without instruments. *That* is why this whole cleansing or circumcising process is so essential. It gets the interference of resentment, guilt, and fear out of our hearts so we can feel and awaken to the realm of the spirit.

Once we become willing to lay our hearts bare before the Lord, with all of our qualities, feelings, and thoughts exposed, we will learn the greatness of God, and will realize that He has the ability to turn our weaknesses to strengths and our mistakes to blessings—if we will come to Him with rigorous honesty.

Thou knowest the greatness of God; and he shall consecrate thine afflictions for thy gain. (2 Nephi 2:2)

Including the afflictions of our own mistakes. I have never felt more "afflicted" than when I have found myself in an unrighteous situation, knowing it was because of my own disobedience the affliction occurred. Under those kinds of circumstances I feel *doubly* afflicted.

I have come to realize that no matter how afflicted I feel by sin, the greatest damage *any* sin or mistake can cause comes through resisting the lesson it could potentially teach me. When I do that, I remain in ignorance and can be sure that life (and God) will orchestrate another chance for me to learn it. In other words, I'll repeat the mistake. Learning good from evil is what this life is all about. It is one of God's main purposes in sending us here.

NO PAIN, NO GAIN

> **Nevertheless, notwithstanding the great goodness of the Lord, in showing me his great and marvelous works, my heart exclaimeth: O wretched man that I am! Yea, my heart sorroweth because of my flesh; my soul grieveth because of mine iniquities. I am encompassed about, because of the temptations and the sins which do so easily beset me. (2 Nephi 4:17–18)**

These words of Nephi illustrate a normal stage of the cleansing process. As we begin to awaken to God's goodness, it serves only to bring us, in one sense, greater pain. Beginning to know his goodness will not only give us hope, but will awaken us to a sense of our own guilt.

At this point many of us stop the process of repentance, choosing to focus on the guilt in *us* instead of the hope in *Christ*. This is a crucial moment of choice, because it demonstrates the current condition of our heart. It takes many of us a very long time of harboring up and avoiding guilt to realize that to do so is one of the highest forms of blasphemy. Guilt is not meant to be stuffed down or covered up. It is meant to be a warning signal to us—like the smoke alarm in our home. One quick "beep" of its piercing influence is all our Designer meant us to bear. Harbored guilt is the source of much "dis–ease"—spiritual, emotional and physical. It is an unspoken testimony that we have not yet accepted the atonement of Jesus Christ in our hearts, where it counts the most.

Thus many turn away, unwilling to openly look at their own guilt, and never come to know the full extent of God's goodness. The rest of **2 Nephi 4** illustrates plainly that Nephi has not let his sins and his guilt cause him to shrink or turn away. He has faced them squarely. And he has faced his fear that he is too wretched, that God might reject him. He then comes to know full forgiveness and remission of his sins, redemption from his "enemies."

Why should I yield to sin, because of my flesh? Yea, why should I give way to temptations, that the evil one have place in my heart to destroy my peace and afflict my soul? Why am I angry because of mine enemy? (2 Nephi 4:27)

Here Nephi demonstrates for us the kind of soul searching we need to apply to ourselves. A fearlessly honest inventory of our past and present behavior will begin to reveal the underlying pattern of our character strengths *and weaknesses*. We should *especially* be searching for our weaknesses.

And if men come unto me I will show unto them their weakness. I give unto men [I have created a time and place—earth–life—where men can have] **weakness that they may be humble; and my grace** [power] **is sufficient for all men that humble themselves before me; for if they humble themselves before me** [admit that they are nothing without me], **and have faith in me** [recognize that I have the answers and the power; that I am the *way*, the *truth* and the *life*], **then will I make weak things** [moments when they thought they were failing, when they were overcome by sin, when they had thought they were lost forever] **become strong unto them** [become their strongest moments]. **(Ether 12:27)**

LET'S GET ON WITH IT *NOW*

Wo unto the uncircumcised of heart [those who won't submit their heart to be revealed and be made clean and sensitive], **for a knowledge of their iniquities shall smite them at the last day. (2 Nephi 9:33)**

I don't know about you, but I would rather have my iniquities be known now than go on for another forty years trying to pretend to myself and others that I don't really have any. If they're going to be known in the last day and spoken upon the housetops **(D&C 1:3)**, then let's get on with it *now*, while I still have time to repent!

Wo unto the liar, for he shall be thrust down to hell. (2 Nephi 9:34)

I must comment on this verse. As He does so often, the Lord has veiled one of the most powerful statements in the scriptures in simplicity and brevity.

As we begin this process of getting *really* honest with ourselves about our past, we will run up against the phenomenon of denial, both in ourselves and in other people, particularly family members. Denial is a coping mechanism that we use when we are physically, emotionally and spiritually too immature, too small and too childish to see an honest way out of our situation. We resorted to it when we thought we were disconnected from the loving protection and guidance of God's power, and we didn't know any other way to get through than to pretend, to deny, to lie to ourselves and others.

The sad part about *any* kind of dishonesty is that it thrusts the pretender down to hell—a state of separation from God—*in the very hour the pretense begins,* and from that hour it just gets worse and worse. Pretending everything's okay when it isn't is a great drain on our energy, emotionally, spiritually and physically.

And, in fine, wo unto all those who die in their sins; for they shall return to God, and behold his face, and remain in their sins. (2 Nephi 9:38)

If I've ever heard a case for "rigorous honesty" and for a "fearless and searching moral inventory," that's got to be it. Put in that perspective, my heart begins to actually ache to get the job done *now,* to get all the "dirty laundry" out now, no matter how large, *or how small,* and get it cleaned up.

In Isaiah the process of searching and inventorying our lives before the Lord is beautifully described:

Wash you, make you clean; put away the evil of your doings from before mine eyes; cease to do evil;

Come now, and let us reason together, saith the Lord: though your sins be as scarlet, they shall be as white as snow. (Isaiah 1:16,18)

That's because weaknesses are weaknesses only until they are turned to strengths, and sins are only sins until they become the stepping stones upon which we learn, repent and mount to godhood. The opportunity to experience separation from God (to sin) isn't outside the Father's plan. It is part of the Father's plan. Our mistakes can be our greatest benefactors, as soon as we allow them to be our greatest teachers.

TRADITIONS OF OUR FATHERS MUST BE EXAMINED ALSO

In the course of this process of doing an inventory of one's past, it will often be revealed to us that the roots of many of our currently destructive behaviors lie in the "traditions of our fathers"—in other words, in the modeling of our parents.

We don't need to be alarmed by this. In fact, it is just as potentially healthy to come unto God, and with his guidance look honestly at the weaknesses of a family, as it is to look at our individual weaknesses. There's a saying that we are only as sick as we are secret. This is just as true of families as of individuals. Families are entities too, each one a "body" with members. It is important that we look squarely and honestly at our family's ways as well as our own. It is not bad or wrong to admit the whole truth. When we begin to relax our resentment or disappointment toward our family, and realize that they, like us, are only mortals, healing begins. We are truly all in this together.

I have found from my study of the *Book of Mormon* that God understands the phenomenon of children growing up and being influenced by incorrect traditions of past generations, and that He takes a pretty merciful view of those so influenced:

Nevertheless, I say unto you, that it shall be more tolerable for them in the day of judgment than for you...

> For it is because of the traditions of their fathers that
> caused them to remain in their state of ignorance...
> (Alma 9:15,16)

CONCLUSION: OUR HONEST NEED FOR THE SAVIOR

And what are the results and rewards of doing such a painful
thing as being rigorously honest about our deepest heartfelt feelings,
both past and present?

I will cite only one scripture here in answer, but next week we
will look at three examples from the *Book of Mormon* of people who
demonstrated this willingness to be thoroughly cleansed.

> *And they had viewed themselves in their own carnal state,*
> **even less than the dust of the earth. And they all cried**
> **aloud with one voice, saying: O have mercy, and apply**
> **the atoning blood of Christ that we may receive forgive-**
> **ness of our sins, and our hearts may be purified; for we**
> **believe in Jesus Christ, the Son of God, who created**
> **heaven and earth, and all things; who shall come down**
> **among the children of men.**
> **And it came to pass that after they had spoken these**
> **words** *the Spirit of the Lord came upon them, and they*
> *were filled with joy, having received a remission of their*
> *sins, and having peace of conscience.* (Mosiah 4:2–3;
> **emphasis added)**

I can't think of words of promise more enticing than these. If we
have these things, how could we want more?

Next week we will continue discussing this process, especially
highlighting and discussing the example set by several *Book of
Mormon* prophets.

ASSIGNMENT FOR THIS WEEK:

1. Read the essay "The Power of His Everlasting Word" (A–28) in
   the appendix at the end of this workbook. It describes one

method of actually doing a personal inventory. I think you'll find it a very practical guide for actually putting this principle into action.

PREPARATION FOR DISCUSSION OF PRINCIPLE FIVE: "I OF MYSELF AM [NOT] MORE THAN A MORTAL" MOSIAH 2:10

Step 5: Honestly shared this inventory with God and with another person, thus demonstrating the sincerity of our repentance, and our willingness to give away all our sins that we might know Him. (Mosiah 26:29; Alma 22:18)

Day 1: 2 Nephi 30:17—"There is nothing which is secret save it shall be revealed." Does this statement give us any idea of how futile it is to try to keep anything a secret forever? Write about something you have kept secret, thinking you would do so forever (to your grave). (You don't have to reveal the actual secret—just write about how it has made you feel to keep it secret.)

Day 2: Mosiah 26:29—In this verse the Lord connects confession not only to Him, but also to another person, with sincerity of heart. Write about how our willingness to confess our mistakes to another person demonstrates the sincerity of our repentance.

Day 3: Mosiah 27:29—Here is an example of a prophet of God who is willing to confess publicly that he has weaknesses and even sins. How does it affect you to know that individuals as advanced in their walks with the Lord as Nephi (see **2 Nephi 4:18** again) and Alma struggled with temptations and sins? How do you think it might help others—your children, for instance—to know that you too have had temptations and even sins similar to the ones they struggle with?

Day 4: Alma 22:18—"And I will give away all my sins to know thee." Write about how being willing to publicly confess our sins is a genuine demonstration of "giving them away." Write about your desire to know the Lord. Is your desire to know the Lord becoming stronger than your fear of being honest?

Day 5: Alma 24:9—"By opening this correspondence, we have been convinced of our sins." To correspond with someone is to communicate with this person. To communicate honestly with another person about our sins is one of the most powerful tools in helping us to own the responsibility for our own choices. Are you ready to take responsibility for all your past choices? Why or why not?

Day 6: 3 Nephi 1:25—"Therefore in this same year were they brought to a knowledge of their error and did confess their faults." One reason we confess our sins is that we want to show the Lord that we recognize the error of our ways. Public confession is the sincerest form of admitting our *need* for His atonement. Write about your personal need for the atonement of Christ. Is it great enough to motivate you to an appropriate confession? Why or why not?

Day 7: D&C 59:12—This verse teaches us that the purpose of the Sabbath is to (1) serve God and our fellow man, (2) partake of the sacrament, and (3) confess our sins before our brethren and the Lord. How do you think it would help our congregations if we shared more openly from our personal experiences and *challenges*? Do you think it would strengthen or weaken us as a people to be more vulnerable and self-disclosing with each other? Why?

I OF MYSELF AM [NOT] MORE THAN A MORTAL
(Mosiah 2:10)

Step Five: Honestly shared this inventory with God
and with another person, thus demonstrating the
sincerity of our repentance, and our willingness to give
away all our sins that we might know Him.
(Mosiah 26:29; Alma 22:18)

Principle Five: I must be willing to tell the whole truth
to another person about my weaknesses and my failings
when I am moved by the Spirit of the Lord to do so.

A friend and I were once discussing the phenomenon of "perfectionism" and how prevalent it seemed to be among the LDS communities we had lived in. She recounted to me that she had heard a General Authority, speaking at a Stake Conference, say that one of the worst things the Saints can do for each other is to *appear* to be too perfect—that by refusing to admit our struggles and maintaining instead the *appearance* of perfection, we sow seeds of discouragement. If an apostle didn't say it, one could have and should have—for it is a truth worthy of prophetic utterance.

My friend and I continued to talk of how we had fallen prey to this lie ourselves. We shared stories of the inhuman amount of commitment and pressure we had taken upon ourselves and exercised upon our families. Tender family relationships had been damaged by our private (and sometimes hysterical) efforts to appear as perfect as possible to others, to hide the weaknesses in ourselves and our families. We thought we were failing the Church, and even the Lord Himself, if we didn't always put our "best foot forward."

As I prayed to understand how I had taken yet another gospel principle, in this case the invitation to be perfect extended by the Savior Himself **(Matthew 5:48)**, and turned it into an indictment and sentence of isolation, a most amazing insight began to enlighten me. I saw the truth that when I had come into the Church many years before, I had been in full flight from the "wicked traditions" of my family of origin—their addictions, and the lies they told to cover them. With these addictions and lies, I had brought a sick sort of secrecy with me. I had spent years learning to keep up an outward appearance of "fineness," when in private, everything was chaotic, even traumatic. Once in the Church, and feeling desperately grateful for its miraculous way of life, I desired with all my heart to live up to the lofty standards it invited me to strive for. I wanted to qualify. I wanted to fit in. I wanted to be worthy. I wanted to be accepted. I didn't want anyone to think the Gospel wasn't working, lest they think it wasn't true. And thus, as crazy and paradoxical as it may sound to some, my *loyalty* to the Gospel, combined with my background of hiding the socially unacceptable "stuff" in my family's private life, forged a prison in which I was to live for many years— the emotional prison of looking good on the outside while suffering in a private "hell" within. While "acting as if," I was perpetuating the condition mentioned in **2 Nephi 9:34**:

> **Wo unto the liar, for he shall be thrust down to hell. (2 Nephi 9:34)**

Wo also to the pretender of anything.

WE MUST OPEN A "CORRESPONDENCE."

And behold, I also thank my God, that by opening this correspondence we have been convinced of our sins. (Alma 24:9)

Step Five encourages us to be totally honest with someone besides God. As long as it is only to God that we do our confessing, we are still prey to the lie that if someone else, someone mortal, knew all about us, they would hate us or shun us in revulsion. Also, opening up to another person helps us to be serious about our repentance. We're not just pretending to be clean. We're willing to be *totally* honest now.

As I heard it so aptly put recently,

Some of you know what it is like to do something that makes you feel as if you just drank raw sewage. You can wash but [inside] you can't get clean." (Stephen E. Robinson, "A Practical Approach to the Atonement: Believing Christ," *BYU Magazine, Nov. 1990,* **p. 26)**

Because of my fear of total honesty about my personal life, I went for years at the mercy of the adversary's tactics to make me feel abnormal and exceptional in my hidden weaknesses and foolish mistakes.

I see today, that living in that solitary confinement of self-imposed darkness was one of the greatest deceptions I ever practiced. As the following verse from James indicates, I was cutting myself off from the supportive prayers of my fellow church members:

Confess your faults one to another, and pray one for another, that ye may be healed. (James 5:16)

Instead of this candid, honest spirit of confession of my own humanity, I had assumed a spirit of fear—fear of the judgement of others, fear of not setting a good example as a member of the Church. Even though part of our common covenant at baptism is **"to**

bear one another's burdens" and to **"mourn with those that mourn; yea and comfort those that stand in need of comfort" (Mosiah 18:8–9)**, I still hid behind a "Sunday smile," refusing to allow others to share and bear my greatest burdens and sorrows—my own fears and feelings of inadequacy. I would accept or give a casserole, all the while hiding from myself and others my deepest need to be known and accepted, despite my weaknesses.

As I internalized the principle in Step Five, I faced one of the most terrifying truths I had ever faced. I had to leave all this pretending and pretense behind. I had to become willing to acknowledge and accept my real self, my "compound" self, my *whole* self—shortcomings, foolish choices, imperfect behavior, and all. And like King Benjamin, I had to be willing to be disclosing in public—to confess to others that I am only a **"mortal man,...subject to all manner of infirmities in body and mind" (Mosiah 2:10–11)**.

IT IS THE WEAKNESS WE MUST ADMIT

Many of us, when confronted with Step Five, are petrified at the idea of being 100% self-disclosing, thinking that means we must dredge up and rehearse all the sins we've ever committed. It's understandable that we would think that. Most repentance processes focus on what we have *done*.

In pursuit of a *heart-deep* and mighty change, however, we in Twelve Step recovery work have come to realize that our behaviors, though they must be admitted and amended if they have harmed others (see Steps Eight and Nine), are only the acting out of *beliefs* and *feelings* we harbor in our hearts. It is these "defects of character" that we really need to own and humbly admit. When and where have we been fearful, resentful, selfish, angry, greedy, self-serving, self-righteous, self-willed, or self-pitying? How have these character defects affected those around us?

TO ADMIT WEAKNESS IS NOT A SIN

There are many "philosophies of men" that would encourage us to never speak negatively of ourselves. My question is: what if speaking "negatively" of myself is the equivalent of speaking *honestly* of myself? Isn't admitting that I have allowed an occasional impulse to grow into a habit, and a habit to grow into a compulsive-addictive behavior pattern admitting the truth? Is that a negative act? Does that tear me down? Or does it open my heart and mind to the truth and to the Spirit of Truth, who can then restore me to the ability to repent and forsake my negative habits and acts? I have lived the reality of the latter. Telling the truth about my weaknesses to the Lord and to the appropriate other people has enlisted His power and theirs in overcoming my weaknesses.

To admit no need of repentance to one another, to thus promote a program of perfectionism to one another, instead of promoting Christ's gospel of repentance, is seriously near an anti-Christ position. We, of all people, should desire never to give this impression to each other.

Let not any man publish his own righteousness, for others can see that for him; sooner let him confess his sins, and then he will be forgiven and he will bring forth more fruit. (Joseph Smith, *Teachings of the Prophet Joseph Smith*, p. 194–195)

We often act as if to *admit* imperfection is a sin, but without that admittance we are not ready—not humble and broken-hearted enough—to allow the Savior to serve us in the very way He was sent by the Father to serve us. I humbly confess, today, that in all those years of not admitting to others my need for repentance, I was promoting the fallacy that Christ's gospel is a program of self-sufficiency and self-perfection, when in reality and truth, it is a program of humility, repentance, personal atonement and remission of sin.

And the seed of Israel...stood and confessed their sins, and the iniquities of their fathers. (Nehemiah 9:2)

If we truly desire to be the "seed of Israel" in our inner hearts, as well as in our outward lineage, we must be willing to do this ultimate soul-cleansing act of humility, being willing to be humble, and even humiliated if necessary, before another person as well as before God.

> By this ye may know if a man repenteth of his sins—behold he *will confess them* and forsake them. (D&C 58:43; emphasis added)

RIGOROUS SELF-HONESTY—EVERY PROPHET'S EXAMPLE

It becomes pretty obvious upon examination of the following examples that the Prophet Joseph, as well as many other prophets knew that a gospel of repentance and not of perfection would be needed to redeem God's children, themselves included. They were constantly acknowledging their own need for repentance. They did not desire to be portrayed on pedestals, but rather on their knees.

> I told them I was but a man, and they must not expect me to be perfect,...but if they would bear with my infirmities and the infirmities of the brethren, I would likewise bear with their infirmities." (Andrew Ehat and Lyndon Cook, *The Words of Joseph Smith*, p. 132)

> I love that man better who swears a stream as long as my arm, and administering to the poor & dividing his substance, than the long smoothed faced hypocrites.
> I don't want you to think I am very righteous, for I am not very righteous. (Ehat and Cook, *The Words of Joseph Smith*, p. 204)

The scriptures are full of the humble admissions of frailties of the prophets: Peter, Paul, Amulek, Ammon, Alma, the brother of Jared, just to name a few. There is probably no more plainly written demonstration of a mortal's willingness to be rigorously honest before others than that of Nephi in the "psalm of Nephi" **(2 Nephi 4)**. Here we find Nephi possessed by the desire to be honest and humble, rather than to appear perfect. He is willing to be remembered as a man, wretched and grieved because of his own personal battle with iniquity. He refers to his mortal tendency to be "easily beset" by temptations and sins.

At the end of verse 19, Nephi speaks words that we all should come to rely on: **"Nevertheless, I know in whom I have trusted."**

Without exception we must *all* come to realize that we are *not* more powerful to "mess up" than Christ is to redeem. We must also come to realize that no human power can alleviate our weakness— not our own power, nor that of any other mortal—no matter how brilliant or close to Christ their solutions may be. We can and most certainly should listen to all such wise counsel, but we must remember that we will someday have to take that leap of faith in Christ *for ourselves.* Not my parents', nor my spouse's rebirth and relationship with Jesus will save me. We must each be able to cry out for ourselves, even as Nephi:

> O Lord, I have trusted in thee, and I will trust in thee forever. I will not put my trust in the arm of flesh; for I know that cursed is he that putteth his trust in the arm of flesh. Yea, cursed is he that putteth his trust in man or maketh flesh his arm. (2 Nephi 4:34)

WE MUST GIVE AWAY ALL OUR SINS TO KNOW HIM

When Aaron, who had gone through the process of **"zealously striving to repair *all* the injuries which [he] had done to the church, confessing *all* [his] sins"** (Mosiah 27:35; emphasis added), began to teach Lamoni's father about this great God, even Jesus Christ who would come, who would have power to repair all sin and redeem all who believed on him, the king fell to the earth and prayed:

> O God, Aaron hath told me that there is a God; and if there is a God, and if thou art God, wilt thou make

thyself known unto me, *and I will give away all my sins to know thee.* **(Alma 22:18; emphasis added)**

We too must be willing to "give away all our sins"; to be clean every whit; to let there not be even a corner of our inner souls that we have not let the pure light of truth penetrate and reveal.

And now, my beloved brethren, seeing that our merciful God has given us so great knowledge concerning these things, let us remember him, and lay aside our sins, and not hang down our heads, for we are not cast off. (2 Nephi 10:20)

This is another of the many paradoxical "inside-out" experiences on the journey to eternal life. We struggle for years thinking that if we were to ever give away any knowledge of our weaknesses, we would die of the shame, but instead we find true fellowship with others and true fellowship in Christ by doing so.

CONCLUSION: LETTING GO OF "SICK" SECRETS

And if all of these examples are not enough to convince us that it is in harmony with the principles of the Gospel to be self-disclosing to others about our weaknesses, let us consider the fact that the Lord included this kind of fearless, moral inventory in His purpose for the Sabbath Day:

But remember that on this, the Lord's day, thou shalt offer thine oblations and thy sacraments unto the Most High, *confessing thy sins unto thy brethren,* **and before the Lord. (D&C 59:12; emphasis added)**

Just who the words "thy brethren" refers to in this quote depends upon who our weaknesses and sins have hurt. We have been taught by our Church leaders that any actions involving moral transgression—sexual sin toward our own self or toward another person, abuse of any kind—need to be confessed to our Bishop or Stake President. Other actions that do not threaten our standing in the Church, but which have been unbecoming of a disciple of Christ, may upon prayerful examination be repented of more fully if we admit them to someone in our life who understands our motive for doing a thorough inventory of our character and our past.

Only in **"bringing to light *all* the hidden things of darkness, wherein we know them"** (D&C 123:13; emphasis added) can we find this sense of release, this sense of being emptied in the inner vessel of our hearts and made ready to receive the new birth of the Spirit. We must die as to the old person, as to the "old man," and become a "new creature in Christ," or in other words in the Spirit of Truth, remembering always that Christ and the Truth are synonyms for one another.

No words can describe the feeling that comes over one's soul when one realizes there is not a single conscious thing left inside that is that sick kind of secret. Only the scriptures could come close to describing this kind of joy. My heart thrilled when I read in **1 John 2:8** these words: **"Darkness is past, and the true light now shineth."**

PREPARATION FOR DISCUSSION OF PRINCIPLE SIX: "LET THIS DESIRE WORK IN YOU" (ALMA 32:27)

Step 6: Became humble enough to yield our hearts and our lives to Christ for His sanctification and purification, relying wholly upon His merits, acknowledging even our own best efforts as unprofitable. (Helaman 3:35; 2 Nephi 31:19; Mosiah 2:20–21)

Day 1: 1 Nephi 15:3—**"...and they being hard in their hearts, therefore they did not look unto the Lord as they ought."** When we turn away from the Lord we are easy prey to resentment, fear and anger—the things that harden our hearts. As they increase, our heart is hardened even more, we turn away from God even more, and a spiritually deadly cycle is set up. Write about any experience you've had with this kind of cycle and its effect on your ability to pray.

Day 2: 2 Nephi 4:31—**"O Lord, wilt thou redeem my soul?...Wilt thou make me that I may shake at the *appearance* of sin?"**

These words describe the only *real* remission of sin, of addiction, of compulsion, of a "bad habit." This kind of remission is not just a change of behavior, it is a change of heart, and only God can accomplish it. Write about how you would feel if you were to be *given* this kind of release, this actual abhorrence of what you used to crave doing? Are you willing to ask God for it?

Day 3: **Enos 1:2**—Enos battled with his desires. The God-given freedom from addiction, or change in behavior that we seek, is always preceded by an inner change of heart (or desire). Even though our weaknesses are painful, we often desire to hold on to them because of the *seeming* benefits. Write about the *seemingly* rational reasons why you hold on to a particular weakness.

Day 4: **Alma 12:10**—When our hearts are hard, we are full of self-will and self-sufficiency. Why might God not be able to share the mysteries or deeper knowledge of the gospel with someone who was self–centered? When our hearts become soft, we are full of humility, knowing we cannot change ourselves *by ourselves*. Why do you think God can share the mysteries only with those whose hearts are softened?

Day 5: **Alma 23:7—"They did lay down the weapons of their rebellion, that they did not fight against God anymore."** The weapons of our rebellion against God are our weaknesses or character defects. When we become willing to lay them down before the Lord, then we cease fighting against His will for us. Write about your desire to do the will of the Lord. Is it stronger than your desire to keep your weaknesses?

Day 6: **Alma 24:11—"It was all we could do to repent sufficiently before God that he would take away our stain."** To repent is to regret those things we have done that separate us from God, and to turn to him. Why is to regret and turn again "all" we can really do? Why can't we remove our own stains? Who is it that can?

Day 7: Helaman 3:35—"…even to the purifying and the sanctification of their hearts, which sanctification cometh because of their yielding their hearts unto God." The program these people adopted for the overcoming of their weaknesses was not a quick-fix approach. Write about what they *did* and their *eventual* results. Write about your willingness to abandon all quick-fix solutions and your desire to rely *wholly* on the power of God or merits of Christ.

LET THIS DESIRE WORK IN YOU
(Alma 32:27)

Step Six: Became humble enough to yield our hearts
and our lives to Christ for His sanctification and
purification, relying wholly upon His merits,
acknowledging even our own best efforts as unprofitable.
(Helaman 3:35; 2 Nephi 31:19; Mosiah 2:20–21)

Principle Six: Only a mighty change in my heart,
a complete change of disposition, of desire,
will ensure any genuine change in my behavior.

So much emphasis in our modern culture over the last century
has been placed on changing or eliminating *behavior* by the use of
external controls. Rewards, punishments, conditioning, habits, envi-
ronmental factors—all have been promoted as determining factors
in the way a person behaves. Meanwhile, factors such as *beliefs* and
values, *desires* and *will* are dismissed and ignored. Under the influence of this philosophy, even many well-intentioned church
members have overlooked or doubted the continual testimony of the
prophets, both ancient and modern, that a person's behaviors
(observable actions) arise from what he (or she) thinks **(Matthew
22:42)**, believes **(Mark 9:23)**, feels **(1 Nephi 17:45)**, intends **(Mosiah
4:24–25)**, and most especially, desires **(Alma 19:33; Alma 32:27)**.

I know this was certainly true of myself. Though I read the scriptures, listened to the modern prophets, and knew well the old adage, "A man convinced against his will is of the same opinion still," I believed in and applied the methods of behaviorism, rather than the truths of Christ's gospel. Deeply entrenched in the "creeds" of my own parents about how to relate to and influence others (by using shame, blame, coercion, manipulation and outright force if necessary), I repeated their "style." It didn't matter what the child thought, felt, believed, or desired—just as long as he or she behaved. I acted as if I was entirely ignorant of the scriptural statement that if a gift (even the gift of obedience) is given grudgingly, it does little or no good for either the giver or the receiver **(Moroni 7:8)**.

I concentrated on *doing* right and making my children *do* right, using my parents' methods and resisting the counsel of the Lord that persuasion, long-suffering, gentleness, meekness, love unfeigned, kindness, and pure knowledge were recommended seven to one over "reproving with sharpness" **(D&C 121:41-43)**. In our home, the ratio was reversed. Sharpness ruled, and there was no thought to consult the Holy Ghost before administering it. Even though we kept up appearances before others and our church attendance "statistics" were high, there was no internal change. Force in all its subtle and outright abusive forms was making a mockery of the truth. We were a troubled, unhappy, "house of strangers," recreating yet another generation of lonely, confused and needy people— church attendance or not—who were sitting ducks for the escape of addiction.

AGENCY: THE HIGHEST TRUTH—THE HARDEST TRUTH

Which gospel principle did I ignore, as I exerted my dominion and enforced my stewardship through unrighteous, un-Christlike means? Agency, of course.

I have to admit, I do not know how Heavenly Father deals with the sorrow generated by this principle. I can only guess that agency must be a principle central to His own eternal progression—one of the principles upon which He attained His exaltation.

There are several places in the scriptures that testify to us that in this business of choice, it is not His will, but our own that is ultimately the "bottom line." We choose what we *will*. It is our will that is final. We get what we truly desire **(Mosiah 26:26, Alma 29:4; Helaman 3:27; D&C 88:32)**.

Agency is the supreme governing law of all eternal progression. It can never be abdicated or controlled with any degree of righteousness. Even God, who cannot look upon unrighteousness with the least degree of allowance (Alma 45:16), cannot cross another's agency in the least degree. He cannot control His children by compulsion or force, not even to achieve His own greatest desire for each of us—to see us become both immortal *and exalted* **(Moses 1:39)**.

> Wherefore the voice of the Lord is unto the ends of the earth, that all that *will* hear may hear. (D&C 1:11; emphasis added)

> Yea, we see that whosoever *will* may lay hold upon the word of God, which is quick and powerful, which shall divide asunder all the cunning and the snares and the wiles of the devil, and lead the man of Christ in a strait and narrow course across that everlasting gulf of misery which is prepared to engulf the wicked...(Helaman 3:29; emphasis added)

> And then shall they know that I am the Lord their God, that I am their Redeemer; but they would not be redeemed. (Mosiah 26:26)

> And they who remain shall also be quickened; nevertheless, they shall return again to their own place, to enjoy that which they are willing to receive, because they were not *willing* to enjoy that which they might have received. (D&C 88:32; emphasis added)

To realize that our own will, our own agency, is actually the supreme last word in what we receive (both from day-to-day and in eternity) can be freeing, but it can also be condemning. Why? Because it means that, just as the prophets have taught, our life is less about what happens to us and more about the way we choose to respond to what happens.

> **Behold, here is the agency of man, and here is the condemnation of man; because that which was from the beginning is plainly manifest unto them, and they receive not the light. (D&C 93:31)**

Someday, for all of us, without exception, our excuses will run out. "I behaved this way because..." will have to be seen as the truth: "I *chose* to behave this way because..." And as incredulous as it may sound, it implies that in nothing, *absolutely nothing*, can we consider ourselves victims.

You may ask in shock, In nothing? How can you say that, when children are abused? And what about the abuse the mentally and physically handicapped, the aged and infirm suffer at the hands of their caretakers? How could you consider them anything but victims? *How could you believe them to be consenting participants?*

The answer, especially seen in the light of the Restored Gospel, stands like a solid granite monolith rising from the fog of mortality, piercing the veil between each stage of eternal progression—*in absolutely nothing are we forced, coerced or manipulated.* This answer is found in careful, prayerful and sincere study of the scriptures and modern prophets. It comes as a personal witness from the Lord to our hearts.

As we allow the beautiful story of the Restored Gospel to become a living history of our own *infinite* reality, we realize that from an eternal perspective, nothing happens by mistake **(Genesis 45:5–8)**, or without the participant's voluntary cooperation **(Abraham 3:27; Isaiah 6:8)**. While it is true that our voluntary consent was given in a veiled and forgotten premortal council, the Holy Ghost can part that veil and confirm this use of our agency to us.

What does this mean to me, as someone who was abused in childhood? It means that I counseled with God and participated in determining my family assignment and birth position, knowing there would be a variety of possible scenarios my life could take, depending upon the choices of those who would serve in this life as my parents, siblings, extended family and so on. It was very likely explained to me that if my parents *chose* to seek God and to live guided by His light, my childhood experiences could be a great blessing to me. If my parents chose differently, my life experiences could be a great challenge. I understood this and I accepted the risk.

Because God's plan is (and *must* always be) based on agency, there are always risks, variables, the possibility that others will make wrong choices, even if we don't. From a premortal vantage point, I knew, as we all did, that allowing individual agency to choose its own course always involves this risk—our loved ones, our caretakers, will be allowed to make wrong choices. Satan knew that, too. He wanted a plan without risk—and he wanted all the glory (**Moses 4:1**).

The difference between one plan and the other can be illustrated by picturing two sheepherders. One has all his sheep bound about the neck, trudging along, tied together like a dog team. The other acts as a shepherd—gently, patiently, long-suffering guiding his flock along, making allowance for their freedom, taking time to go back and search out the lost ones, redeeming and repairing the inevitable injuries.

SERENITY TO ACCEPT WHAT I CANNOT CHANGE

What does all this have to do with the sixth principle? *Everything!* Before God can apply His atoning power—His power to make us one with God, with the fellowship of God and Christ—we must *want* Him to. We must be *willing* to be so changed. <u>*Our will is the determining factor in any change we make, for ill or good*</u>.

> I ought not to harrow up in my desires, the firm decree of a just God, for I know that he granteth unto men *according to their desire,* whether it be unto death or unto life; yea, I know that he allotteth unto men, yea, decreeth unto them decrees which are unalterable, *according to their wills,* whether they be unto salvation or unto destruction. (Alma 29:4; emphasis added)

Let me say it again: our will is the determining factor. It is the bottom line. It is the final word. Often we hear the saying "God grant me the serenity to accept the things I cannot change." That serenity will come to each of us only when we realize that "the things we cannot change" are things we already agreed to in the premortal life, and thus, even in those things we are not being subjected or victimized.

With this realization comes the freedom to hold up our heads with dignity, to step free of the anger, the blame, the shame. We are not victims. We never were. We are conquering heroes and heroines, given nothing we are not equal to *in Christ.* Do you realize what that says about some people's spiritual powers—their ability to connect with and draw on the powers of heaven?

Just ask them (or yourself), "How deep did you descend into a world of darkness and sin as an innocent child? How much were you abused? How much have you, in reaction, abused yourself?" Then with that sad and sometimes terrifying vision so well described in **D&C 123:13, 7** of **"the hidden things of darkness... urged on and upheld by the influence of that spirit which hath so strongly riveted the creeds of the fathers, who have inherited lies, upon the hearts of the children"** still fresh in your mind, declare the good news of the gospel of Christ to them or to yourself. Pray about this truth, seek its confirmation: know that you have the strength spiritually, in direct and more than equal proportion, to rise above that abuse—*if you desire it.* Remember, He will not and *cannot* **(D&C 121:41)** force this good news upon you.

GOD CAN ONLY OFFER YOU HIS WORD

"You'll have to take my word for it." We've all heard that phrase before. All too often, however, we want *more* than another person's word for something; we want proof. And so it is in our attitude toward God and His word. We resist His word to us, wanting proof before we trust Him, thus resisting the eternal process of the seed of faith becoming the tree of knowledge.

Through modern revelation we are taught that while it is absolutely true that God has *all* power both in time and eternity, He will wield that power only in obedience to the principles of righteousness. He cannot force more light and knowledge on us than we are willing and spiritually ready to receive. Thus His word, either written in scripture or whispered directly to your heart and mind through the Holy Spirit, is *all* He can rightfully offer you. In no way can He righteously "control" you. He revealed this truth to us when He allowed these words to be penned:

> **No power or influence *can* or ought to be maintained by virtue of the priesthood, only by persuasion, by long–suffering. (D&C 121:41; emphasis added)**

If we had a heart to understand the true character of God, we would hear in these words the admission of a gentle, tender, loving, patient Father—that He suffers for our choices and sorrows at our rejection of Him. If we were wise, we would realize that He has just shown us one of His limitations—maybe His *only* one. He *cannot force* another.

> **For they *cannot* be redeemed from their spiritual fall, because they repent not. (D&C 29:44; emphasis added)**

Even when He "commands" the tiny intelligences which modern prophets have taught us give life and motive to the atomic structure of earth and air, He must wait upon their obedience. He does not have to wait long, however, for they obey Him immediately **(Helaman 12:7–13)**. Why? Because they love and trust Him explicitly—*in all things*. It is this same kind of absolute letting go and trusting of God in *all* things, going to any length to obey His word, that marks the *mighty* change of heart we must all experience.

And so He speaks to us through his prophets, through men and women who have gone before us into *certainty*, who call back to us, inviting us, even as He invites us, to come and partake. He speaks to us directly through the Light of Christ, and if we are willing to receive it, through the gift of the Holy Ghost. But He only whispers. His communication is still and small, so easily ignored or disbelieved. Listen to Alma's words:

> **Now, we will compare the word unto a seed. Now, *if ye give place*, that a seed may be planted in your heart, behold, if it be a true seed, or a good seed, *if ye do not cast it out by your unbelief*, that *ye* will resist the Spirit of the Lord, behold, it will begin to swell within your breasts... (Alma 32:28; emphasis added)**

In a powerful Sunday School manual, *Teach Them Correct Principles*, on page 24, we find these words under the heading "The Heart of the Matter":

> **A person, and especially one who has been commanded to receive the Holy Ghost, must *actively resist* the promptings of the Spirit in order not to have the Spirit strive with him. (John 13:2, 26–30; Alma 3:26, D&C 11:25; emphasis added)**

We must acknowledge the truth that we are all "hearing" the "voice" of the Spirit all the time, either through the Light of Christ, which is our "conscience" and which has been with us since we entered into this world; or through the magnified and enhanced Gift of the Holy Ghost. If we do not hear it, it is not because we *cannot*, but because we *will* not. We are even as these people:

> **But there were many among them *who would not* hear his words; therefore they went their way. (Alma 19:32; emphasis added)**

It is our own vanity or unbelief in God's mercy and goodness—that it should include even *us*—that causes us to resist turning to Him, and to instead go our own way. In our prideful, willful hearts, we are so vain as to imagine ourselves more powerful to mess up than God is to make right; we imagine ourselves somehow beyond the power of Christ's atonement. Thus, no matter what we profess with our lips, claiming belief in Christ, we deny Him in the single most personal way we can—for ourselves.

But if we will finally give up this perverse form of pride and prejudice, if we will finally give place in our hearts to receive the word of God—especially directly—then we can trust that what Alma promises will happen:

> **And when you feel these swelling motions, ye will begin to say within yourselves—It must be that this is a good seed, or that the word is good, for it beginneth to enlarge my soul; yea, it beginneth to enlighten my understanding, yea, it beginneth to be delicious to me. (Alma 32:28)**

CONCLUSION: ONLY WHEN WE'RE READY

When Lehi clung to the rod of iron, which represented the *word of God*, he was eventually led to the tree of life, which represented the *love of God*, and once tasting it, he exclaimed that it was **"sweet, above all that** [he] **ever before tasted" (1 Nephi 8:11)**. There is nothing as sweet and delicious to the experience of man than this coming to God. No amount of food, money to spend, or physical demonstration of desire or affection from another mortal can even hint at it **(1 Corinthians 2:9)**.

When something is "delicious" to people, that means they have acquired a "taste" for it. Their likes, their *desires*, have changed. They have become entirely ready to be different. Only when we are *ready* can God begin His work with us.

PREPARATION FOR DISCUSSION OF PRINCIPLE SEVEN: "AND NEVER, UNTIL I DID CRY OUT" (ALMA 38:8)

Step 7:   Humbly cried unto the Lord Jesus Christ in our hearts for a remission of sins that through His mercy and His grace we might experience a mighty change of heart, lose all disposition to do evil, and thus be encircled about in the arms of safety because of His great and last sacrifice. (Alma 36:18; Alma 38:8; Moroni 10:32; Mosiah 5:2; Alma 34:15–16)

Day 1:   **1 Nephi 14:1–2—"He shall manifest himself unto them...in power...unto the taking away of their stumbling blocks."** If we will turn to the Lamb of God and not harden our hearts against Him, He will manifest Himself unto us by using His infinite and yet gentle power to remove our stumbling blocks. Nothing has been more of a stumbling block to me over the years than my tendency to feel sorry for myself and think I have to take out my "weapons" (anger, sarcasm) to defend myself. I have witnessed God cleansing me of this tendency more in the last three years than I was ever able to accomplish on my own in the previous 25 years. Write a letter to your Heavenly Father or the Savior, expressing your desire to be healed by *Him* rather than by your own efforts.

Day 2:   **Mosiah 4:10**—Sometimes we pray for forgiveness, but the sincerity isn't totally there. Write about a prayer in your past that you realize now wasn't totally sincere, even though you went through the motions of offering it to God.

Day 3:   **Mosiah 4:21**—This verse tells us that God will grant unto us whatsoever we ask that is right. Is it right to ask God to change our hearts? Is it necessary? (See **Mosiah 5:2** and **Alma 5:7**.)

Day 4:   **3 Nephi 27:28–29**—In whose name must we ask for this great change? Why?

Day 5: **Alma 36:18**—*Who* will cleanse us? Does it bother you to think of approaching Christ directly for this blessing of healing as Alma did? Write about your feelings as you ponder this need to literally "come unto Christ."

Day 6: **D&C 10:21**—According to this verse, what often stops people from asking God for what they need? Knowing (or thinking) that our deeds are, or have been evil, stops us from approaching the Lord—yet who needs Him more? Write about how much you need Him today, and whether guilt is keeping you from reaching out to Him.

Day 7: **Mosiah 7:33**—Once we have asked to be healed (cleansed), whose timetable must we be willing to trust? What do you think the Lord's "own good will and pleasure" is? (See **Moses 1:39** for a clue.) Can you think of some reasons why His timetable is usually so slow and patient, while ours is so "quick fix" and impatient?

AND NEVER, UNTIL I DID CRY OUT
(Alma 38:8)

Step Seven: Humbly cried unto the Lord Jesus Christ in our hearts for a remission of sins that through His mercy and His grace we might experience a mighty change of heart, lose all disposition to do evil, and thus be encircled about in the arms of safety because of His great and last sacrifice. (Alma 36:18; Alma 38:8; Moroni 10:32; Mosiah 5:2; Alma 34:15–16)

Principle Seven: The mighty change of heart is a gift from God that I must desire and ask for.

Wouldn't it be wonderful to stop overeating simply because you have no more desire to do it? Wouldn't it be a miracle if you could stop losing your temper, not because you bit your tongue or went somewhere alone and slugged a pillow, but because you have no more disposition to strike out at others? Wouldn't it be wonderful if you could live on a budget, not because you had no charge cards, but because you didn't desire to overuse them? Or to stop looking at pornography on the Internet, not because you've installed a content filter or cancelled your service, but because you have no more desire to look at it. And finally, to return to the place where Twelve Step recovery began—wouldn't it be wonderful to know that "peace which passeth understanding" **(Philippians 4:7)** which takes away all desire to use alcohol or drugs. No longer do any of us need to run from life, but we can face and embrace *the Life*—even the gift of Christ's coming into our lives.

In the very first discussion we considered these questions:

Do you have a problem? An insurmountable problem of any nature? Is there some aspect of your life in which you are out of control, unable to "govern" yourself or your life? Is it alcohol or some other drug, legal or illegal? Is it a compulsive sexual behavior pattern? Is it your weight or a disordered behavior towards food and eating? Is it compulsive use of money? Or excessive work commitments that consume you and your family's lives? Or is your downfall a desperate obsession with trying to help and control and fix other people and their mistakes, cover all their needs or die trying?

These questions were previously asked with the hope they would focus our longing, the very *desires of our hearts*, on finding and beginning to practice the eternal principles that could bring us solutions. Then we began this course of study, discussing and hopefully acting on twelve powerfully correct principles.

We are halfway through that course and find ourselves being challenged to be humble once again; to relinquish once and for all any thought that we can perfect or even improve ourselves, and then to *ask God* to remove our weaknesses.

PRIDE—THE UNIVERSAL SIN

The reason there is so much resistance in the mortal character to this idea of reliance on God can be summed up in one word: *pride*. As President Benson so bluntly put it, **"there is no such thing as righteous pride" (Ensign, May 1989, p. 4)**. Let me reiterate: *No such thing*.

Step Seven is a call to another level of inventory, even deeper than Step Four—the deepest one yet. This principle asks us to lay our heart bare and open its very core to the Lord, so He can reveal to us the subtle way pride keeps us separated from Him. Pride is the **"universal sin,"** and represents, in all its forms, nothing less than **"enmity toward God and our fellowmen"** (Ezra T. Benson, *Ensign*, May 1989, p. 4). It is in every mortal heart in some form.

This is pretty strong language, but then this is a pretty powerful principle—this humbly asking God to change our whole character; to burn us clean of the last vestiges of self-will and self-importance and to make us new creatures in Christ **(2 Corinthians 5:17)**, still ourselves, but now one with Christ.

"But I only want to do it myself. I mean, shouldn't I do everything I can to make sure I need as little of Christ's atonement as possible?" If we were truly fearless in facing the deepest implications of this cherished train of thought, we would see that it is the same as saying: "And if I could be *really* successful at this determination to keep myself on the straight and narrow, I wouldn't have need of *any* of His sacrifice at all." Admirable attitude or anti-Christ?

Where do we get the power to face our pride, to search it out and let it go? From the same Source as all other power to do good—from God.

> I thank my great God that he has given us a portion of his Spirit to soften our hearts.
> And I also thank my God, yea my great God, that he hath granted unto us that we might repent of these things, and also that he hath forgiven us...and taken away the guilt from our hearts, through the merits of his Son. (Alma 24:8, 10)

The antidote for pride is the same as for guilt: to come to Christ and seek His Spirit, His counsel, His grace.

THE RESULT OF THIS TOTAL HUMILITY

What happens when we are finally willing to admit that *only* God has the power and *only* God deserves the glory for our redemption; when we finally stop trying to fix ourselves and turn our lives, weaknesses and all, over to Him? Listen to the very promise of God Himself, implicit in His charge to us to **"harden not** [our] **hearts against the Lamb of God"** (1 Nephi 14:2):

> **He shall manifest himself unto them in word, and also in power, in very deed,** *unto the taking away of their stumbling blocks.* **(1 Nephi 14:1; emphasis added)**

What does it mean to have Christ manifest Himself unto us in (1) word, (2) power and (3) in very deed? I believe it means that (1) we will begin to hear His words in personal revelation to teach us our weaknesses; (2) we will be given *His* power to transform these weaknesses into strengths; and (3) we will see the effect of this change in our inner self in the **"very deed[s]"** of our lives **(Ether 12:27)**.

The changing of our deeds will be an automatic result of the first two portions of this process:

(1) receiving His word—

> **Counsel with the Lord in all thy doings, and he will direct thee for good (Alma 37:37)**

(2) receiving His power—

> **And again, if ye by the grace of God are perfect in Christ, and deny not his power, then are ye become holy, without spot. (Moroni 10:33)**

In fact, through this process we can come to the place that we can **"shake at the appearance of sin,"** the very sin that we once embraced.

> **O Lord, wilt thou redeem my soul? Wilt thou deliver me out of the hands of mine enemies? Wilt thou make me that I may shake at the appearance of sin? (2 Nephi 4:31)**

This change of character, inclination—our very neuropathways—that causes us to "shake at the appearance of sin" is a gift from God. On our own, the best we can accomplish is a sort of "white knuckle," uptight feeling of resistance to our desire to sin. The *fact* is that internally, nothing has been changed, and we still want to "do it" (whatever our sin is) just one more time. This state of constant struggle is not the best we can hope for. Life was not meant to be a long, slow, torturous journey of constant tension, fear and guilt. A God-given remission of sins (in contrast to a self-imposed, self-powered effort) brings periods of unspeakable peace and comfort, best described as the "rest of the Lord."

> **Therefore, whosoever repenteth, and hardeneth not his heart, he shall have claim on mercy through mine Only Begotten Son, unto a remission of his sins; and these shall enter into my rest. (Alma 12:34)**

Many people interpret the expression "enter into my rest" as a promise of heaven after we die. It is not the Lord's will, however, that we must wait until death to receive Him and His peace. Listen to His promise of the coming of "heaven" within you, right here and now, as soon as you have transferred your hope to Him:

> **Wherefore I would speak unto...the peaceable followers of Christ, [ye who] have obtained a sufficient hope by which ye can enter into the rest of the Lord, *from this time henceforth*. (Moroni 7:3; emphasis added)**

WHAT CAN WE DO TO FIND "HIS REST"?

The answer is not new. *Repent!* Truly repent.

"But I have!" we cry. "Over and over again I make the resolve to stop this addiction, this sin, this destructive action, but I can't sustain my resolve."

You're right. You can't. Why? Because as noble as all those re-starts are—they are not true repentance, but only half-measures, as evidenced by the return to sin (**D&C 58:43**). True and total repentance doesn't merely involve turning away from sin. True repentance must also involve turning to God. It takes exercising faith in His atoning power to redeem and repair us.

Faith is a principle of action. We must take action in order to have faith take deep root in us. As we act in faith—in Christ—we are empowered to continue to respond righteously. True faith, combined with true repentance, is internalizing and living by the very principles we have discussed so far. It is coming down into the depths of humility **(2 Nephi 9:42)**; admitting our nothingness without God **(Mosiah 4:5, Moses 1:10)**; acknowledging that He has *all* power both in heaven *and* on earth **(Mosiah 4:9)**; and being humble and **"in a preparation to hear the word" (Alma 32:6)**.

This course of ever-deepening humility, of a willingness to acknowledge that all power and all glory for all good works belongs to the Father and the Son, is in truth and reality, **"all that we** [can] **do" (Alma 24:11)**. And it will bring forth the grace of Christ.

We must become so humble that we realize we are relying **"*wholly* upon the merits of** [Christ]**" (2 Nephi 31:19**; emphasis added). We must awaken to the fact that Christ's contribution to this effort is so much greater in comparison to ours that it can truly be said that we are **"relying *alone*"** upon His merits **(Moroni 6:4; emphasis added)**.

> Yea, humble yourselves, and continue in prayer unto him. (Alma 34:19)

Once we have done all we can to humble ourselves and continue in prayer, we can then trust His word that we actually have a "claim" upon Him for this mighty change:

> **Therefore, whosoever repenteth, and hardeneth not his heart, he shall have claim on mercy through mine Only Begotten Son, unto a remission of sins; and these shall enter into my rest. (Alma 12:34)**

We have **"claim on mercy"** but *we* must choose to exercise that claim.

WE MUST ASK

While it is incorrect to ask without taking any thought beforehand **(D&C 9:7)**, that does not describe the circumstances of someone who has sincerely pursued this course of study and action to this point. This is the point at which it is absolutely appropriate and *essential* to ask God.

God will always respect our will. He will send the Holy Spirit to guide us. He may inspire others to help us. Over and over, He will attempt to persuade us to His truth, but He will do nothing to, or even *for*, us without our permission, without our consent. He will never force us. We can trust this eternal truth. I believe that if we cannot remember giving permission for certain circumstances to occur in our life, we can remind ourselves that we don't remember all there is to remember. And we can *know* that He does nothing against our will.

He will not even help us against our will. We must ask.

> If ye cannot understand [these words] it will be because ye ask not, neither do ye knock. (2 Nephi 32:4)

We have His own promise:

> For every one that asketh, receiveth; and he that seeketh, findeth; and to him that knocketh, it shall be opened. (3 Nephi 14:8)

We need not fear that He will not answer or that we're asking for something amiss. He *will* answer because He loves us.

> Or what man is there of you, who, if his son ask bread, will give him a stone? Or if he ask a fish, will he give him a serpent? If ye then, being evil, know how to give good gifts unto your children, how much more shall your Father who is in heaven give good things to them that ask him? (3 Nephi 14:9–11)

EXAMPLES FROM THE SCRIPTURES

And my soul hungered; and I kneeled down before my Maker, and I cried unto him in mighty prayer and supplication for mine own soul; and all the day long did I cry unto him; yea, and when the night came I did still raise my voice high that it reached the heavens.

And there came a voice unto me, saying: Enos, thy sins are forgiven thee, and thou shalt be blessed.

And I, Enos, knew that God could not lie; wherefore, my guilt was swept away. (Enos 1:4–6)

And they had viewed themselves in their own carnal state, even less than the dust of the earth. And they all cried aloud with one voice, saying: O have mercy, and apply the atoning blood of Christ that we may receive forgiveness of our sins, and our hearts may be purified. (Mosiah 4:2)

And it came to pass that as I was thus racked with torment, while I was harrowed up by the memory of my many sins, behold, I remembered...the coming of one Jesus Christ.

Now, as my mind caught hold upon this thought, I cried within my heart: O Jesus, thou Son of God, have mercy on me. (Alma 36:17–18)

I was...in the most bitter pain and anguish of soul; *and never, until I did cry out unto the Lord Jesus Christ for mercy, did I receive a remission of my sins. But behold, I did cry unto him and I did find peace to my soul.* (Alma 38:8; emphasis added)

WE MUST ASK AND THEN TRUST GOD'S TIMETABLE

Sometimes we get caught up in our own "all or nothing" perception of perfection, totally forgetting that becoming perfect is a *process*. God wants us to become perfect, but not any faster than we can *genuinely* do so. He has some pretty tough words to say about "acting as if."

To "act as if" might be a good temporary tactic, but it cannot be a permanent resort. "Acting as if" is the equivalent of "being willing to be willing." It is not capable of sustaining any long-term change or maintaining a change under severe stress. Eventually we must all come to a place where we aren't just "acting as if," but actually being genuine in our motivation.

> **For if [a man] offereth a gift or prayeth unto God, except he shall do it with real intent it profiteth him nothing. For behold, it is not counted unto him as righteousness. For behold, if a man being evil giveth a gift, he doeth it grudgingly; wherefore it is counted unto him the same as if he had retained the gift. (Moroni 7:6–8)**

> **For it is not requisite that a man should run faster than he has strength. (Mosiah 4:27)**

And thus God does not grant us a greater degree of recovery until we are ready for it. He knows and sees far more than we do, and we gave Him permission to direct and conduct our lives while we are under this veil of forgetfulness. We have forgotten the eternal principles that motivated us to take on the challenge and pain of this mortal life—but He hasn't. We gave Him permission to guide our lives by these principles, even when we kick and scream at Him for doing so.

> **But if ye will turn to the Lord with full purpose of heart, and put your trust in him, and serve him with all diligence of mind, if ye do this, he will, according to his own will and pleasure, deliver you out of bondage. (Mosiah 7:33)**

What is His will and pleasure? It is the same as His work and his glory—to bring to pass our immortality and eternal life (Moses 1:39). We can trust that that is what *everything* is for. We can trust Him and thank Him in *all* things **(Mosiah 7:33, D&C 59:7).**

CONCLUSION: WE CAN TRUST THE PROCESS

Let us come again to that very same conclusion that we have come to in every lesson—*Christ*. Christ is the answer, He is the solution, and He is the conclusion. He is both the **"author and finisher of** [our] **faith" (Moroni 6:4)**, the beginning and the end of our recovery from any compulsion or addiction. Our hope is bright only in Him and in His own words to us:

> **For it is I that taketh upon me the sins of the world. (Mosiah 26:23)**

> **Yea, and as often as my people repent will I forgive them their trespasses against me. (Mosiah 26:30)**

We can trust the process. It's not a process of beeline perfection. It's a process of learning by our own experience the good from the evil. It isn't how many times we fall down that counts. *It's how many times we get up.*

ASSIGNMENT FOR THIS WEEK:

Read "Beauty for Ashes, the Atonement of Jesus Christ," by Bruce C. Hafen (*Ensign*, April 1990) or "A Practical Approach to the Atonement: Believing in Christ," by Stephen E. Robinson (*BYU Today*, Nov. 1990). Capture in writing at least one thought from either of these articles and come willing to share it with the group next week. (Or at least be willing to be willing!)

PREPARATION FOR DISCUSSION OF PRINCIPLE EIGHT: "THEY BURIED [THEIR] WEAPONS OF WAR, FOR PEACE" (ALMA 24:19)

Step 8:   Made a list of all persons we had harmed and became willing to make restitution to all of them (even those we had harmed in what we might have considered righteous anger), desiring instead to be peacemakers and to do all that we could to come unto God by being first reconciled to others. (3 Nephi 12:9; 3 Nephi 12:24; 3 Nephi 12:44–45)

Day 1: **1 Nephi 7:21**—We too must **"frankly forgive them all that they** [have] **done."** Usually when we have harmed someone else, we feel that we are justified in doing so. We rationalize our behavior to ourselves. Someone once said that the word "rationalize" could be broken into the two words: *rational/lies*. Write about someone you have hurt, and why you felt justified in doing so.

Day 2: **Mosiah 26:29–30**—We already considered this scripture in the context of the fifth principle as we discussed the need to confess to another person. Now let's think of it in terms of repenting in the "sincerity" of our heart. How would being willing to actually go and make restitution to all others demonstrate our sincerity?

Day 3: **Alma 7:15**—This verse tells us that baptism is one way that we **"show unto** [our] **God that** [we] **are willing to repent."** How is being willing to make restitution to others another powerful way to "show unto your God that ye are willing to repent"? (See **Matthew 5:23–24**.)

Day 4: **Alma 24:18–19**—**"…it being in their view a testimony to God, and also to men, that they never would use weapons again."** When we are finally humble enough to go to all persons we have harmed and acknowledge our part of the past pain and conflict, we are laying down our weapons of war. Why is it important that we carry through with this public action, rather than just saying to ourselves and God that we're sorry and letting "bygones be bygones"? Do the words of this scripture, **"a testimony to God, and also to men,"** give us a clue?

Day 5: **Alma 27:29**—**"They would suffer death…before they would take** [up] **the sword."** When we go to others to make amends or restitution for past wrongs, we must be willing to suffer their rejection, even if it makes us feel like we're going to die. This willingness is part of going down into the very *depths* of humility to be made whole. Do you have anyone on your list that you fear will reject or belittle your efforts to make peace? If so, write about them and about whether you feel that their negative reaction is more important than your life being cleansed of regret and pain.

Day 6: **3 Nephi 12:9—"Blessed are all the peacemakers."** Our physical parents pass on physical traits to us. When we are born again we become the children of Christ, and we inherit or are blessed with His godly traits. Most of us have been involved in the lifelong business of trying to *make* ourselves have these traits. Write about the blessing it would be in your life to *be* a peacemaker through the power of Christ.

Day 7: **3 Nephi 12:23–24—"If ye shall come unto me,...first be reconciled to thy brother."** Until we are able to make amends, our hearts are not able to completely center on the Lord. Instead they wander, due to the unresolved pain we have received from or given to others. When we become "reconciled" (friendly or settled) with our "brothers," then more and more of our hearts and the purpose of our hearts can be given to the Lord. Write about how past hurt causes you to separate yourself from the Lord.

THEY BURIED [THEIR] WEAPONS OF WAR, FOR PEACE
(Alma 24:19)

Step Eight: Made a list of all persons we had harmed and became willing to make restitution to all of them (even those we had harmed in what we might have considered righteous anger), desiring instead to be peacemakers and to do all that we could to come unto God by being first reconciled to others.
(3 Nephi 12:9; 3 Nephi 12:24; 3 Nephi 12:44–45)

Principle Eight: The mighty change of heart brings a willingness to make amends for all past wrongs, to seek a spirit of peace and oneness with everyone, including those I have hurt or been hurt by.

First a few words about *willingness*. In the last discussion we emphasized the place of *willing action* in our recovery. In this discussion we acknowledge that our willingness usually precedes a change of action. First our belief and our will changes, then—sometimes quickly, sometimes gradually—our actions change.

Meanwhile, we have a tendency to demean and underestimate the power of simply being *willing* to do something. For example, take a morning in which our teenagers sleep in *again*. When we finally discover them amidst the bedclothes an hour after school has started and awaken them, they moan woefully, "I meant to get up. I *really* did." We often reprimand them disbelievingly.

We have been taught to scorn the small, delicate, trembling honesty of such a lament and reply sternly, "Well, that's fine that you *wanted* to get up, but where's the action? Don't forget that the road to hell is paved with good intentions." Then, as if that isn't enough of a put-down, we are sure to also remind them that "faith without works is dead."

Thus we slam and slander the very beginnings of a soul's potential change. Good intent, willingness—these are not always enough for us. But should they be? We would be wise to learn how God feels about intentions and willingness, even when they are still so small as to be only the embryo of change.

Speaking to those who *wanted* to give to others but were too poor at the time to do so, King Benjamin taught these words:

> **I would that ye say in your hearts that: I give not because I have not, but if I had I would give.**
> **And now, if ye say this in your hearts ye remain guiltless. (Mosiah 4:24–25)**

Those of us who discourage and dishearten others, as well as ourselves, by turning the scriptural statement "Faith without works is dead" into an instrument of shame need to be taught and never forget that as far as the Lord is concerned, *works without faith are just as dead.* In language too plain to mistake, Moroni conveyed God's feelings about works that are done grudgingly:

> **For behold, God hath said a man being evil** [in a state of not being genuinely willing to do God's will] **cannot do that which is good** [he can go through the motions but in truth, his actions are empty]**; for if he offereth a gift, or prayeth unto God, except he shall do it with real intent it profiteth him nothing. For behold, it is not counted unto him for righteousness. (Moroni 7:6–7)**

It appears that God holds the willingness to do something in a lot higher regard than we do. Often I have heard myself say to my children as they complain that they don't want to do something, "I didn't ask you to want to do it. I just asked you to *do* it." I have thought myself so clever to come up with such a smart answer. (We would do well to always examine an answer that feels "smart.") In this case, for instance, I was displaying an appalling lack of understanding of God's ways. Truly, when the day comes that we can honestly say, "I'm willing," the heavens rejoice over us, for they know we have finally come to the "winter solstice" of our life. From that hour our days will get warmer and brighter as the light of God's Son increases daily. The heavens have known all along that the power of God was not waiting as much for us to become worthy, as for us to become willing.

The power in being willing cannot be stressed enough. Sincere willingness is the equivalent of the "mustard seed" beginning of faith in Christ's own parable, and the flickering spark of desire that Alma claimed as the nearly invisible beginning of a mighty change. Let's look at what they both had to say.

> **And Jesus said unto them, Because of your unbelief: for verily I say unto you, If ye have faith as a grain of mustard seed, ye shall say unto this mountain, Remove hence to yonder place; and it shall remove; *and nothing shall be impossible unto you.* (Matthew 17:20; emphasis added)**

> **But behold, if ye will awake and arouse your faculties, even to an experiment upon my words, and exercise a particle of faith, yea, *even if ye can no more than desire to believe,* let this desire work in you, even until ye believe in a manner that ye can give place for a portion of my words. (Alma 32:27; emphasis added)**

Ultimately, it is in the sacrament prayer that willingness is given its rightful place of preeminence:

> ...that they may eat in remembrance of the body of thy
> Son, and witness unto thee, O God, the Eternal Father,
> *that they are willing* to take upon them the name of thy
> Son. (Moroni 4:3; emphasis added)

WILLINGNESS TO BE HEALED—TO ONE ANOTHER

When the Lord walked upon the earth during His mortal
ministry there was never a shortage of people willing to have Him
heal them physically. They sought Him everywhere, even lowering
their sick down through the roof of a building where He sought
respite. They pressed Him on every side and dogged his every step,
until the middle of the Sea of Galilee became His only sure refuge.

Meanwhile, Jesus tried with all His heart to play down the
physical side of his healing powers, to emphasize that the physical
was only symbolic of the far more significant healing of heart and
mind. Few would listen to Him. Even many of His apostles thought
that when He spoke of redeeming and restoring Israel, He meant
that He would free them politically from the tyranny of Rome.

As typical mortals, we tend to see things the same way. We think
that to be healed in body is sufficient for our needs. If everything is
going well in our lives temporally, we have a tendency to be content
and even complacent toward things of the spirit. As the old saying
goes, "Out of sight, out of mind."

Despite the people's clamor and insistence on physical relief,
Christ was sent to offer us a spiritual healing, a oneness and whole-
ness with God. Becoming reconciled to God and at peace and
oneness with His mind and will is to become whole again on a scale
we can hardly comprehend. It means not only to become one with
the Father, the Son, and the Holy Spirit, but also one with all those
with whom they hold communion. It is to become one with the
fellowship of Christ, a fellowship that includes every willing,
obedient intelligence, from the smallest atomic particle to the most
complex and greatest of all, even God. Once in this fellowship, once

conscious of it, a person is never alone again and is always aware of God's encircling presence and power.

Wouldn't you think that people would flock to the chance to be so restored, to be reunited with such a degree of power and peace? What would stop them? What would stop us? If Christ held out to you the riches of eternity (and He does), what would stop you from coming to Him to claim His offer?

I propose that one of the major hurdles for many of us is this: Deep inside we all know our Father. We know that it is impossible to be healed to God without being healed to all other living souls. It is impossible to come into the arms of God's love without finding all your enemies encircled about in His embrace also. God's love encircles us all, everyone, *without exception*. To come unto Him and remain with Him, we must be willing to become like Him—holding no grudges, no resentments or feelings of estrangement toward anyone. All those "kinks" will eventually have to be worked out.

> **Therefore, if ye shall come unto me, or shall desire to come unto me, and rememberest that thy brother hath aught against thee—**
> **Go thy way unto thy brother, and first be reconciled to thy brother, and then come unto me with full purpose of heart, and I will receive you. (3 Nephi 12:23–24)**

A PARABLE

One day I dreamed a dream and saw myself in a scene that was almost like something out of *Gone with the Wind*. I was walking up a long, tree-lined lane, and though I was ragged and wounded and still using a crutch to steady myself, I was full of excitement. I had just entered into the last stretch in what had been a long and perilous journey home. Just over the next rise was "the green, green grass of home" and my family waiting to greet me. Even there along the lane, every tree was filled with yellow ribbons. And when the breeze carried just right, and I had my good ear turned, I could hear the music and smell the feast at the great party they were having.

Suddenly I noticed that another figure was hobbling along just ahead of me. Whoever this poor soul was, I could tell that he was in at least as bad a shape as I was. But even with all his wounds, he had made it this far too. My heart went out to him in fellowship, and quickening my pace, I hurried to overtake him, calling out to him, "Brother, wait! Wait for me!"

He stopped and turned. My heart went chill as all feelings drained from it. I recognized his face. He had been my enemy, the very one who had inflicted the deepest wounds—wounds that had made my journey so slow and painful—wounds that I still bore unhealed. Not him! How could he be here too?

I halted my steps, unable to approach him any further, unwilling to say anything. As he called out "Who's there? I can't see you," I realized that he was blind. Rather than answer his plaintive cry, I held my breath. Soon he turned, dejected, and shuffled on his way.

I didn't have far to follow him, for just ahead of us was a shining, glorious gate. The boundary that it marked was as definite as if it were guarding night from day. Even though the beauty of the country through which the lane passed was exquisite, what lay beyond the gate was beyond description, but not recognition. It was Home. Upon my seeing it, childhood memories seemed to flood my mind. Every path and byway was familiar to me. The longing to be there once more became an overwhelming ache within me. It caused me to totally forget my reluctance to approach my enemy, who was even now standing at the gatehouse, speaking to the gatekeeper.

The gatekeeper had his back to me. Still I recognized Him immediately as my Lord and Good Shepherd, He who had carried me throughout much of my journey, ministering to my stubborn wounds. Just as He had promised, He employed no servant here. Still I could see only my enemy's face. There was light shining either from it or on it. I could not tell which. Suddenly I realized that his eyes were bright and clear, focused upon the face of the Gatekeeper. I realized he was not blind anymore! Then I noted how straight he stood. Eagerly I threw down my crutch and rushed forward. Maybe I too could be made whole!

Before I could take more than a step or two, I was suddenly aware of the Gatekeeper's words to my lifelong enemy. "There is only one last thing before you are ready to enter in, one last question I must ask."

My enemy! This person who had been responsible for my deepest wounds? He was about to enter in?

The Gatekeeper continued, breaking through my shock, "Are you a friend to every man?"

Taking his gaze from the Gatekeeper's face, the man looked steadily into my eyes, and I knew that he was seeing me, *really* seeing me, for the first time. Somewhere inside I trembled. I had known all along that I would have to face the Lord to enter in, but my enemy?

His words pierced my soul. "I am willing to be," he said quietly. Healed and no longer blind, he loved me. Could I, still maimed and crippled as I was, say the same? Could I answer this one last question with an honest yes?

The Gatekeeper seemed to disappear from between us, though I knew He was near. Nothing stood between my enemy and me. He waited for my response with longing meekness in his eyes, unable to enter in without my approbation. And just as surely, I knew I could not enter in without him. My long-harbored resentment and bitterness, or all that lay beyond this last barrier—which would it be? Which would I choose? Why had I waited so long? How had I thought I could avoid this moment?

My first step toward him was still halting, as if crippled, but with each step my strength grew greater and greater. I could feel my wounds healing as I reached for his hands and then his embrace.

And as the dream ended, I saw us wrapped in more than each other's acceptance and forgiveness. The Gatekeeper and still another figure stood with us. With shining countenance the Gatekeeper turned to the other; and speaking my name in unison with that of my former adversary, He said, "Father, these are my friends." As I awoke from the dream, the last impression I had was hearing the voice of the Father, so long awaited, *"Well done. You may all enter in."*

Speaking of those who would gain only a portion of glory and not a fullness, the Lord said:

> **Nevertheless, they shall return again to their own place** [the one *they* choose], **to enjoy that which they are willing to receive, because they were not willing to enjoy that which they might have received. (D&C 88:32)**

CONCLUSION: ONLY COMPLETE SURRENDER BRINGS COMPLETE PEACE

> **And this they did, it being in their view a testimony to God, and also to men, that they never would use weapons again for the shedding of man's blood; and this they did, vouching and covenanting with God, that rather than shed the blood of their brethren they would give up their own lives; and rather than take away from a brother they would give unto him...**
> **And thus we see that, when these Lamanites were brought to believe and to *know* the truth, they were firm, and would suffer even unto death rather than commit sin; and thus we see that they...buried their weapons of war, for peace. (Alma 24:18–19; emphasis added)**

We too must be willing to bury our weapons permanently—our weapons of pride (self-will, competition, and enmity), fear (self-pity), and self-righteousness. We must not allow ourselves to use them *ever* again, even in the guise of helping another person: "I'm just doing this for his own good."

We must come to a day when we are willing to practice Christ's complete trust in God's will, in order to have His complete peace. Even as our Lord and exemplar did, we must also see through the seeming victory of evil in our lives and the lives of others, to the glorious and inevitable triumph of good and God.

> Therefore, they would suffer death in the most aggravating and distressing manner which could be inflicted by their brethren, before they would take the sword or cimeter to smite them. (Alma 27:29)

It was their perspective that gave these people the power to let go absolutely and to trust God's will in *all* things.

One last word, and that a word of warning. These people of Anti-Nephi-Lehi were fanatics by normal standards. They were different. They were a peculiar people who had to find their comfort in the esteem and goodwill of God rather than the esteem and goodwill of men. No matter how crazy their choices seemed to others, they cared only for the love of God. There was definitely no codependency among them, no caring more what people thought of them than what God thought. They were willing to come down into depths of humility that few of us ever know.

We'll talk more in our next discussion about what keeps us from putting this willingness into action.

ASSIGNMENT FOR THIS WEEK:

Read "Beware of Pride," by President Ezra Taft Benson, *Ensign*, May 1989, p. 4. Underline and capture some quotes from it.

PREPARATION FOR DISCUSSION OF PRINCIPLE NINE: "BLESSED ARE ALL THE PEACEMAKERS" (3 NEPHI 12:9)

Step 9: Made restitution directly to those we had harmed, confessing our own wrongdoing in each instance except when to do so would further injure them or others. (Mosiah 27:35; 3 Nephi 12:25; Mosiah 26:30)

Day 1: Mosiah 3:19—What do the phrases **"becometh as a child"** and **"willing to submit to *all* things"** mean? How old is the child you visualize? Are there any exceptions to the "all" to which you are willing to submit?

Day 2: **Mosiah 27:35**—Alma and the sons of Mosiah went about **"zealously striving to repair all the injuries which they had done."** If you were "zealous" about making amends, who would you go to? Make a list.

Day 3: **Alma 24:21**—In the course of making our amends we will sometimes meet people who do not react favorably to our efforts, who choose to retain their negative feelings toward us. What does this verse teach us about our resolve to be "defenseless" even in the face of such hostility?

Day 4: **Helaman 10:4**—**"thou...hast not sought thine own life, but hast sought my will."** To make amends requires us to lose our fear of other people and declare what we know we must to them, no matter what the results. How does being willing to make amends equate with not seeking our own life? With being willing to lose our own life?

Day 5: **3 Nephi 12:25–26**—**"Agree with your adversary quickly while you are in the way with him lest he cast you into prison."** Into what prison are we immediately cast if we have adversarial feelings toward someone else? What are the character weaknesses that keep us in bondage?

Day 6: **3 Nephi 14:2–4**—Describe your understanding of the "mote/beam" disease. Why is it that your eye is always the one with the beam when you see any fault in another?

Day 7: **3 Nephi 14:12**—There is a secret or mystery of human behavior in this injunction of the Savior's. It is that we always do unto others as we believe we deserve to have done unto us. What is revealed about a person's feelings of self–acceptance if that person cannot forgive and accept another's imperfections and weaknesses?

BLESSED ARE ALL THE PEACEMAKERS
(3 Nephi 12:9)

Step Nine: Made restitution directly to those we
had harmed, confessing our own wrongdoing in
each instance except when to do so would further
injure them or others. (Mosiah 27:35; 3 Nephi 12:25;
Mosiah 26:30)

Principle Nine: The establishment of Zion begins with a
mighty change in my own heart and then extends
to others as I act to amend all past wrongs.

Living the principles we have covered so far in this course will
have the effect of establishing Zion within each participant's heart.
In fact, that establishment began back in the first three principles
through which we dethroned ourselves and any other earthly idols,
and enthroned in our hearts the Lord God of Israel, even Jesus the
Christ.

Then we moved on through the next five principles, each
requiring some change either in heart or in action, or both, which
cleansed this newly consecrated kingdom within us. During this
process, quietly and automatically, Zion has been established within
each willing heart. There is an ever-growing desire to be of one heart
and one mind within oneself—and to have that one heart and one
mind be one with God. While the "multitude" of "voices" that a

person has always been subject to hearing within are allowed to remain, the individual actually heeds only those that profess love of God and oneness with His mind and will.

In the last principle, we discussed willingness, especially willingness to let go of pride and fear and to approach all those whom we have wronged or who have wronged us with the offer of forgiveness and healing. In the principle we are considering in this discussion, we will have the opportunity to act upon that willingness. We will have the opportunity to participate in "healing the nations" and spreading Zion beyond the confines of our own heart. More about that in a minute. First let's recheck the condition of Zion within ourselves.

\ THE ABILITY TO WALK PEACEABLY WITH OTHERS BEGINS WITHIN

One of the most curious phenomena I have experienced as I've gone through this process of change is to realize that I no longer fight with anyone, not even the dissident voices within me. I don't heed them, but at the same time, I don't fight with them either. I used to think I had to throw them all out or even wrestle to the death with some of them.

You know which voices I mean, don't you? I mean the "voices" on that "committee" that participates in all our thoughts. Lots of people sit on that "committee." Every significant other from our past (father, mother, siblings, friends, teachers, etc.) has left a voice behind. I spent the better part of my first 37 years wrestling with those voices, being blown about, in a sense, by every "wind of opinion"—and none of them mine, or God's. Little did I know that in my zealous *fighting* of evil, I was doing exactly what evil wanted me to do. I was ignoring the joy along the way. I was like a person who spent the whole trip through the breathtaking splendor of the Grand Canyon focused on an annoying fly in the car. Halfway through the journey I realized that if I didn't let go of the fly, I would miss the whole reason for being here—to participate in the joy of God's purpose.

I ceased trying to eliminate the "fly" or the dissident voices on my committee. I even allowed them their turn to speak. To deny them would not be Zion—for Zion loves all, accepts all as they are. I just didn't argue with them anymore. I just plain didn't heed their input.

And so inner peace must be established first. We must go around to each voice on our committee, and say something like "I recognize you have a right to be, to exist. God allowed you to be on my committee. There must be something I can benefit from by having had you established in my memory. God accepts you the way you are, allows your attitudes and choices to be just as you want them, but He doesn't pay any attention to the lies you still believe and speak. He recognizes them for what they are and goes on with His own work. I desire to be like Him in every way. I see today that I cannot bind you with force, with hand-to-hand combat. As I struggle to destroy you, I have wasted my precious time, when instead, I should be preparing to meet God, preparing to live in a state of peace and joy."

Thus a mighty change of heart automatically changes people's dispositions. They no longer want to "fix" other people. They no longer desire to do evil (separate themselves from the Spirit of God) by taking the privilege of judgment unto themselves, by making themselves the judge, jury and executioner of justice toward other people. Their walk with others becomes peaceable, not adversarial. It becomes accepting and understanding.

Moroni taught that this is one of the ways you may know those who have "a sufficient hope" and have entered into "the rest of the Lord."

And now my brethren, I judge these things of you because of your peaceable walk with the children of men. (Moroni 7:4)

In so many words he is saying: "I can recognize those of you who have been born again in Christ, who have obtained sufficient hope for yourselves and others, because you *know* His atonement is great enough to redeem all as soon as they're ready. I recognize you because you walk peaceably with others, loving them, accepting them as they are, and not judging them."

As we go forth to make amends to others, we need to retain this spirit in our hearts. We need to remember plainly that we are not out to "clean their plow" but to clean our own. We have stopped judging others and fixing others, setting them straight, taking their inventory. We are about our own business, and that is to become in deed what we are inside—the children of God. Our objective is not to go to others and say, "You have hurt me and I forgive you" in a condescending manner. Our objective is to say, "I have retained a lot of self-pity and defensiveness over this problem between us, and I need to apologize for that."

THERE'S PEACE AND THEN THERE'S PEACE

As we pursue this process of seeking peace through amends, we must beware of Satan's counterfeit peace. Believe me, he has a counterfeit, and he does a good job of passing it off as sufficient. It's the peace that *seems* easy, that *seems* cheap, and that's really a lie. It's the kind of peace where you cover up, pretend, and "act as if" indefinitely. It's the outward peace that we're willing to purchase at the price of Christ's true inner peace. Satan's brand of peace is the kind that has a veneer of "fineness," which covers up a lifetime of pain and regret with obsession and compulsion.

Many of us have lived our lives, either consciously or unconsciously, by the philosophy that we need to maintain "peace at any price." The only problem is that when that outward peace has been purchased by denying and avoiding our real feelings, we have paid far too high a price. As we have discussed before, the suppression of feelings is an across-the-board phenomenon. If we turn down the volume on some feelings, then all are affected; those that are the stillest and smallest, the most refined, are often lost entirely. And since feelings are the channel through which we receive the words or whisperings of the Spirit, Satan has us right where he wants us—hiding feelings of shame, anger, pain, and resentment, and thus tuning ourself out from the personal experience of God's love and guidance.

We should always beware of *any* voice, whether internal or external, that counsels us to deny our true feelings, that would advise us to be dishonest in the name of keeping peace, of caring what others might think, that twists the meaning of "avoiding the appearance of evil" to suppress honesty and truth.

We each need to ask ourselves honestly, if in the attempt to avoid the appearance of evil, we have settled for only the appearance of peace.

The voice of the Lord will always admonish you to be gentle, but never, *never* dishonest. The spirit of lying and the Spirit of Christ are *never* compatible.

BRASS TACKS—WHO DO WE GO TO?

Old-timers at this process have discovered three categories of amends to make; there are three lists to be made. The third one is short if not easy, so we'll leave it until last. The first two are usually longer. These two lists are easily generated from the inventory process we did in principle four. One list is of all the people we have harmed; the other is a list of all the people who have harmed us.

We come prayerfully before the Lord, seeking the Holy Ghost to teach us the truth, and we ask for personal revelation to guide us. We ask for the gifts of discernment and wisdom, and we begin to write our list. We include everyone we can think of, no matter how small the transgression, no matter how much the rational part of our mind wants to say, "Oh, that's no big deal." Even the little boy in third grade who pulled our ponytails all the time or called us "fatty" or "four-eyes." Or maybe it was we who were pulling hair or calling names. We put *everyone* on these lists. Why? Because we are going to make amends directly where possible and indirectly otherwise. We're going to sit down and write that little boy a letter:

Dear Little Boy,

You probably don't remember me and I don't even know where you are, but I know you are somewhere. I need to tell you I forgive you. I need to tell you that I know today that you were probably hurting inside yourself when you said those things to me. In fact, now I recall how angry your dad looked all the time, how your mom was sick all the time.

You see, if we want to be thorough, we need to be *thorough*. In fact, it might be a good idea to save all these letters we write as a sign of our faith and our willingness to make amends if the chance should ever present itself in the future.

I'M SCARED. I'M STUCK. WHERE DO I GET THE POWER?

Hopefully, going through this course of study has shifted your dependency for power from yourself to God. Hopefully, by now you automatically think of God first when you come upon a situation where a lack of power is obvious.

Only *love of God* will give us the power to approach other people in this amends process. It is love of God that motivates people to do this kind of peacemaking—not love of other people. When we love and want His good favor more than the favor of others, we will lay aside all our fear and prejudice and go to any length to thoroughly right all wrongs.

Yea, I say unto you come and fear not, and lay aside every sin, which easily doth beset you, which doth bind you down to destruction, yea, come and go forth, and show unto your God that ye are *willing* to repent of your sins [and take action based on your repentance]. **(Alma 7:15; emphasis added)**

Charity is the pure love *of* Christ. It is to love Christ purely, and in return, to receive the gift of His love for others. This gift of love and power from Christ Himself will overcome our fear of going to others. If we will pray for the gift of His love, to be able to feel about others the way the Lord does, we will be able to transcend any barrier that keeps us from coming to peace with everyone.

OBSERVE THEIR COVENANTS BY SACRIFICE

Even with God's power it is not necessarily a painless or fearless experience to put our heart's desires into actions. Even our Lord Himself did not do the task He was sent and empowered to do without pain or fear. He too wished **"not [to] drink the bitter cup" (D&C 19:18)**. He too would rather "shrink." But He came to sacrifice His own comfort and His own will upon the altar of truth and honesty. He knew His honest answers would condemn Him to a most ignoble result, but He gave them anyway **(Matthew 26:64–65)**.

Our Lord knew well what each of us must learn: that pain and fear are two of those elements of opposition we must allow to exist, but not allow to hamper our journey of recovery.

> **Verily I say unto you, all among them who know their hearts are honest, and are broken, and their spirits contrite, and are willing to observe their covenants *by sacrifice*—yea, every sacrifice which I, the Lord, shall command—they are accepted of me. (D&C 97:8; emphasis added)**

We too must be willing to observe our covenants by sacrifice—the sacrifice of our "comfort zone," as it is often called.

We cannot postpone this work of making amends forever. As was illustrated with the parable of the enemies at the gate in our last discussion, the day will come when we must choose either peace or pride. How wise it would be for us to follow through with applying these eternal principles now, and allow ourselves to be prepared to meet God even while yet in this life.

> For behold, this life is the time for men to prepare to
> meet God; yea, behold the day of this life is the day for
> men to perform their labors. (Alma 34:32)

WE MUST LET GO OF RESULTS

As we go out to make amends where it is possible and where it
will not cause even greater injury, we must prepare ourselves thoroughly to let go of the results. We must realize that how other people
choose to react to our efforts is not our business, but their own. We
must remember that the only salvation we can obtain is our own; the
only person I can bring to Zion is myself.

It's very tempting when we get some sort of negative reaction to
our efforts, either on the spot or later through the grapevine, to
resort to our shields of resentment and blame again. We are tempted
to unbury our swords and go back to hacking and slicing in our own
defense. We are tempted to reassume the lie that we must *make*
others see the light. We would do well to remember Alma's advice:

> Therefore, O my son, whosoever will come may come
> and partake of the waters of life freely; and whosoever
> will not come *the same is not compelled to come;* but in
> the last day it shall be restored unto him according to his
> deeds. (Alma 42:27; emphasis added)

Letting go of results is synonymous with the counsel given by
King Benjamin:

> ...and becometh...submissive, meek, humble, patient,
> full of love, willing to submit to all things which the
> Lord seeth fit to inflict upon him. (Mosiah 3:19)

It takes a special brand of humility to trust that as we go out to
make peace with others, whatever their reaction is, it will be within
the will of the Lord, and it will be something that he sees fit to allow
to be inflicted upon us—even if it is a cold shoulder or sarcastic
rebuttal.

But behold I say unto you, love your enemies, bless them
that curse you, do good to them that hate you, and pray
for them who despitefully use you and persecute you.
That ye may be the children of your Father who is in
heaven; for he maketh his sun to rise on the evil and on
the good. (3 Nephi 12:44–45)

CONCLUSION: MAKING AMENDS FREES US

In case you think I forgot the third list we need to make in our
amends process, I haven't. Remember I said that it would be short,
if not easy to make. That's because there's only *one* person on it—
you.

This is often the hardest list for many of us to make. It's a hard
thing for each of us to acknowledge that the person we've hurt the
most by harboring up all these sins and not getting on with this
thorough repentance sooner has been ourselves.

Often we view making amends as a form of punishing ourselves.
The truth is that making amends is really a major milestone in
forgiving and finally loving ourselves, in *freeing* ourselves. We are
finally going to let our single greatest prisoner go free through this
process. It matters not what others choose to do or feel; whatever
they do, we can't control or help.

But this much I can testify of, because I have lived it. As we work
through our amends list, we will be free, free at last—free to enter
into the rest of the Lord, or in other words, free to receive and trust
revelation; free to know we have done all that *we* can do to "heal the
nations" and establish Zion; free to feast upon the "good of the land
of Zion" even while the world is still reeling in the predawn
darkness of the Saturday night of time.

Behold, the Lord requireth the heart *and a willing mind;*
and the willing and obedient shall eat the good of the
land of Zion in these last days. (D&C 64:34; emphasis
added)

We will be free to join that chorus of voices who can say, "[We] **that walked in darkness have seen a great light" (2 Nephi 19:2).**

May I take the liberty of orchestrating several beautiful verses together in order to leave us with a message of supernal hope?

> **And blessed are all the peacemakers, for they shall be called the children of God. (3 Nephi 12:9)**
>
> **Children of Christ, his sons, and his daughters,...ye are born of him. (Mosiah 5:7)**
>
> **...to retain [His] name written always in your hearts,...that ye hear and know the voice by which ye shall be called. (Mosiah 5:12)**
>
> **...that have obtained a sufficient hope. (Moroni 7:3)**
>
> **And what is it that ye shall hope for? Behold I say unto you that ye shall have hope [that] through the atonement of Christ and the power of his resurrection, [you will be able] to be raised unto life eternal, and this because of your faith in him according to [His] promise [to you]. (Moroni 7:41)**

PREPARATION FOR DISCUSSION OF PRINCIPLE TEN: "RETAIN A REMISSION OF YOUR SINS" (MOSIAH 4:12)

Step 10: Realizing that the weakness to be tempted and to sin is a part of the mortal experience, we continued to take personal inventory and when we were wrong promptly admitted it, being willing to repent as often as needed. (2 Nephi 4:18; 2 Nephi 10:20; Mosiah 26:30)

Day 1: **2 Nephi 4:17–18—"encompassed about, because of the temptations and sins which do so easily beset me."** As you read Nephi's humble confession of human weaknesses, does the word "easily" suggest a feeling of his ongoing struggle being somewhat like Paul's **(2 Corinthians 12:7–9)** or your own? Look up Paul's words and write something of your own struggle.

Day 2: **2 Nephi 4:27**—In this scripture Nephi demonstrates his willingness to continue to take a personal inventory. We too must be willing to keep our inventory process current each new day. When we are wrong, we must be willing to admit it immediately. Write about an "enemy" (bad habit) that weakens your strength.

Day 3: **2 Nephi 4:31**—When it becomes obvious that we have slipped back into some of our old ways, we must remember who caused our previous successes. Who gave us the power to obtain forgiveness of sin? Look up **Mosiah 4:30** and write about our powerlessness to keep ourselves from sin.

Day 4: **2 Nephi 10:20**—**"Let us remember him and lay aside our sins, and not hang down our heads, for we are not cast off."** Christ's gospel is a gospel of repentance, not perfection. It was Lucifer who was all for not leaving any room to learn from our own experience. Write about a time when you learned by your own experience the good from the evil and are better off for it.

Day 5: **Jarom 1:12**—**"...continually stirring them up unto repentance."** Are you ashamed that you have to be stirred up unto repentance over and over again? Did God make allowances for us to be human and to be able to repent often? By what means?

Day 6: **Omni 1:3**—**"...we had many seasons of peace; and we had many seasons of serious war and bloodshed."** Has it become obvious to you yet that progress doesn't happen in a perfectly straight, unwavering line? Can you relate this "ebb and flow" process to your own life's history? Note some periods of peace and some periods of serious "war" in your life.

Day 7: Mosiah 26:30—"As often as my people repent will I forgive them." So many scriptures reveal the loving and merciful face of God. How has your perception of the degree of His personal love for you changed in the course of these discussions?

Retain A Remission of Your Sins
(Mosiah 4:12)

Step Ten: Realizing that the weakness to be tempted and to sin is a part of the mortal experience, we continued to take personal inventory and when we were wrong promptly admitted it, being willing to repent as often as needed. (2 Nephi 4:18; 2 Nephi 10:20; Mosiah 26:30)

Principle Ten: The mighty change of heart does not bring me to a state of perfection but rather to a state of continual repentance and abhorrence of sin.

Once a person has consciously and sincerely entered into the mighty-change-of-heart process through living the first nine principles of this program, it does not mean that he or she is suddenly removed from the ability to be tempted or even to sin. Even having many undeniable spiritual experiences and knowing the presence, the voice, and even the face of the Lord Himself does not exempt a person from the tests of mortality. Listen once more to Nephi's words, remembering that he was the ultimate example of a man reborn in Christ:

> **I am encompassed about, because of the temptations and the sins which do so easily beset me.**

> And when I desire to rejoice, my heart groaneth because
> of my sins; nevertheless, I know in whom I have trusted.
> (2 Nephi 4:18–19)

As we have rehearsed again and again, the mighty change of heart does not bring us to a state of perfection, but rather convinces us of our own powerlessness to be perfect, and turns us to know and trust Him who is perfect enough for us all. The word repentance means literally to "turn again." As that process of turning again to God and to the principles of truth and righteousness becomes more and more consistent and continuous, our lapses from it grow shorter and shorter. They go from being years, months, weeks or even days in length to only hours, eventually minutes, and ultimately nothing more than the turn of a thought, which is discarded instantly.

RETAINING WHAT WE HAVE OBTAINED

The first nine principles we have covered are really the whole program. By the time we have finished implementing the ninth, we have come to a place where we have done all we can do to receive a mighty change of heart and a remission of the effects of past sins, both our own and others. The challenge of the future is to live these principles over and over again, both in order and randomly, whenever and wherever our current circumstances call for their application.

It sounds easy enough, doesn't it? And I suppose it would be if we could just stay suspended at that point, in a sort of vacuum, not having to interact with others.

The problem is, we can't stay suspended. Life is not a frozen, stationary thing. It is a fluid, motion-filled and emotional experience, made up entirely of relationships with others and the constant reaffirming of our previous choices. Life is always changing, growing, progressing, learning, and teaching over and over again.

The last three principles we will cover—ten, eleven and twelve— will give us the ability to *retain* what we have *obtained* in the first nine.

YOU MEAN IT'S NOT OVER?!

You mean we could come to a place of mighty change and still have to deal with imperfection, even in ourselves?! Oh, how we are challenged and repelled by that realization.

Yes, people can come to a place of mighty change, in fact even a sealing up by the Holy Spirit of Promise to a sure place with Him in Eternity, and still be vulnerable, even able to sin (think, speak, or act in a way that separates themselves from God).

Speaking of those who have come to a place of knowing they are sealed up by the Holy Spirit of Promise, Elder Bruce R. McConkie wrote:

> **The prophets and apostles from Adam and Enoch down, and all men, whether cleansed and sanctified from sin or not, are yet subject to and do in fact commit sin. This is the case even after men have seen the visions of eternity and been sealed by the Holy Spirit of Promise...**
>
> **Obviously the laws of repentance still apply, and the more enlightened a person is, the more he seeks the gift of repentance, and the harder he strives to free himself from sin as often as he falls short of the divine will...It follows that the sins of the godfearing and the righteous are continually remitted because they repent and seek the Lord anew every day *and every hour.*" (*Doctrinal New Testament Commentary*, Vol. III, pp. 342–343; emphasis added)**

IS HEAVEN ALL VANILLA?

I remember so well how I once pictured heaven as a place we might eventually reach where there would never be any more challenges, never be any more heartache or sorrow. Only a "vanilla" state of bliss—a Nirvana. Then noting such scriptures as **Mosiah 14:3** and **Luke 22:42 & 44,** I began to wonder if my dream of "arriving" at a place where no sorrow could tempt me, where I would be free from the necessity of having to make choices, was a little off-center or at least premature. Apparently even God suffered and was tempted, and his ability to feel pain and suffering extends beyond mortality.

> **Which suffering caused myself, even God, the greatest of all, to tremble because of pain,…and to suffer both body** *and spirit—and would that I might not drink the bitter cup, and shrink—*(D&C 19:18; emphasis added)

> **And it came to pass that the God of heaven looked upon the residue of the people, and he wept.**
> **And Enoch said unto the Lord, How is it that thou canst weep, seeing thou art holy, and from all eternity to all eternity? (Moses 7:28–29)**

THERE MUST NEEDS BE OPPOSITION— ELSE GOD WOULD CEASE TO BE GOD

God himself, through His prophet Lehi, taught us that there must needs be opposition (in other words, choices) in *all* things, and if there were not, then even *He* would cease to be God. Listen to the *present* tense of Lehi's very plain, straightforward statement.

> **Wherefore, this thing** [lack of opposites] **must needs** [would] **destroy the wisdom of God and his eternal purposes, and also the power, and the mercy, and the justice of God.**
> **And if these things are not there is no God. (2 Nephi 2:12,13)**

In other words God is not if these things (the opportunity to choose between opposites) *are* not. God has not come to a place of cessation of free agency, a place where there is no need to make choices, to exercise faith. He made choices to get to where He is, and *He consciously makes choices to stay where He is.*

I have come to realize the truth that *agency* must *always* exist, and for agency to exist there *must* be the possibility of wrong choices. The *probability* of God making a wrong choice is *zero*; the possibility, however, cannot be removed from Him, or He would cease to be God. By the constant renewal of His commitment to these Eternal truths, He too retains what He has obtained. In fact, the force of His *faith* in eternal truth and His constant recommitment to truth holds all of creation together. Consider deeply these words of Joseph Smith:

> **By this we understand that the principle of power which existed in the bosom of God, by which the worlds were framed, was faith; and that it is by reason of this principle of power *existing in the Deity*, that all created things exist; so that all things in heaven, on earth, or under the earth exist by reason of faith as it *existed in HIM*.**

> **Had it not been for the principle of faith the worlds would never have been framed neither would man have been formed of the dust. It is the principle by which Jehovah works, and through which Jehovah works, and through which he exercises power over all temporal as well as eternal things. Take this principle or attribute— for it is an attribute—from the Deity, *and he would cease to exist*. (Joseph Smith, *Lectures on Faith*, pp. 8–9, emphasis added)**

Goodbye Nirvana. Goodbye "easy street." Goodbye vanilla. Hello choices. Hello *agency*—yesterday, today and *forever*.

(For a more in-depth discussion of the verses in **2 Nephi 2** that cover the absolute necessity of opposite choices, read "Discussion on Opposition" (A–36) in the appendix at the back of this workbook.)

CONSTANCY FROM CHANGE—LIFE FROM DEATH

Oh, how our perfectionistic hearts reel from this idea that there's no end to becoming, to being! No, no! It can't be, we cry. You mean to say that I have come all this way, and I have to go on repenting; I will have to go on being forgiving and accepting of even myself?

Yes, I'm afraid so. At least as long as you're mortal. Remember with me again the honest admission of Benjamin, an aged prophet, and yet another of the Lord's closest friends:

I have not commanded you to come up hither that ye should fear me, or that ye should think that I of myself am more than a mortal man. But I am like as yourselves, subject to all manner of infirmities in body *and mind*. (Mosiah 2:10; emphasis added)

We as a people are so enamored of the lie that perfection is a place, a somewhere, that we can arrive at or achieve and then be done with it. We are averse to the idea that instead, it is a state of choice that is always subject to either being retained or lost in each new instant. We would much rather it be more concrete, something absolute, from which we can never fear falling, ever again.

We are such "all or nothing" creatures. It nearly devastates us to deal with the idea that our environment won't ever be all or nothing. If only we realized that what we're wishing for is that very condition of no choices that Lucifer himself proposed long ago.

He wanted earth life to be a perpetual summer of perfection—no ebb and flow, no seasonal ups and downs for him, thank you. And oh, how like him and his philosophy we often yearn for life to be. We too, like him, tend to abhor the ebb and flow of life. We get impatient with the transitional weather of spring or fall for instance. "Why doesn't it just get on with it?" we lament when a few warm days are followed by a return to clouds and cold.

And yet everywhere we look, the creation of God mirrors the eternal truth of life's transcendent, pulsating rhythm—ever wavering and yet ever progressing.

The seasons are only one example. Our very heartbeat and the resulting ebb and flow of the blood in our veins is yet another. I will never forget when I discovered that without the ups and downs on the monitor of a cardiogram or electroencephalogram, the person being monitored would be dead. *Life's very presence is reflected in the heights and depths printed on the tape emerging from those machines. The last thing anyone would want to see is a straight line.*

We as mortals are finite and limited in our viewpoint. We need to pull back and take the perspective of God. He watches the seeming devastation, for instance, of great forest fires, knowing that from the clearing away of the old will come a whole new wave of life. He watches all these changes and knows that they are simply a part of the constancy of eternal progress and life.

THE CHALLENGE OF LEARNING TO LIVE BY THE SPIRIT

Repentance is an essential tool in our lives as we learn to recognize and obey the words of Christ through the gift of the Holy Ghost **(2 Nephi 32:3)**. It is a process of learning, of trial and error, of correcting and recorrecting, as Joseph Smith explained:

> **A person *may* profit by noticing the first intimation of the spirit of revelation; for instance, when you feel pure intelligence flowing into you, it may give you sudden strokes of ideas...thus by *learning the Spirit of God* and understanding it, you may *grow into the principle of revelation*, until you become perfect in Christ Jesus. (*History of the Church* 3:381; emphasis added)**

If we could not repent, learning to live by the Spirit would be like trying to do an algebraic equation, or take an essay exam, without an eraser. Because we are imperfect and do not always listen, nor always hear the Spirit's instructions perfectly when we do listen, we need repentance to give us the opportunity to reestablish our hold on the rock of revelation from Christ.

THE CONSTANT REESTABLISHMENT OF HUMILITY

In the ten years in which I have been consciously trying to apply these principles, I have observed that all other wrongdoing or sin I get into begins when I forget that I of myself am nothing. The minute I start insisting that *my* will be done, I lose my peace and serenity.

Then I begin to think, speak, and act in ways that make it obvious that I have become separated from God again. I lose my temper. I resort to criticism, sarcasm, and whining to get *my* way. I find myself resorting to little white lies again in order to manipulate and please people, forgetting that I'm not powerful enough to always be perfect and honest at the same time. Thus today, whenever I find myself needing to repent, I can always trace any outward behaviors such as these to feelings of wanting to be in charge.

If we would retain a remission of our sins and always rejoice (have joy renewed in each new moment), we must remember the teachings of King Benjamin. He reduced this whole process into a very tight formula. Consider how many of the principles we've discussed can be found in his counsel.

> **And again I say unto you as I have said before, that as ye have come to the knowledge of the glory of God, or if ye have known of his goodness and have tasted of his love, and have received a remission of your sins, which causeth such exceedingly great joy in your souls, even so I would that ye should remember, and *always retain in remembrance*, the greatness of God, and your own nothingness, and his goodness and long-suffering towards you, unworthy creatures, and humble yourselves even in the depths of humility, calling on the name of the Lord daily, and standing steadfastly in the faith of that which is to come.**
>
> **And behold, I say unto you that if ye do this *ye shall always rejoice*, and be filled with the love of God, and *always retain a remission of your sins*. (Mosiah 4:11–12; emphasis added)**

CONCLUSION: THE MERCY AND GRACE OF CHRIST

So we come again to the only conclusion there is, to the only solution—the mercy and grace of the Lord Jesus Christ. Literally, there is *no* other lasting or genuine solution to *any* problem we face, including the problem of not being able to maintain a state of purity. We cannot maintain our own purity any more than we were able to obtain it by ourselves. He was our way *to* the mighty change, and He is the way to *maintain* it. The depth and breadth and height of His willingness to work with us are infinite, limited only by *our* willingness (or lack of willingness) to work with Him. Again and again in the scriptures we find the testimony that His love will outlast the process of perfecting us, no matter how long it takes.

> **But as oft as they repented and sought forgiveness, with real intent, they were forgiven. (Moroni 6:8)**

> **Yea, and as often as my people repent will I forgive them their trespasses against me. (Mosiah 26:30)**

> **And if any man hear my words, and believe not, I judge him not: for I came not to judge the world, but to save the world. (John 12:47)**

The truth is that God takes into account *every* factor that affects a person's behavior. He doesn't just judge the behavior itself, out of context. Even on the cross, dying one of the cruelest deaths invented by man, Christ pled with the Father for our sakes, citing ignorance as sufficient reason to extend forgiveness.

> **Then said Jesus, Father, forgive them; for they know not what they do. (Luke 23:34)**

And again in the *Book of Mormon* we can find the understanding, all-considerate judgement of a God of love, which Jesus is:

> **For it is because of the traditions of their fathers that caused them to remain in their state of ignorance; therefore the Lord will be merciful unto them and prolong their existence in the land.**
> **And at some period of time they will be brought to believe in his word, and to know of the incorrectness of the traditions of their fathers; and many of them will be saved, for the Lord will be merciful unto all who call on his name. (Alma 9:16–17)**

What a blessing it is to know that the Lord is merciful and willing to support and comfort us in our effort to discover the incorrectness of some of the traditions of our fathers. When we begin to turn from the unrighteous traditions of our fathers, He will empower us to live our lives according to His word.

As a final thought for this lesson on learning to be like the Lord in His willingness to forgive and restore His people (us), may we ponder the precious, hope-filled words of **Hebrews 8:10–12**:

> **For this is the covenant that I will make with the house of Israel after those days, saith the Lord; I will put my laws into their mind, and write them in their hearts: and I will be to them a God, and they shall be to me a people: And they shall not teach every man his neighbor, and every man his brother, saying, Know the Lord: for all shall know me, from the least to the greatest.**
> **For I will be merciful to their unrighteousness, and their sins and their iniquities will I remember no more.**

We have labored too long under the fallacy that in our sins we have cut the Lord off from us. The truth is, we have cut ourselves off from the Lord. He is *always* "with" us, in the sense that He is always aware of us and awaits our genuine, heart-deep turning to Him. Even in our unrighteousness we can turn to Him and find mercy and grace. *Mercy and grace are not forgiveness. Mercy and grace are gifts of power beyond our own, extended to us from God even while in our sinful or darkened state, thus enabling us to repent.* Without these gifts we have no power to turn again, no matter how much we might want to. Our will *must* be joined to His power. *Will-power = OUR will + HIS power.*

PREPARATION FOR DISCUSSION OF PRINCIPLE ELEVEN: "COUNSEL WITH THE LORD IN ALL THY DOINGS" (ALMA 37:37)

Step 11: Sought through prayer and meditation to improve our conscious contact with God, seeking the words of

Christ through the power of the Holy Ghost that they might tell us all things that we should do, praying only for a knowledge of His will for us and the power to carry that out. (2 Nephi 32:3; Alma 37:37; Helaman 10:4)

Day 1: **1 Nephi 2:11**—When we make this mighty change and become people who conduct our lives by the Spirit, or in other words by personal revelation, we run the risk of being thought of as a "visionary." Would you be ashamed to be called this? Why or why not? How would you react to others accusing you of "following the vain imaginations" of your own heart?

Day 2: **2 Nephi 8:7**—Once we've experienced the mighty change of heart, once our hearts have been purified and made clean, we are ready to have God write His law in us. He does this by the continual tutoring of the Holy Spirit, and through the words of His Son, Jesus Christ, as they are whispered into our minds. Write about not fearing the reproach of others more than we desire to do God's will ever more continually in all things.

Day 3: **2 Nephi 9:39**—"to be carnally-minded is death, and to be spiritually-minded is life eternal." To have a mind that dwells on the things of this world, the "carnal" things, is death—spiritual death. To give our mind up, to put God and the spiritual life first *is* life eternal. Notice the present tense of the verb "is." Describe the characteristics of your life on a day when your thoughts have been predominantly on physical reality. Now describe the characteristics of a day when you were focused primarily on spiritual reality.

Day 4: **Alma 26:22—"prayeth continually without ceasing."** How can a person pray continually without ceasing?

Day 5: **Helaman 3:35—"Nevertheless, they did fast and pray oft, and did wax stronger and stronger in their humility, and firmer and firmer in the faith of Christ."** Here is the opposite condition from the downward cycle of hardening our hearts, turning from God and practicing compulsive/addictive behaviors. Do you think abstaining from a character weakness and its resulting destructive habits is a form of fasting? Write about your willingness to magnify your prayers with the commitment to abstain from your primary addiction. This is one of those good and "of God" cycles or spirals: abstaining brings increased need to pray in order to maintain our abstinence, and increased praying brings more genuine, long-lasting abstinence.

Day 6: **3 Nephi 19:9**—When these people prayed for the gift of the Holy Ghost, it being what "they most desired," they revealed their mighty change; they revealed that they desired to know and do God's will more than *anything* else in their lives—more than wanting to be prospered financially, more than wanting to have good health. Why do you suppose having the Holy Ghost would be the single greatest possession to have? (See **2 Nephi 32:3** and **Moroni 10:5** before you start writing.)

Day 7: **3 Nephi 20:1—"And he commanded them that they should not cease to pray in their hearts."** We have been given very clear instruction in the Church on offering formal prayer, in which we speak aloud, addressing our Heavenly Father, in the name of Christ, using the most reverent prayer language we are familiar with—head bowed, eyes closed, arms folded, often on bended knee. The act of "praying in our hearts" is not always that formal. The "prayers" of our hearts are often our deepest yearnings expressed in an immediate "crying out" from a deep sense of neediness, as when Alma cried out to "one Jesus Christ" for a remission of his sins. Other times, these "prayers" are silent, deeply personal efforts to "converse" and "counsel" with the Spirit of the Lord **(Alma 37:37)**, as we ponder and study things out in our own mind, seeking to receive His words through the impressions and whisperings of the Holy Ghost **(2 Nephi 32:3)**. It is possible to practice the state of surrender necessary to be in more and more consistent consciousness of the Saviour's availability and approachability, until you come to the perfect day, the day when you are "perfected in Him" **(Moroni 10:32)**, a day when you are aware of His Spirit and His love every hour, just as in the Sacrament prayers promise. For just one day (or even part of a day), try pausing to record how many times you think of Jesus.

Counsel With the Lord In All Thy Doings
(Alma 37:37)

Step Eleven: Sought through prayer and meditation to improve our conscious contact with God, seeking the words of Christ through the power of the Holy Ghost that they might tell us all things that we should do, praying only for a knowledge of His will for us and the power to carry that out. (2 Nephi 32:3; Alma 37:37; Helaman 10:4)

Principle Eleven: The mighty change of heart brings me an awareness of Christ's living presence in my life through the gift of the Holy Ghost, as I learn to receive and believe the voice of the Lord in my own mind.

When I first heard the phrase "conscious contact with God" it sounded unfamiliar and a little jarring to my ear. I was used to hearing phrases like "living by the Spirit" or being "in tune with the Holy Ghost." Eventually I came to realize that while the words were different, they captured perfectly the goal of the entire recovery process. The reason these Twelve Steps (or principles of truth) are so powerful to deliver us from addiction is very simple: *they deliver us into conscious contact with God.* The Steps are like keys. If we insert them into our hearts and minds, they will open the prison doors of shame, fear, guilt, anger, regret and sorrow that have kept us from feeling the Spirit of God and His love for each of us. These steps "liken" the principles of the gospel and the teachings of the scriptures directly to us and awaken us to our need to be involved with God.

> ...what [receiving personal revelation] **means to us is that we need** *religious experience,* **we need to become personally involved with God....***What counts in the field of religion is to become a personal participant in it."* **(Elder Bruce R. McConkie, "How to Get Personal Revelation,"** *New Era,* **June 1980, p. 46, original italics.)**

THE PURPOSE OF THIS COURSE OF STUDY

By taking these steps and practicing these principles in our lives, we are doing "all that we can do" to demonstrate our willingness to cleanse the "inner vessel" and thus become a fit companion for the Holy Ghost. This course has taught us to turn our will and our life completely over to God, to be one with His holy mind and will. The *Book of Mormon* has taught us plainly that there are no exceptions to this requisite of going down into the **"depths of humility" (2 Nephi 9:42)** and needing a rebirth experience **(Mosiah 27:25)**. It is required of everyone sooner or later.

Just how important is this conscious contact with God? According to President Benson, it is most important.

> **The** *constant* **and** *most recurring* **question in our minds, touching every thought and deed of our lives, should be, `Lord, what wilt thou have me to do?' (Acts 9:6) The answer to that question comes only through the Light of Christ and the Holy Ghost.** *Fortunate are those who so live that their being is filled with both.* **(Ezra T. Benson,** *Ensign,* **Dec. 1988, p. 2; emphasis added)**

In a First Presidency message in the January, 1999 *Ensign,* President James E. Faust bore this powerful testimony of the importance of "conscious contact" with God:

Some time ago in South America, a seasoned group of outstanding missionaries was asked, "What is the greatest need in the world?" One wisely responded, "Is not the greatest need in all of the world for every person to have a personal, ongoing, daily, continuing relationship with Deity?" Having such a relationship can unchain the divinity within us, and nothing can make a greater difference in our lives as we come to know and understand our divine relationship with God and His Beloved Son, our Master. As Jesus said in the great Intercessory Prayer, "This is life eternal, that they might know thee the only true God, and Jesus Christ, whom thou hast sent." (John 17:3).

We should earnestly seek not just to know about the Master, but to strive, as He invited, to be one with Him (see John 17:21), to "be strengthened with might by his Spirit in the inner man" (Eph. 3:16). We may not feel a closeness with Him because we think of Him as being far away, or our relationship may not be sanctifying because we do not think of Him as a real person. (President James E. Faust, January, 1999 *Ensign*, p. 2.)

It is essential that we acknowledge our great need, even our hunger and thirst for God. We are through with other, half-measures. They have availed us nothing—at least, nothing permanent. Now we're here wanting what only God can provide, freedom from the bondage of our compulsive/addictive behaviors and victory over our worst enemies (our character weaknesses)—not by killing them, but by allowing the Lord to convert them into strengths **(Ether 12:27)**.

And blessed are they who do *hunger and thirst* after righteousness, for they shall be filled with the Holy Ghost. (3 Nephi 12:6; emphasis added)

And they did pray for that which *they most desired;* and they desired that the Holy Ghost should be given unto them. (3 Nephi 19:9; emphasis added)

MY HEART PONDERETH CONTINUALLY— A PERSONAL CONFESSION

When I first attended a Twelve Step support group, I went because I was desperate for a place to admit that I was staggering under the weight of the sorrow and sin of addiction. I hoped that practicing these steps would relieve me of that weight and the yoke of heavy bondage. I have not been disappointed. Those things have been removed. Instead, another yoke has been placed on my shoulders—the yoke of being completely alive in Christ and filled with His joyful rest:

Come unto me, all [ye] that labour and are heavy laden, and I will give you rest. Take my yoke upon you, and learn of me; for I am meek and lowly in heart: and ye shall find rest unto your souls. For my yoke [is] easy, and my burden is light. (Matthew 11:28-30)

I have become like Nephi when he said,

Behold, my soul delighteth in the things of the Lord; and my heart pondereth continually upon the things which I have seen and heard. (2 Nephi 4:16)

Today, I attend recovery meetings because I need a place where I can confess I am in such total need of the Lord that I must continue to pray always in my heart. I have finally come to realize that my only safety is in *continuous* conversation with Him.

These [ideas] are incomprehensible to some but are the first principle of the gospel—to know that we may converse with him as one man with another. (Joseph Smith, *The Words of Joseph Smith,* Ehat and Cook, p. 357)

To remain free of my addictive behaviors, I must, just as President Faust stated in an earlier quote, "have a personal, ongoing, daily continuing relationship with Deity." Every day I must be willing to get up early, to use the scriptures, personal prayer and journal writing as tools to make conscious contact with God. And from there I must be willing to walk through my day's activities picturing the Savior by my side, counseling with Him in all my doings, looking to Him in every thought.

At first I was suspicious of this process. It seemed too simple: I always remember Him; He is always with me in Spirit. But as I have experimented upon His word, I have found He will do even as He promised:

I will tell you in your mind and in your heart, by the Holy Ghost, which shall come upon you and which shall dwell in your heart. Now, behold, this is the spirit of revelation. (D&C 8:2–3)

To keep this spirit of revelation, my life must be a continuous walk with the Lord. I must get up every day and set my feet anew on the road to Emmaus **(Luke 24:13–32)**. And even as these travelers, I need not walk along in silence. In the thoughts of my heart, I find a sweet communion with Him. He answers my questions, stills my fears, comforts my sorrows and regrets. He continually reveals to me the meaning of my life—its hours and its days. Feeling His presence in my heart and perceiving His words in my mind does not distract me from my mortal commitments or obligations, but guides me in all things and enhances my willingness to participate in everyday life, free of my addiction.

Often as I go through my day, I actually picture myself walking those hot, dusty, rocky roads of Judea with Him. He has become a familiar companion and friend. His presence doesn't paralyze me with awe and unfamiliarity as I had thought it would. I am intent on my journey, watching the road before me, but very aware of His patient, tender presence, ever ready to give me counsel if I am humble enough to ask for it.

> Yea, humble yourselves, and continue in prayer unto him. (Alma 34:19)

> And Alma and his people did not raise their voices to the Lord their God, but did pour out their hearts to him; and he did know the thoughts of their hearts. (Mosiah 24:12)

As *children* in the gospel, three years old or thirty, we face a challenge when presented with the goal of having personal prayer even twice a day. But when we have seen enough of this life to know the truth about our own need for constant interaction with the powers of heaven, the following entreaty of Alma begins to make sense to us:

> Yea, and when you do not cry unto the Lord, let your hearts be full, *drawn out in prayer unto him continually for your welfare, and also for the welfare of those who are around you.* (Alma 34:27; emphasis added)

REVELATION MAKES UP FOR ANY AND EVERYTHING ELSE

> I, Nephi,...having seen many afflictions in the course of my days, nevertheless, having been highly favored of the Lord in all my days; yea, *having had a great knowledge of the goodness and mysteries of God.* (1 Nephi 1:1; emphasis added)

How generous and considerate and loving our God is! Note how He did not bury the secret to making it through this life deep in the middle of some voluminous amount of scripture, where we would have to scratch and scrape to find it. He put it right in front of us, in the very first verse of the *Book of Mormon*. Listen once more to Nephi tell you and me the exact formula, the exact "how-to" for being able to live a life filled with affliction and yet still know that we are highly favored of the Lord: **"Having had a great knowledge of the goodness and mysteries of God"**—in other words, having been able to obtain and retain an open channel of revelation. That is what I believe Nephi meant when he said he was **"highly favored of the Lord."**

> My God hath been my support; and He hath led me
> through mine afflictions in the wilderness. (2 Nephi 4:20)

You see, to be "highly favored of the Lord" does *not* mean, as much as we would like it to, to have a life of "vanilla" peace (as we discussed in the last lesson). Nor does it mean to have a life of wealth and comfort. (Note the words "afflictions" and "wilderness" in that last quote from Nephi.) It does not even mean to have a family that hangs together no matter what (remember, Nephi's didn't either).

To be "highly favored of the Lord" means one thing and one thing only to Nephi and all others who have known the experience. It is to have the gift of personal revelation. It is to have the "lights on," so to speak, through the "night" of this life. It means to walk this mortal journey with a flashlight, and occasionally even a floodlight, illuminating our way. And since, as the saying goes, "It's always darkest before the dawn," we can be sure that no people have ever walked in greater darkness or have ever had more need of "further *light* and knowledge" than we do at this point in the earth's history. We are no longer simply in the Saturday evening of time; we are entering the darkest period known on earth—the dark before the dawn. We need not be in despair, however, if we walk in the light and with the light, even Christ.

Wouldn't you, after some honest thought, agree with this statement: I could get through *any*thing if I just knew what God wanted of me, and that He was there for me. There is a perfectly simple formula for having that very blessing:

> Nevertheless they did fast and pray oft, and did wax
> stronger and stronger in their humility, and firmer and
> firmer in the faith of Christ, unto the filling their souls
> with joy *and consolation*, yea, even to the purifying and
> the sanctification of their hearts, which sanctification
> cometh because of their yielding their hearts unto God.
> (Helaman 3:35; emphasis added)

It isn't the *events* of this life that make it a trial, a confusing mystery; it's having our "faces covered." The obstacles on this course don't make us stumble, fall, crash, and burn, over and over—it's trying to negotiate the course blindfolded that does it.

So why don't we open our eyes and awaken to God? We're don't *have* to be blindfolded, you know.

Hearken unto me, and open your ears that ye may hear, and your hearts that ye may understand, and your minds that the mysteries of God may be unfolded to your view. (Mosiah 2:9)

A better analogy would be that we are sleeping—stumbling around half-asleep, afraid to open our eyes for fear of what we'll see (our own weaknesses and powerlessness); we're the ones who *choose* to be blind. As soon as we're ready to look, He'll begin to show us the lessons, the reasons, the principles behind all this. As soon as we're ready to listen, He'll start to explain.

Yea, he that repenteth and exerciseth faith, and bringeth forth good works, and prayeth continually without ceasing—unto such it is given to know the mysteries of God. (Alma 26:22)

Therefore, blessed are they who will repent and hearken unto the voice of the Lord their God; for these are they that shall be saved. (Helaman 12:23)

Anyone who has come to recognize the voice of the Lord as a direct teacher, through the power and gift of the Holy Ghost, will never lack for what to do, if he or she will but believe and receive His word **(2 Nephi 32)**.

So if personal revelation makes up for everything else and can get us through everything else, are we ready to "suit up and show up" for class (life) each day to receive it? Are we willing to get up early and get in conscious contact with Him?

How do you do that? You take the first three steps *every* morning of your life. (1) I'm powerless to know the right things to do this day, but (2) God knows *exactly* what the right thing is for me and for everyone, so (3) I'll turn my will and my life over to Him and trust in Him in all things this day—including His power to direct my life. I will trust His voice to me. I will pray—not for this thing or that thing, for I do not know if this or that is the best policy. I will pray only for a knowledge of His will for me and the power to carry that out.

REVELATION MUST BE PERSONAL TO BE PERMANENT

> ...that they were depending on the Prophet, hence were darkened in their minds, in consequence of neglecting the duties devolving upon themselves [to search and study and receive personal revelation]. (*The Teachings of the Prophet Joseph Smith*, p. 238)

The people were depending on the Prophet and hence were darkened in their minds?! Did I hear that right? Aren't we supposed to rely on the prophet in all things?

> I am more afraid that this people have so much confidence in their leaders that they will not inquire for themselves of God whether they are led by Him. I am fearful they settle down in a state of blind self-security, trusting their eternal destiny in the hands of their leaders with a reckless confidence that in itself *would thwart the purposes of God in their salvation*...Break not the spirit of any person, but guide it to feel that it is its greatest delight and highest ambition to be controlled [directly] *by the revelations of Jesus Christ;* then the will of man becomes godlike...and God shall reign within us to will and do of his good pleasure. (Brigham Young, *Journal of Discourses*, 9:150, emphasis added.)

I once heard the saying "A good mother works herself out of a job." In other words, a good mother teaches her children "to fish" for themselves and does not keep them dependent on her for their ability to live. So it is with a good prophet: he will do everything he can to "work himself out of a job," to encourage and train up a whole people capable of sustaining the kind of relationship he has with the Lord.

When the fact was brought up to Moses that others besides himself were receiving revelation in the camp of Israel, he expressed his *and* God's opinion on the issue plainly.

> **Would God that all the Lord's people were prophets, and that the Lord would put his spirit upon them! (Numbers 11:29)**

> **We talk about latter-day prophets; we think in terms of prophets who tell the future destiny of the Church and the world. But in addition to that, the fact is that *every person should be a prophet for himself and in his own concerns and in his own affairs.* (Elder Bruce R. McConkie, "How to Get Personal Revelation," *New Era,* June 1980, p. 46)**

And if this wondrous circumstance were to come to pass, and all the Lord's people were prophets, would that mean there would then be no need for a prophet to preside and direct the whole church? Of course not! As long as there is an organized church upon the earth, there will be order in the kingdom; and all true prophets (see the definition of prophet in the Bible Dictionary) will recognize and uphold the prophet, as no doubting, wavering, slumbering member could.

> **And there are *many* among us who have many revelations, for they are not all stiffnecked. And as many as are not stiffnecked and have faith, have communion with the Holy Spirit, which maketh manifest unto the children of men, according to their faith. (Jarom 1:4; emphasis added)**

It is God's goal to have a "peculiar," "redeemed" people **(Deuteronomy 7:6, Titus 2:14, 1 Peter 2:9)**, a people whose absolute conversion to Him and His way of life is based in undeniable spiritual experiences, even as Nephi's. But first we must believe that God can and will do these things, even for us.

> For it came to pass after I had *desired* to know the things that my father had seen, and *believing that the Lord was able to make them known unto me*, as I *sat pondering in mine heart* I was caught away in the Spirit of the Lord, yea, into an exceedingly high mountain, which I never had before seen, and upon which I never had before set my foot. (1 Nephi 11:1; emphasis added)

First, we must believe that God can and will make these same things known even to us. And after we believe, then we must *desire* Him to do so.

> I, Nephi, *was desirous* also that I might see, and hear, and know of these things, by the power of the Holy Ghost, which is the gift of God unto *all those who diligently seek him*, as well in times of old as in the time that he should manifest himself unto the children of men. (1 Nephi 10:17; emphasis added)

And once believing and desiring, we must also be humble and willing enough to *ask*. Apparently Laman and Lemuel's lack of light was due to their prideful, stubborn, negative estimation of themselves and God.

> And I said unto them: Have ye inquired of the Lord?
> And they said unto me: We have not; *for the Lord maketh no such thing known unto us.* (1 Nephi 15:8–9; emphasis added)

Fortunately for all of us, Enos did not have that same prideful resistance to desiring and asking diligently for himself.

> And my soul hungered; and I kneeled down before my Maker, and I cried unto him in mighty prayer and supplication *for mine own soul*; and all the day long did I cry unto him; yea, and when the night came I did still raise my voice high that it reached the heavens. And there

came a voice unto me, saying: Enos, thy sins are forgiven thee, and thou shalt be blessed...And while I was thus struggling in the spirit, behold, *the voice of the Lord came into my mind again.* (Enos 1:4–5, 10; emphasis added)

PRAYER *AND MEDITATION:* CONSCIOUS CONTACT— THE COIN OF THE REALM

For so many years in my past, even as a very active member in the church, I thought of prayer as a rote exercise over meals, at the beginning and end of meetings, and once in a while, in private. I was, in all these moments, only "doing" prayer. I was not *being* prayer–full. I am humbled to admit that it took the devastation that addiction brought to my life to teach me to fill myself with prayer. I was like the people Alma described, who were *compelled* to be humble, *compelled* to cry out to God (Alma 32:13).

Another false idea I had about prayer—mainly because it was just an obligatory thing for me to do—was that you just say it, and then it's over. I didn't give any time or consideration to the possibility that if I lingered—if I meditated (or "pondered," as we call it in LDS terms)—I might actually receive and *perceive* answers from God. I thought you just *did* this prayer–thing—and then you got up and stumbled on, as confused and lost as before, hoping an answer would eventually come along and hit you over the head.

Today, though, I have come to realize that prayer and meditation (or pondering) are two sides of the same coin; the "coin of the realm" of the Spirit and spiritual life. In the actions of praying and meditating, whether we use a form of traditional meditation or *do* something to focus our attention and thoughts, such as studying the scriptures or writing in our journals, we are actually opening a channel of communication involving all three members of the Godhead—our Heavenly Father, the Savior, and the Holy Ghost. It is through this sacred channel that we are restored (recovered) into the presence of God.

COMING TO CHRIST AND BEING PERFECTED IN HIM

In **Moroni 10:32**, we are invited to come unto Christ and "be perfected in Him." We have all wrestled with this invitation. Come unto Christ and be *perfected in him*? How does a person become perfected in Christ? Too often, we have gone away puzzling. Joseph Smith gave the answer:

> **...by learning the Spirit of God and understanding it, you may *grow into* the principle of revelation, until you become perfect in Christ Jesus." (***Teachings of the Prophet Joseph Smith***, p. 151, emphasis added)**

We "learn the Spirit of God" by praying unto the Father and listening to the counsel of our Savior, delivered to our hearts and minds by the sanctifying companionship of the Holy Ghost. It is a process, a learned skill. Like any other skill, we develop it by practice until we reach perfection.

To all my fellow prodigals (mortals), I offer this entreaty: reread Step Eleven. Desire conscious contact with God, however falteringly. Practice this step, however clumsily. Come to God: pray unto the Father. Come to Christ: let Him into your mind and heart. Let Him teach you the truth of all things and quiet the storms of the lies you've inherited in mortality. And above all, trust and believe in the Savior's willingness to help your unbelief.

> **And straightway the father of the child cried out, and said with tears, Lord, I believe; help thou mine unbelief. (Mark 9:24)**

If we will do this, our Heavenly Father, our Saviour Jesus Christ, and the Holy Ghost will—as one—teach us to deny ourselves of all ungodliness, as the rest of Moroni 10:32 promises us. We will come to know it is by *God's* power, and *not* our own, that this has been accomplished. No more will we be able to ignore or deny that God has power enough to heal and repair and redeem *even us*. This is the most central and personal revelation we can ever receive from God. He will carry us home, like lost and weary lambs, in His own bosom if we will stop running from the truth of our lives. If we will give up our addictions and compulsions, and be still and let Him own us, He will lift us and lead us Home. I bear my testimony with the Prophet Joseph concerning God's willingness and eagerness to recover each of us.

> **Having a knowledge of God, we begin to know how to approach him, and how to ask so as to receive an answer. When we understand the character of God, and how to come to him, he begins to unfold the heavens to us, and to tell us all about it.** *When we are ready to come to him, he is ready to come to us.* **(*Teachings of the Prophet Joseph Smith*, p.349, emphasis added.)**

REVELATION SELDOM BRINGS POPULARITY

One of the biggest deterrents and distractions from living by our own personal revelation is worrying about what others will think, say or do. However, if we would live by **"every word that proceedeth out of the mouth of God" (Matthew 4:4)**, we must come to a place where we do not care about (or fear) man's favor more than we do God's.

> **Hearken unto me,** *ye that know righteousness,* **the people in whose** *heart* **I have written my law, fear ye not the reproach of men, neither be afraid of their revilings. (2 Nephi 8:7; emphasis added)**

This fear of other people's opinions or choices is the phenomenon currently known as "codependency." Unfortunately, one of codependency's most powerful strongholds is in family relationships. While truly the most potentially sacred and supportive of relationships, family ties can often serve as the **"very handcuffs, and chains, and shackles, and fetters of hell" (D&C 123: 7–8).**

If we have made sure that our conscience, our own inner guide, is as Christ-centered (truth-centered) as possible through sincere personal prayer, then we must sometimes let go of what even our close family members think of us and our choices.

> **For behold they did murmur in many things against their father, because he was a visionary man, and had led them out of the land of Jerusalem…because of the foolish imaginations of his heart. (1 Nephi 2:11)**

We can be sure that Laman and Lemuel didn't call their father a "visionary man" with respect, but rather with disdain and sarcasm. They regarded his "spiritual experiences" as the "vain imaginations of his heart." Where would we be if Lehi had given heed to the opinions of his *older* sons?

We must be willing to be challenged by others, and we should accept their challenges as opportunities to examine our own convictions, our own feelings and spiritual life. To be challenged is really an invitation to us to keep our "inventory" current. Are we sincere? Are we guilty of any of the charges made to us or about us? Prayer and honest evaluation are always the companions of the truth-loving soul. And if after such consideration, our honest yearning is to still pursue the course we have felt guided by the Spirit to pursue, then we must let go of what even our closest loved ones think, even if in response they choose to become angry or detach themselves from us.

> **Behold, it came to pass that I, Nephi, did cry much unto the Lord my God,** *because of the anger of my brethren.* **And it came to pass that the Lord did warn me, that I, Nephi,** *should depart from them* **and flee into the wilderness, and all those who would go with me. (2 Nephi 5:1, 5; emphasis added)**

To come to a support group is to admit a need for support. This takes a lot of humility and the overcoming of our fear of other people's opinions. It takes wanting to dedicate our lives more to what God thinks of us than what other people think of us.

> And thou hast not feared them [the people], and hast not
> sought thine own life, *but hast sought my will,* and to
> keep my commandments. (Helaman 10:4; emphasis
> added)

CONCLUSION: REVELATION = CHRIST

For many years I puzzled over the third member of the Godhead
and the expression "the gift of the Holy Ghost." I read many
wonderful books about Him and His work and power, and I learned
a great deal. Never, though, did I read words that caused me to want
to qualify and obtain His gift more than these that I found in the
"most correct book ever written":

> Angels speak by the power of the Holy Ghost; where-
> fore, they speak the words of Christ. Wherefore, I said
> unto you, feast upon the words of Christ; for behold, *the*
> *words of Christ will tell you all things what ye should do.*
> (2 Nephi 32:3; emphasis added)

Reading these words from the *Book of Mormon* made me feel as if
a great burning light filled my inner vision and feelings. Suddenly I
saw what the "gift of the Holy Ghost" meant for me. The gift of the
Holy Ghost was, as we've always understood, His constant companionship, but suddenly I saw *why* it was valuable to me to have Him
as a constant companion. *Because He conveyed to me the words of Christ.*
Through Him and His mediation I could have the words of my Lord
with me to instruct me in **"all things what [I] should do."** Never
again would I have to blunder around alone. The counsel of Christ
Himself could and would be with me if I but asked, believing.

No longer did I have to rely upon my own mortal understanding
and perspective. For me, self-reliance has been replaced by God-
reliance.

> Behold, I say unto you...ye have not come thus far save it
> were by the word of Christ with unshaken faith in him,

relying wholly upon the merits of him who is mighty to save. (2 Nephi 31:19)

As I said in the discussion on principle two, we must be willing to let the following words from Isaiah apply to us *personally.*

For unto [me] a child is born, unto [me] a son is given; *and the government [of my life] shall be upon his shoulder;* and his name shall be called, Wonderful, *Counselor,* The Mighty God, The Everlasting Father, The Prince of Peace. (2 Nephi 19:6; emphasis added)

He must become our Messiah, our own Holy Child, our own precious Son, our own Wonderful Counselor, our Everlasting Father **(Mosiah 5:7)**, our very own Prince of Peace **(John 14:27)**, which peace no one can take away. He must become, through a life of revelation about Him and from Him, our friend, our confidant—our Jesus **(2 Nephi 33:6)**.

No final thought could conclude this discussion better than this by President Ezra Taft Benson:

May we be convinced that Jesus is the Christ, choose to follow Him, be changed for Him, captained by Him, consumed in Him and born again. (*Ensign,* June 1989, p. 5)

PREPARATION FOR DISCUSSION OF PRINCIPLE TWELVE: "I [WAS] DESIROUS THAT MY FAMILY SHOULD PARTAKE" (1 NEPHI 8:12)

Step 12: Having experienced a mighty change and having awakened unto God as a result of our sincere repentance demonstrated in taking these steps, we were willing to become instruments in carrying this message to others and to practice these principles in all our affairs. (Alma 5:7; Mosiah 27:36–37; Moroni 7:3)

Day 1: Enos 1:9—"When I had heard these words I began to feel a desire for the welfare of my brethren, the Nephites;

wherefore, I did pour out my whole soul unto God for them." Reread the context of this statement by Enos. Enos had just had a spiritual awakening to the glory and goodness of God. How has coming to know the goodness and mercy of God affected your desire to share these truths with others?

Day 2: **Mosiah 27:36–37**—Many beautiful phrases in these two verses could be captured. Thoughts such as **"instruments in the hands of God," "knowledge of the truth,"** and **"the Lord reigneth"** have much to do with living these principles. Choose at least one or two of these and record your thoughts.

Day 3: **Alma 5:7**—**"Behold, he changed their hearts; yea, he awakened them out of a deep sleep."** Consider this state of being spiritually asleep and then awakened. Who awakened you? Why did you awaken? What was the first thing you had to awaken to or acknowledge? What have you since become awakened to?

Day 4: **Alma 7:14**—**"Now I say unto you that ye must repent, and be born again."** Think about the process of physical birth— the conception, period of "hidden" growth (in the womb) and then the active labor, transition and delivery. Liken the physical process to the stages of spiritual birth.

Day 5: **Mosiah 27:25**—**"Marvel not that all mankind...must be born again; yea, born of God."** This concept of being "born again" is as central to The Church of Jesus Christ of Latter-day Saints as it is to *any* pentecostal Christian faith. Encouragement to seek and obtain this "mighty change" is the very plea of the *Book of Mormon*. All too often we equate being born again with being baptized. Do you feel that the act of baptism, while being a symbolic and essential ordinance, is really the actual "rebirth" itself? Write about your thoughts and feelings concerning your own baptism.

Day 6: **Alma 37:47—"Go unto this people and declare the word, and be sober."** It is a fundamental premise of the Twelve Step program that a recovered addict *must* share the principles they're learned in order to stay "sober," or in other words escape their addiction. Ponder and then write about how and why you think this sharing with others would keep you "sober."

Day 7: **Alma 58:40—"But behold, they have received many wounds; nevertheless they stand fast in that liberty wherewith God has made them free."** "Practicing these principles in all our affairs" will often bring other people's respect, but not always. There are times when we are attacked for our commitment to these principles, and sometimes we feel wounded by others' negative reactions. How must we respond to these "wounds" if we would **"stand fast in that liberty** [freedom from our compulsion/addiction] **wherewith God has made [us] free"?**

I [WAS] DESIROUS THAT
MY FAMILY SHOULD PARTAKE
(1 Nephi 8:12)

Step Twelve: Having experienced a mighty change and having awakened unto God as a result of our sincere repentance demonstrated in taking these steps, we were willing to become instruments in carrying this message to others and to practice these principles in all our affairs. (Alma 5:7; Mosiah 27:36–37; Moroni 7:3)

Principle Twelve: The experience of being born again, of being changed from the inside out, causes two spontaneous reactions in me: (1) an irrepressible desire to share with others the good news of God's reality and availability, and (2) an ever-increasing willingness to practice these principles in every area of my life.

Here we are with only one more principle to discuss! It seems as if we've barely begun this journey and now we're nearly finished. As we've turned to the *Book of Mormon* and written our way through the scripture study exercises, we've experienced some amazing changes in our sense of the Savior's nearness and availability. Leaning on His grace, we've plunged into the depths of humility, explored the inner places of our own hearts, made a personal pilgrimage to God's altar with the things we found there, and finally, admitted our total need for the Savior and His atonement in our lives. Hopefully, we have experienced a huge paradigm shift, making us 100% dependent on Him and His strength, His wisdom and His love. At the very least, we've come to realize that there is no other name, way or means (power) that can take us all the way to a state of healing and peace equal to the challenges of life in these last days.

If you've been involved in a study–support group such as Heart t' Heart or LDS Family Services Substance Abuse Recovery Services (SARS), you've been blessed by the friendship of other LDS people who have also been learning to practice these principles in their lives. You may have already done some personal inventory (Step Four) and some Fifth Step work. It's my hope and prayer that you've not only read this book, but have turned to the *Book of Mormon* and allowed it to bring you closer to Heavenly Father and the Savior as you've pondered, prayed and written your way through the "capturing" exercises. And now, here we are so close to the end of our journey together. I'm afraid I don't do goodbyes very well. I've put off writing this discussion for that very reason. How do I wind it up, cap it off, say "I love you" one last time?

I can only exercise faith and continue on. And so, though I am sad to be so close to the end of this chance to share with you, I will plunge ahead and address this final step. It actually consists of three distinct gospel principles, two of which we are very familiar with in the Church. First, there is carrying this message to others who still suffer (what we are used to calling "member-missionary work") and second, there is practicing these principles in all areas of our life for the rest of our lives (similar to the prophets' entreaty to "endure to the end"). The third concept, however, that of having a *"spiritual awakening"* of such a magnitude that it could be referred to as being "born again," or having a *mighty* change of heart, is unfortunately a little more obscure to many members of the church, even though the prophets, throughout the scriptures, have described it as the culminating and most *essential* experience in every disciple's life.

For many years, before I personally experienced this undeniable and monumental awakening to the reality and goodness of God, I was only "walking through the motions" of much of my activity in the church. I desperately wanted to *know* enough and *do* enough so I could *make* the promises of the Gospel come true for me. Nevertheless, year after year I came away from talks on concepts like "being a member-missionary" and "enduring to the end," more bored than born again. Today I realize this was another example of "spiritual dyslexia" on my part (See "Benjamin's Promises" A–5). I was putting the "cart" (the work to be moved along) before the "horse" (the power to move it.) It was only when I stopped trying to fix myself and admitted my need for the Savior that I began to experience such love and kindness, such empowerment and redemption from Him, that changes—heart-deep changes—began to happen. With this much love—His *love*—pure love for and from Christ, I had to share this message of His reality and availability to all who would live these principles.

In all humility, I can say that the following words of President Joseph F. Smith perfectly express the truth of my own testimony:

> **My brethren and sisters, I desire to bear my testimony to you; for I have received an assurance which has taken possession of my whole being. It has sunk deep into my heart; it fills every fiber of my soul; so that I feel to say before this people, and would be pleased to have the privilege of saying it before the whole world, that God has revealed unto me that Jesus is the Christ, the Son of the living God, the Redeemer of the world. (*Gospel Doctrine*, 5th ed. (1939), 501)**

Practicing these principles in the format of the Twelve Steps as adapted for LDS people and originally presented through Heart t' Heart (A–44) has opened this degree of witness to my mind and heart.

YE MUST REPENT UNTO A REMISSION OF SINS

Repentance comes in more than one form or degree.

There is the minimal form or degree of repentance that a person manifests simply because he or she is caught in the act of wrong behavior. This is a surface repentance and basically amounts to being sorry that you got caught and were forced to stop your incorrect behavior, *temporarily*. On the opposite end of the spectrum there is a full repentance that is genuine and heart-deep. The scriptures contain many references to this degree of repentance. (See Topical Guide under "Remission of Sin.")

In between these two forms of repentance, I have discovered there is a "half-measure" degree of repentance. This form of repentance is more than just being sorry we got caught, but it's not quite deep enough or sincere enough to turn us *to* the Lord and *away* from sin. It's a sort of "half-baked" repentance. It's like saying, "Well, okay. I'll stop doing this, but I don't want to get rid of the possibility entirely. I'll just lock it up in the back of my heart and mind, but I don't want the Lord to actually eradicate it completely. You never know. I might need to return to it some day."

This degree or level of repentance might be the most pitiful of all—even worse than that of the obvious backslider or reprobate. Why? Because this repentance holds a person in "limbo"—not really out there being a prodigal, but also never able to enter into the Lord's living presence and feel of His reality and peace. This is the degree of repentance I practiced almost exclusively for the first 25 years I was a member of the Church. Good as far as it went, but it just didn't go far enough. It didn't go *deep* enough.

This "half-measure" repentance was fueled by *my* power, and therefore destined for eventual failure. The abstinence it brought to me was a constant, white-knuckled struggle to maintain. My addictions still lurked in the back of my heart and mind, creating a sense of foreboding that some new situation or turn of events would unleash it. I developed more "coping devices" (a nice expression for bad habits or addictions) to take the edge off my anxiety. But gradually, my efforts failed and I realized I couldn't live in this half-measure effort to repent. I thank God that I was brought to this state of "failure." Not only did I have to *turn away* from my foolish, sinful, faithless behavior, but I finally had to *turn* to the Savior—even one Jesus Christ, a Son of God **(Alma 36:17)**. By doing this, I came down into the depths of humility, accepted my foolishness and admitted it before God, bringing my weaknesses to Christ **(Ether 12:27)**. Only then was I prepared to receive His gift: a *remission* of my sinful *nature,* a complete change of *disposition* and *desire* to do harm to myself or others **(Mosiah 5:2; Alma 19:33)**.

Heart-deep, full repentance takes a person out of the *cycle* of repentance and brings a remission of sin, such as Enos experienced when he received the testimony of Christ concerning his own salvation **(Enos 1:5–6)**. This is the most precious testimony of Christ any one of us can ever receive. It is the witness *from* Christ that your life is redeemed and has been made acceptable to the Father through the Savior's individual love and atonement for you. And every one of us, without exception, can exercise this degree of repentance and receive this *remission* of sin. We can be encircled about in the arms of safety from sin because of His last and great sacrifice **(Alma 34:15–16)**. That's what this course of study and change is about!

> **And it came to pass that after they had spoken these words the Spirit of the Lord came upon them, and they were filled with joy, having received a remission of their sins, and having peace of conscience, because of the exceeding faith which they had in Jesus Christ who should come, according to the words which King Benjamin had spoken unto them. (Mosiah 4:3)**

As President Benson once said:

> **When we awake and *are born of God,* a new day will break and Zion will be redeemed.**
> **May we be convinced that Jesus is the Christ, choose to follow Him, be changed for Him, captained by Him,**

> consumed in Him, *and born again*. (*Ensign*, July 1989, p. 5; emphasis added)

This is His greatest gift to us, our greatest reward! To preach repentance to people and encourage them along its path without also teaching this amazing gift of remission of sin—of loss of desire to do evil, of rebirth as its intended destination—is sort of like giving a person a map to a treasure without an "X" marked on it.

> **"Men are, that they might *have* joy." (2 Nephi 2:25; emphasis added)**

We need to realize that while *feeling* joy comes from repenting, *having* joy, possessing it as a permanent resource in our inner being which no external circumstances can affect comes from being born again in Christ. We have to get over our fear of these kinds of expressions, fear of sounding like born-again Christians. We need to start sounding like born-again *Christian* Mormons.

> **And those who did belong to the church were faithful; yea, all those who were true believers in Christ took upon them, gladly, the name of Christ, or Christians as they were called, because of their belief in Christ who should come. And therefore, at this time, Moroni prayed that the cause of Christians...might be favored. (Alma 46:15–16)**

There is not a soul, who desires to return home to the God who gave them life, who can or will circumvent or avoid this process or experience of being born again as a child, a new creature in Christ. Baptism, even by proper authority, is not its equivalent, neither is confirmation or any other physical ordinance. All the ordinances, absolutely essential as they are, are but actions to pattern us, guideposts to guide us along the path to our eventual awakening to Him **(2 Nephi 11:4)**.

AND BE BORN AGAIN, BECOMING HIS SONS AND DAUGHTERS

I would pray with all my heart that we who have thoroughly studied these materials no longer cringe at the concept of being born again, but realize it is the very bulls-eye, the very core of God's purpose for His children and the central message of the *Book of Mormon*.

> And the Lord said unto me: Marvel not that all mankind, yea, men and women, all nations, kindreds, tongues and people, must be born again; yea, born of God, changed from their carnal and fallen state, to a state of righteousness, being redeemed of God, becoming his sons and daughters. (Mosiah 27:25)

"*Becoming* his sons and daughters?" If you're like me, you may have read that phrase and wondered at the seemingly strange way to describe being redeemed. Aren't we already sons and daughters of God since before the world began? Then how is it that the scripture says that this process of being born again causes us to "become" the children of God? I believe the following verses of scripture clear away the confusion.

> And now, because of the covenant which ye have made ye shall be called the *children of Christ, his sons, and his daughters*, for behold, this day he *hath spiritually begotten you*; for ye say that your hearts are changed through faith on his name; therefore, ye are born of him and have become his sons and his daughters.
> And under this head ye are made free, and there is no other head whereby ye can be made free. (Mosiah 5:7–8; emphasis added)

The whole reason our Heavenly Father sent us here was to reconfirm our relationship with His Son, Jesus Christ. It is not offensive to the Father, or incorrect in His sight, for us to establish this loyalty, this friendship, even a parent-child intimacy with His Son. In fact it is the *only* thing that will save us. Christ *must* become our *head*, not just someone whose name we use as we brush past Him on our way. *He is our way.*

> [Another] sense in which Jesus Christ is regarded as the "Father" has reference to the relationship between Him and those who accept His Gospel and thereby become heirs of eternal life. ...
>
> That by obedience to the Gospel men may become sons of God, both as sons of Jesus Christ, and, through Him, as sons of His Father, is set forth in many revelations given in the current dispensation [see D&C 11:28-30; D&C 34:1-3; D&C 35:1-2; D&C 39:1-4; D&C 45:7-8] (*Teachings of Presidents of the Church: Joseph F. Smith,* 40.)

Again in the *Book of Mormon,* we read:

> And now I say unto you, who shall declare his generation? Behold, I say unto you, that when his soul has been made an offering for sin he shall see his seed. And now what say ye? And who shall be his seed?
>
> Behold I say unto you, that whosoever has heard the words of the prophets, yea, all the holy prophets who have prophesied concerning the coming of the Lord—I say unto you, that all those who have hearkened unto their words, and believed that the Lord would redeem his people, and have looked forward to that day for a remission of their sins, I say unto you, that these are his seed,... (Mosiah 15:10–11)

In allowing the principles of truth in this course of study to lead us through heart-deep repentance and preparation to receive the Lord Jesus Christ into our lives, we are each, individually, answering the inquiry of Mosiah 15:10, **"And now what say ye? And who shall be his seed?"** with this declaration: I will declare myself a part of "His generation." I will accept the offer of His soul as a sacrifice for all the sins from which I have suffered—my own and others. I will be "His child"—"His seed."

ONE FAMILY IN CHRIST—THE MOTIVE FOR CARRYING THE MESSAGE

With Christ as our father–figure, divinely appointed to that role by our equally universal Father in Heaven, and each of us changed by Him, Lehi's words spoken as he partook of the fruit of the tree of life take on new meaning:

> **And as I partook of the fruit thereof it filled my soul with exceeding great joy; wherefore, I began to be desirous that *my family* should partake of it also; for I knew that it was desirable above all other fruit. (1 Nephi 8:12; emphasis added)**

In that time before being born again in Christ, we may have been content or maybe even overwhelmed at trying to teach the gospel to our immediate family, but now we have been born again with a new heart and a new spirit—Christ's own. I believe that each of us in our own way, with our own unique talents, will awaken to the desire to participate in this great effort to help others come to Him and acknowledge His complete supremacy.

As the Prophet Joseph Smith expressed it:

> **Love is one of the chief characteristics of Deity, and ought to be manifested by those who aspire to be the sons [or daughters] of God. A man [or woman] filled with the love of God is not content with blessing his [or her] family alone, but ranges through the whole world, anxious to bless the whole human race. (*History of the Church*, 4:227)**

This desire to carry the message to others who still suffer—those who still do not know the Savior's reality—is essential to those who have been redeemed. In the original Twelve Step program, Bill Wilson, A.A.'s founder, realized that along with applying all the other principles that were to eventually become the basis for the other eleven steps, he had to also carry the message to others or he would lose his own sobriety.

I add my testimony to his. It is an absolute fact: if we do not share our new life in Christ in one way or another, we cannot retain it. In giving it away and watching others begin to recover, our recovery is continually renewed.

And behold, when I see many of my brethren truly penitent, and coming to the Lord their God, then is my soul filled with joy; then do I remember what the Lord has done for me, yea, even that he hath heard my prayer; yea, then do I remember his merciful arm which he extended towards me. (Alma 29:10)

TWELFTH STEP WORK BLESSES OUR IMMEDIATE FAMILY, TOO

Does this mean that we use our recovery work as another excuse to neglect our immediate family? Sometimes it may seem that way, at least at first. If our previous style of interacting with our family was to be enmeshed—caring or controlling beyond righteous bounds—our newly mended definition of "family" might actually be a blessing. It might give our closest loved ones some much-needed space in which to practice their own moral agency. When we put God and His will first in our life, how much we need to be there for and do for our immediate family, and how much God would have us extend ourselves to help to our Eternal family, begins to fall into place also. Here again, as in all other areas of our life, we must turn our will and life to God and trust His direction in all things— including this.

I have experienced this phenomenon in my own life. As I have done "twelfth-step work" (carrying the message) with others, I have witnessed a miracle in my home. It is an absolute fact that when I go out to do this work (as opposed to just "getting away" for money or for pleasure), I come home a more Christ-centered person, a far more sober person. I come home to my family with the words of eternal truth in *my* mind. The kind of spirit that possesses me and its effect on my household is perfectly expressed in these words by Nephi:

> **Therefore, the redeemed of the Lord shall return, and come with singing unto Zion; and everlasting joy and holiness shall be upon their heads; and they shall obtain gladness and joy; sorrow and mourning shall flee away. (2 Nephi 8:11)**

There is no way to describe the difference in the spirit that fills my home since I have dedicated my life to this work. There is now peace and joy where there once was a spirit of sorrow and mourning. The dreadful abuse my children lived with from both their parents has ended, and a gradual but steady healing is taking place.

If I did not share the good news of Christ's power to do these things, I know it would gradually slip away from me. I would lose it, and my family and I would be right back where we were before—I would be "drunk" and they would be neglected and abused. It is the nature of this telestial sphere to wear away at our commitment to God if we do not continually remember and renew it through sharing it with others.

> **And now, O my son, ye are called of God to preach the word unto this people. And now, my son, go thy way, declare the word with truth and soberness, that thou mayest bring souls unto repentance, that the great plan of mercy may have claim upon them. And may God grant unto you even according to my words. Amen. (Alma 42:31)**

GO AND DECLARE THE WORD WITH SOBERNESS

I have long realized that to be "sober" from my destructive, addictive behaviors, I must first be "sober" from any thoughts of fear, anger, resentment, doubt, self-pity, or other negative emotions. I used to think that meant I must somehow totally eliminate those thoughts and emotions from my mind—that I should just simply stop having them; that if I had them, that meant I was bad, that I had somehow failed God, that I was essentially unworthy and defective. I did not realize that to be tempted is *not* a sin.

You can imagine my amazement when, in prayerful scripture study, I began to realize that my emotions are a part of me—*all* my emotions, both positive and negative. I began to understand that *no* part of me can be destroyed because I, as a whole entity, am eternal. Then how do I stay sober of these things, since I can't just eliminate them? I learned that I must look unto the Lord in every thought, counsel with Him in *all* my doings **(Alma 37:36–37)**. I have come to realize that negative emotions only made me "drunk" and set me up for a binge of acting-out behavior if I don't take them to the Lord *as soon as they appear.*

What an amazing and revolutionary idea! I could take my fears, my anger, pride, jealousy, resentment, envy, greed, lust—all my negative thoughts to Christ *while they were still thoughts!* Instead of trying to resist the fact that I was having these thoughts and feelings—instead of trying to stuff them down and hide them, pretending I could eliminate them, I could take them to Christ.

I tried it. When I was tempted, I turned to the Savior in my mind. I cried out in my heart to my Redeemer and to my Father and sought the Savior's intervention. "Lord, I'm being so tempted to feel…, or think…, or do…I have no hope but Thee. O Jesus, Thou Son of God, deliver me! Father, apply the Atoning Power of Thy Son." Some version of one or all of these thoughts became my first reaction to temptation. I began to get past the lie that to be tempted was a sign I was bad. I wasn't bad. I was mortal. I found there was a time between temptation and action—enough time to call upon the Savior's power and surrender the fact of my mortality and weakness to Him. I began to realize that soberness was a condition in which I needed to look to the Lord every hour—or at least, be willing to practice doing so. Lo and behold, it worked!

When I first began to practice soberness, I would often be challenged by another human being who was filled with fear, anger, resentment, etcetera; sometimes, before I knew it, I was staggering "drunk" again. Just like the original alcoholics who shared their stories in *Alcoholics Anonymous*, I would find myself shaking my head, wondering how I had "lost it" so easily. It was literally as if someone had come waving a bottle under my nose, filled with one of these "intoxicating" negative emotions, and crying, "Here, listen to this tale of resentment and offense. I am reeling drunk with anger or bitterness! Don't you want some too?" And I would succumb.

How then, under the circumstances of living with others who are still **"drunken and not with wine," (2 Nephi 8:21)** can we, who are so recently recovering ourselves, stay "sober?" We practice these principles of recovery—one day at a time, one hour at a time and sometimes, one minute at a time. As we practice, our ability to remain sober grows. Each hour in which we invite the Lord to be "in our midst," at the absolute center of our lives, is an hour of sobriety, an hour of remission, an hour in which we inhabit Zion.

> **And again I ask, were the bands of death broken** [in that hour], **and the chains of hell which encircled them about, were they loosed? I say unto you, Yea, they were loosed, and their souls did expand, and they did sing redeeming love. And I say unto you that they are saved** [at least for that hour]. **(Alma 5:9)**

There is only one way the drug addict can stay out of drugs permanently, one hour at a time. There is only one way that the depression addict can stay out of depression, and the food addict can stay out of Twinkies, or the perfection addict can stay out of the life-damaging tenseness and desire to control which their compulsion creates. Listen now to Alma as he explains what that way is. I invite you to become as a little child and to listen to the words of a prophet/father to his own son and to receive them to yourself, into your own heart:

> **And now, my son, see that ye take care of these sacred things, yea, see that ye** *look to God and live.* **Go unto this**

people and declare the word, and be sober. My son,
farewell. (Alma 37:47; emphasis added)

LOOK TO GOD AND LIVE

We are living in a time in the history of the world when the
power of Satan's lies is spreading over the earth as the black plague
once did over Europe: *There is no God; Money and things are all that
matter; Eat, drink, drug, have all the sex you can get, for tomorrow you die.*
These lies pull at us nearly every waking moment, threatening to
wrench loose our hold on any form of hope or recovery. With
increasing frequency these lies rip our closest loved ones, spouses,
children and even parents from our arms and fling them to their
death spiritually and sometimes temporally. We feel alone and
racked with fear in the blackest period of time ever foretold.
Desperately we grasp at something dependable, something
predictable, something we can count on and even control. Thus
dependency on earthly things increases.

Is it any wonder that we are all, every one, turning to *something*,
anything, to distract and numb us. Busy, busy, busy—we must work,
work, work. Or in some other way, in some other form we must
"use." At first it seems to help—the new diet, the new furniture, the
new hobby, the new plan, the new commitment or project; but it
cannot last. Eventually we crash again, even more destitute than
before. We need not despair, however, when we experience these
feelings or watch someone else experience them. It's all part of the
grand journey of mortality as we learn by our own experience what
works and what doesn't. Someday we will have all tried enough
alternatives, none of which bring lasting peace, to finally realize that
there is *no* hope but in God.

You see, that is the bottom line, my friends: There is no way to
stay sober except by *looking to God*. Only then can we live, and only
then can we be alive to carry the message of this single hope to
others who are still suffering, still dying.

> Blessed art thou...for those things which thou hast done;
> for I have beheld how thou hast with unwearyingness
> declared the word, which I have given unto thee, unto
> this people. And thou hast not feared them, and hast not
> sought thine own life, but hast sought my will, and to
> keep my commandments. (Helaman 10:4)

SAY UNTO ZION, "THY GOD REIGNETH!"

Once we have been born again and have come to know the
joyous reality of nearly continual conscious contact with the Lord,
what is it that we will have the *desire* and *the call* to share with
others? The first four principles of the Gospel. They are the message
we are awakened to share. The mighty change in our sharing is our
focus—the Savior's central place in salvation.

Where we once may have rattled off the first four principles of
the Gospel as "faith, repentance, baptism, and gift of the Holy
Ghost," we now ground each of these principles in Jesus Christ. In
other words, we testify continually that the first principle of the
Gospel is *not* simply "faith," but "faith in the Lord Jesus Christ." We
know by our own experience that "repentance" and "baptism" can
and will result in a *remission of sin* through the Savior's atoning
power and grace if we will renew our faith in Him every day. We
come to appreciate that the greatest gift of the Holy Ghost—the
greatest gift He is authorized to bestow upon us—is conscious
contact with the words of our beloved Lord and a sure witness of His
and the Father's *living* presence in our lives.

The public message of the person born again in Christ is plain
and direct. It is simply this:

> And then shall they say: How beautiful upon the moun-
> tains are the feet of him that bringeth good tidings unto
> them, that publisheth peace; that bringeth good tidings
> unto them of good, that publisheth salvation; that saith
> unto Zion: Thy God reigneth! (3 Nephi 20:40)

> And thus they were instruments in the hands of God in bringing many to the knowledge of the truth, yea, to the knowledge of their Redeemer. And how blessed are they! For they did publish peace; they did publish good tidings of good; and they did declare unto the people that the Lord reigneth. (Mosiah 27:36–37)

This then is the message of the born-again person: "The Lord reigneth! Lift up your heads and droop no longer in sin. Repent and come unto Him, come unto Christ. He has more power to redeem than anyone (including you) has to be lost. Repent, turn to Him, and with His power, turn from sin. It's possible! It works! It's true!" You will desire to say **"nothing but repentance unto this generation" (D&C 6:9)**, to bear testimony of His power and His mercy, and to invite others to come and partake of His grace. This is *all the message there is.*

FIRM IN THE FAITH OF CHRIST UNTO THE END

And finally, the last concept in the twelfth principle: enduring to the end—practicing these principles in *all* our affairs, until the end of our lives. Now that we have the "horse" (the power of Christ), before the "cart" (enduring in righteousness), we are assured we can do this thing. In fact, we can do it joyfully, with gladness, with zeal.

> And they were also distinguished for their zeal towards God, and also towards men; for they were perfectly honest and upright in all things; and they were firm in the faith of Christ, even unto the end. (Alma 27:27)

And this zealousness, this enthusiasm (the root *entheos* derives from the Greek expression meaning "God in us"), will not leave us, even though life might go on to administer more "wounds."

> But behold, they have received many wounds; nevertheless they stand fast in that liberty wherewith God has made them free; and they are strict to remember the Lord their God from day to day; yea, they do observe to keep

his statutes, and his judgments, and his commandments continually; and their faith is strong in the prophecies concerning that which is to come. (Alma 58:40)

That which is to come is the same as it has always been: There is only one sure conclusion to this world, and to this life, for each of us personally—to receive Christ. Whether joyfully as a dearest friend, or in terror because we never knew Him, is our own choice, and no one else's.

CONCLUSION: THERE IS STILL ONLY ONE

And now it's time for that good-bye, for that conclusion I was putting off, for that one last "I love you." I don't know why I dreaded it so much; it's really pretty simple once I realize the conclusion will never change, and "good-bye" still means "God be with you."

I hope by now you realize that I did not attempt this work in order to "fish for you," as the old story goes, but to teach you how to fish for yourselves. You have my complete permission to forget me, along with all these other sources, but I pray with all my heart you will never forget the message: all power, wisdom, and authority reside in the Lord Jesus Christ. He waits for you to open the doors of your heart and to allow Him to become your best friend, your ultimate Sponsor—your Jesus.

If you have been reading quickly through this material in order to get an overview, I plead with you to go back now, and leave absolutely no scripture reference unread or uncaptured (see "What Is Capturing?" [A–3] in the appendix). Your own personal willingness to come unto Him and His word ensures your freedom from the bondage of compulsive addictive behaviors.

I know beyond a shadow of a doubt that if you will do this study seriously, your life will be changed forever, not by the material you study, but by Jesus Christ Himself. If, during the course of these discussions you have felt your heart lighten, *please be assured that it is Christ who brought you that light*. If you have felt instructed, please realize that it is *He* who has given you instruction through the Holy Spirit. If you feel different, changed somehow, somewhere deep inside, remember that He, and He only, can change hearts.

> **Behold, *he* changed their hearts; yea, *he* awakened them out of a deep sleep, and they awoke unto God. Behold, they were in the midst of darkness; nevertheless, their souls were illuminated by the light of *the everlasting word*. (Alma 5:7; emphasis added)**

We need to always remember that God's "everlasting word" is Christ Himself, and the revelation that pours into our minds is *His* word, *His* counsel, *His* comfort. We have no other source to look to for heart-deep healing. Other programs which promote self-help, self-affirmations, taking control of your life, and "you can do it" seminars, workshops, etcetera— are good as far as they go, but they *do not* go far enough. Not even the testimony of the prophets themselves will suffice. Only your relationship with Christ will change your life and unlock His power to redeem you.

ASSIGNMENT (FOR THE REST OF YOUR LIFE)

1. Scripture study (Genesis 1:1 through the end of the *Pearl of Great Price*). Take at least one verse a day and capture it—make it your own.

2. Prayer (*two-way* communication), not just daily, but continuously in your heart. If you will believe and receive His counsel, He will teach you *all things* whatsoever you should do.

3. Ordinances (sacrament and temple rites). Return often, weekly if possible. When Peter questioned the Savior, **"Lord, to whom shall we go? thou hast the words of eternal life"** (John 6:68), he was not just talking about the truths Christ taught to the public generally. These "words of eternal life" Peter spoke of are not ordinary words; they are the words of the ordinances, and valid only when received from one having been commissioned of

Jesus Christ. These precious words are the only "letter of the law" that is absolutely irreplaceable and unalterable.

4. Personal revelation through journal keeping (capturing). Take up the tool of writing and never lay it down. Our journals can be filled with far more than just names, dates and facts. They can be filled with God's word to us, personally and individually. We all have the ability to write by the spirit of revelation.

Well, I guess this is it for now. Thanks for blessing my life with your love of the Lord. I hope the blessing has been mutual. One more time: *I love you.*

EPILOGUE

Dear Reader,

As I sit here, this morning, I struggle, once again, as I did when *He Did Deliver Me from Bondage* was completed the first time, twelve years ago, to find the appropriate words to put closure on a never-ending story. In all humility, I must decline the task, today. There is no end to this amazing adventure of eternal progression, filled as it is with both unspeakable sorrow and unspeakable joy! There is no end to the amazing grace and joy found in continually using these principles to keep us in a "right relationship" with God.

I must admit to you that in the twelve years since I originally attempted to finish *He Did Deliver Me from Bondage*, my life went from hard to worse as these principles and my closeness to our dear Savior saved me one horrendous day at a time. When I first published these discussions in 1990, I thought that coming to know these truths was a reward for my previous faithfulness in facing my life's challenges. Instead, I found they were preparation for the challenges yet to come—challenges which included the death of my oldest daughter, the loss of my 23 year marriage, and the heart-ache of watching every one of my children inherit the family tradition of coping with life through compulsive or addictive behaviors.

However, I re-discovered the timeless truth of the adage "it's always darkest before the dawn." In the last six years, I have been blessed with health and strength and love greater than in all the years of my previous life. I have been blessed to marry a man who shares my love of the Savior and His grace in recovery. We are both anchored deeply in the Lord, and in Him and His love we come together as one. It is the most amazing experience, to be one with another person through mutual oneness with the Savior Jesus Christ.

As the years pass, I watch my children have their own adventures, and I feel the continual assurance that these words from Elder Boyd K. Packer are so true:

Save for the exception of the few who defect to perdition, there is no habit, no addiction, no rebellions, no transgression,...exempt from the promise of complete forgiveness. That is the promise of the Atonement of Christ. (*The Brilliant Morning of Forgiveness*, Ensign, Nov. 1995, p. 20)

I have been so blessed by and grateful for the chance to testify of the power in the Twelve Step program to open the principles of the Gospel to our hearts and minds and make them alive and practical. I have rejoiced in watching both Heart t' Heart and LDS Family Services Substance Abuse Recovery Services grow. This growth represents "my brethren"—other LDS members who have come to realize our only hope is in Christ.

With President Gordon B. Hinckley, I bear this testimony:

Each of us has burdens. Each of us has challenges and confusing options...Strength to do battle against destructive habits, or the battle toward personal purity...begins with enlisting the strength of God. *He is the source of all power*. (*Standing for Something*, p. 115, emphasis added.)

Someone once told me that this book should be subtitled, "A Survivor's Manual for the Last Days." I laughed, but I had to agree. In these principles, there is peace that passeth understanding, there is rest in the midst of tragedy, and hope in the midst of discouragement, because in these principles there is the formula for coming (home) to Christ. I bear this testimony with all my heart and soul and pray continually for all of you, "my beloved brethren," in the Name of Jesus Christ, Amen.

— *Colleen H.*
May 2002

APPENDIX

What Is Capturing?

What does "capture" mean? It means to get hold of something, *really* get hold of it, and make it your own. Here's how you capture thoughts from any source.

1. If your source is in the form of written material, underline the words or phrases that stand out to you. If it's in the form of a lecture, take notes as you listen. (Remember, taking notes is not the same as taking dictation. The goal is not to recreate every word the speaker says. The goal is to note those single thoughts that stand out to you.)

    Most people think that this is the entire procedure, that this constitutes "capturing." Sorry. This is only the step of identifying what it is that you *want* to capture. (If you were an old-time cowboy and were sitting up on a ridge watching a herd of wild mustangs below you, just picking out the ones that look good to you is not the same as making them your own.)

2. Get a notebook of some sort (maybe a journal) and a pen and then rewrite the words, phrases, sentences or whatever you underlined or noted into that notebook. When I copy quotes, I usually underline them as well as put quote marks around them so they stand out from the rest of what I write.

    Now are you done? After all, you have written the thought down in your own notebook or journal. Sorry, this still does not make it your own. There is a third and final step. Without this last step you are only a *collector* of thoughts, not a captor.

3. Now write all that comes into *your* mind about the thought or quote that you have previously copied into your notebook. Why was it important to you? How did it connect for you? What does it say to you? How do you see that it applies to your life? This is capturing.

For me, this process of capturing thoughts, scripture and quotes has also become a way of praying. I often find that I have just naturally entered into a prayer mode somewhere during this process, writing prayerful thoughts, expressing myself directly to God. And in just as easy and simple a manner I nearly always find myself realizing that what I am hearing in my thoughts is the voice of the Lord, through the Holy Spirit's mediation, speaking to my mind and heart.

BENJAMIN'S PROMISES:

"...If ye do this ye shall always..."

INTRODUCTION

I wonder if King Benjamin lay awake as many nights in anticipation of his discourse as I have this presentation. May I preface my remarks, even as Benjamin did, with a disclosure of my background and a declaration of my motive and intent.

I am a forty-one-year-old Orem housewife and mother of twelve. I joined The Church of Jesus Christ of Latter-day Saints at the age of fourteen, the only member of my family to do so. An only child, I was raised in a severely alcoholic background. I am a recovering addict myself, having practiced my addiction for twenty-two years, while at the same time being a feverishly active member of the Church in good standing.

You might wonder how a person can do that. It's easy. One just has to find addictions that are acceptable, or at least tolerable, in our Latter-day Saint culture. My choices of addictions were just that. One was compulsive eating and the other was perfection*ism* (which I define as the obsession to *appear* perfect to others). They were strange bedfellows, I must admit. The one drove my weight up over 300 pounds, approximately twice what it is today, and the second drove me to the gates of insanity and spiritual death.

I stand before you this day, however, healed on both counts. I am eager and excited to share by what power I was delivered from those invisible bonds that were truly **"the very handcuffs, and chains, and** shackles, and fetters of hell" **(D&C 123:8)** despite the fact that they were woven of the **"flaxen cords" (2 Nephi 26:22)** of my own finite self-will (wanting life to come on my terms) and self-righteousness (thinking that I was responsible for everything and must make everything right), masquerading as the ever-popular self-mastery and self-sufficiency.

No message of self-sufficiency or self-mastery was Benjamin's, and neither is mine. Even as Benjamin, I have not come here to boast of myself, but rather to rehearse to you and rejoice with you in those correct principles which, if taken *in the correct order,* will cause such a mighty change to be realized.

SPIRITUAL DYSLEXIA

In the last few decades a curious learning disability has been defined and given the title *dyslexia.* It has been found that individuals suffering its effects often perceive letter and word sequence in reverse. Even the plainest and simplest of statements can become frustrating puzzles to these otherwise bright people. Children so afflicted will often exhibit dysfunctional, self-defeating behaviors symptomatic of this underlying frustration and inability to understand.

I propose that many Latter-day Saints are *spiritually* dyslexic. The symptoms of this "dis-order" (literally) and the "dis-ease" it causes vary among us in outward severity and yet spring from the same genesis: this tendency to reverse the order of the written and spoken word of God. Thus we **"have eyes to see, and see not...ears to hear and hear not" (Ezekiel 12:2).**

Stricken with this disorder of perception, we, like ancient Israel, find the gospel neither easy nor simple **(1 Nephi 17:41).** Instead, we are frustrated and bewildered, wandering in a modern wilderness of stress, anxiety, discouragement and depression. Only occasionally do we glimpse the promised land of joy and peace that is potentially ours. Like those ancient (adult) children of Israel, we too cling to a dyslexic solution. Reversing the order of these words, **"the letter** killeth, but the spirit giveth life" (2 Corinthians 3:6), we act as if they teach us that the "letter," the outward activity, "giveth life." We desperately try to alleviate our disease by escalating and intensifying our performances and seeking to improve our appearances.

In **Moroni 10:32** is yet another example of a mystery of godliness veiled, not in God's delivery, but in our dyslexic perception. Though it plainly states **"come unto Christ, and be perfected in him,"** before it continues with the otherwise impossible charge to **"deny yourselves of all ungodliness,"** some Latter-day Saints may perceive and believe thusly: **"Deny yourselves of all ungodliness and [then] come unto Christ."** Having read it in that order, we launch off on a campaign of self-improvement, sincerely striving, knuckles white, to deny ourselves of all ungodliness. With set jaw and a countenance that would scare a child (and often does), we set about to "clean house," ourselves, meanwhile ignoring the gentle knock of Him who is like **"a refiner's fire, and like fuller's soap"** (3 Nephi 24:2).

WE REVERSE THE PROCESS

At this point may I invite you to look at the diagrammed model provided (page A–24). They say a picture is worth a thousand words. I hope then that a picture with a thousand words written on it is worth a whole lecture series because that is what it would take to do the fourth chapter of Mosiah justice.

Condensed into the core of this solitary chapter of the *Book of Mormon* is nothing less than the nucleus of the entire gospel of Jesus Christ. If we had no other words on earth to live by than these, we would have the seed, which if planted and nourished would bear fruit, **"precious...sweet above all that is sweet...and [we] shall feast upon this fruit even until [we] are filled"** (Alma 32:42).

To reverse the order of what Benjamin teaches in this chapter is as spiritually devastating as comprehending it correctly is exalting. To focus on the circumstances described on the right side of this diagram, trying to make them happen before giving our whole heart to the relationship with God set forth on the left side, is the spiritual equivalent of reversing the very process of exaltation. It is to put the cart before the horse, the destination before the journey, the gift before the Giver.

We would never even consider attempting to accomplish a journey in a car that had no fuel. Yet trying to perfect *ourselves* is as exhausting and discouraging as if we were doing just that! No wonder so many people give up part-way through and don't endure to the end. They've been pushing their own cars the whole distance!

MANDATE OR PROMISE?

For example, how many of you, like me, have sat in a lesson on parenting and had someone rehearse the words of **Mosiah 4:14** out of context? **"And ye will not suffer your children that they go hungry, or naked; neither will ye suffer that they transgress the laws of God, and fight and quarrel one with another..."**

Then, with those infamous words (that become more infamous the more kids you have) still ringing in your ears, you drive home with a van full of children who can't make it out of the parking lot before World War III erupts. As each discordant sound falls on your ears, this seemingly impossible mandate falls on your head like a pile driver—driving your sense of pleasing God ever further from you and you ever further from Him. You feel confused, befuddled, discouraged, or you feel frustrated, angry, determined to *force* this unrighteous behavior to cease. In confusion we are left to wonder, "Why would God give us such an impossible mandate and then call His gospel the `good news'?" Honestly, we find better news on television or in the Sunday newspaper. No wonder we spend the rest of the Sabbath day studying them instead of any more scriptures.

I am here to declare that the gospel, if read in the correct order, is always *good news!* To all my fellow beleaguered and bewildered parents I bring glad tidings of great joy. I'm about to share with you how God, having healed my spiritual dyslexia, gave me not only eyes to see, but also ears to ear and a *heart to understand* **(Mosiah 2:9)**.

With this understanding both God and Benjamin were transformed from stern task-masters to my greatest benefactors and friends.

When read in context, **Mosiah 4:14** is not a mandate or a command; it is actually a promise! No wonder it seems impossible by our finite, mortal understanding! God's promises usually are: manna from heaven, life after death, garments washed white in blood.

ALL THINGS FALL INTO PLACE

The truth is that the things on the right side of our model (page A–25) are promised results that will begin to happen *automatically* if we are willing to put all our effort into establishing and developing the relationship outlined on the left side. How can I make such a bold statement? I am in good company. Recently, President Benson repeated the same message to us: **"When we put God first in our lives, all other things fall into their proper place, or drop out of our lives" (President Ezra Taft Benson, *Ensign*, May 1988, p. 4, italics added).**

Notice the words "fall into their proper place." Feel the easiness and simpleness of the way. The gospel, when approached in the right order, can be successfully lived, and with such a lack of struggle as to seem like it's happening automatically. Notice I didn't say effortlessly. To live correct principles takes great effort on our part, most certainly—the effort of overcoming pride and self-will; the effort of seeking to know and then trust God's will for us above our own.

"FOR WE BELIEVE IN JESUS CHRIST"

Before we use our model, along with our scriptures, to rehearse the central verses of **Mosiah 4** and the detailed relationship principles it sets forth, we need to look at the first few verses of the chapter.

Here we find King Benjamin looking out over a great number of people who are bowed down to the earth in overwhelming reverence for God. Benjamin's previous words have found their place in ready and willing hearts. In godly sorrow and from the depths of sincere humility, the people honestly face and admit their weaknesses and failings. Convinced of their own hopeless and helpless state without Him, they come to a place of genuine surrender to their need for God. En masse, they cry out unto the name and personage of the Son of God, even *Jesus Christ*, that His atoning blood be applied to them.

And immediately they receive a remission of their sins, a cessation of the resentment and guilt that festers in unremitted sin. They are overwhelmed in a sense of peace—even His own peace. And all this because **"of the exceeding faith which they had in Jesus Christ," (v. 3)** that He could deliver them.

Seeing this mighty change from self– and sin–centeredness to God– and good– centeredness, Benjamin begins to rehearse to them again the conditions upon which they can retain what they have now obtained. His is the classic example of the perfect teacher—He tells his students what he's going to teach them, teaches them, and then, seeing they are taught, repeats his message again. Beginning in verse 6 we will rehearse with him what has not only brought on this mighty change, but also what will retain for them what they've so recently been given.

SALVATION COMES TO HIM WHO TRUSTS THE LORD

1. *"That salvation might come to him that should put his trust in the Lord"* (v. 6). Recognize and trust the Lord Jesus Christ specifically.

Jehovah of the Old Testament, Christ of the New Testament, and the Lord of the Book of Mormon are the same individual **(Helaman 14:12, 3 Nephi 15:5).** Nephi, Jacob, Enos, Benjamin, and later Alma, the brother of Jared, Mormon and Moroni—all these men, even like Adam, Abraham, Moses, Peter, James and John had a "working, walking," intimately personal relationship with Him, even the Lord Jesus Christ. While they kept the supremacy of the Father always in perspective, they realized full well that the Savior was the One they counselled with and conversed with in their hearts and minds **(Enos 1:2, 4, 10; Alma 36:18)**.

Each discovered in turn (even as we must) that the Son is the member of the Godhead sent by the Father to represent Him in full authority and power, as the **"mediator of the new covenant" (D&C 107:18–19)**, and that it is the *Son* whose words are conveyed to us by the Holy Ghost **(Moses 5:9)** and will lead us along in *all* things whatsoever we should do **(2 Nephi 32:3)**.

For us to work with the Son, to talk to Him, visualize Him, walk with Him, love Him with all our heart, might, mind and strength, *delights* the Father **(Colossians 1:19)**. He knows full well that the Beloved Son will attribute all glory, honor and power to the Father **(Matthew 6:13)**. There is no jealousy between them. They are, along with the Holy Spirit who administers for both of them, even as one **(John 10:30)**. They think as one, work as one, and rejoice as one when we become **"born of God" (Mosiah 27:28)** and become one with Christ **(D&C 50:43)**.

2. *"Salvation, through the atonement...for all mankind"* (v. 7). Accept and apply the atonement of Jesus Christ to all mankind, including myself.

To retain guilt for my own sins past the point of contriteness and confession or to continue to resent (much less to be angry with or bitter towards) another for his sins is to be in an even greater state of "sin" (separateness from God) than that caused by the original transgression. Why? Because to harbor guilt or resentment is to reject the very atonement of Christ. It is to make His gift, His offering, for nothing.

The Lamb of God offers us the gift of cleansing **(John 1:29)**, the gift of "at-one-ment" with Himself and the Father who sent Him. This is the gift of "good cheer" **(D&C 78:18)**, joy **(Alma 22:15)**, and peace that **"passeth understanding"** (Philippians 4:7). Yet we go about as if there were no atonement made. Filled with fear and anxiety, guilt and shame, we act as if there is a power that is greater to make wrong than Christ is able to make right, meanwhile totally ignoring the assurances of the scriptures that He retains **"all power, even to the destroying of Satan"** (D&C 19:3). Truly, as it has been so plainly said, **"For what doth it profit a man if a gift is bestowed upon him, and he receive not the gift?"** (D&C 88:33).

3. *"There is none other salvation save this"* (v. 8). Acknowledge that *all* salvation [improvement] from any source comes [though anonymously] from Jesus Christ.

Christ is the light **"that giveth light to every man that cometh into the world"** (D&C 84:46). A lecture on any subject, if it be good and uplifting, faith and hope producing, is coming from Jesus Christ, who is the origin of all truth (D&C 84:45), no matter what source the speaker gives for his material. The fact is that Christ is willing to work anonymously for now. He is calm and secure, knowing that ultimately, not by compulsion, but by enlightened choice, **"every knee shall bow and every tongue shall swear"** (Isaiah 45:23). Someday He will stand revealed as the saving force, the original source of everyone's journey toward salvation, whether they began to realize that saving power through Buddha, Mohammed, or the **"Great Spirit"** (Alma 18:28).

4. *"Believe that he is"* (v. 9). Believe that Jesus Christ *is* a *living* entity, available to each of us personally *this very day and hour,* through both the light of Christ and the Holy Ghost.

We must get over the holding pattern mentality that Christ was amongst us in the meridian of time or will yet be in His second coming. We must come unto Him even now so that He might come unto each of us personally, or we will not "remain" when he comes to the world generally (Ehat and Cook, *The Words of Joseph Smith*, p. 4). He must become a living reality to us today.

While the past is to be learned from, and the future to be hoped for, we have only this day to live, and **"sufficient unto the day is** [not only] **the evil** [the need, the challenge] **thereof" (Matthew 6:34)**, but also the strength, which we can renew each morning in and through Christ. Even like manna, His companionship must be sought each new day. We must learn to trust Him whose way is the way of manna and not of worry. After all, Christ Himself declared His own position in time and power by His very name **"I AM" (D&C 29:1)**.

5. *"That he created all things"* (v. 9). Believe that Christ created all things and that He is the instrument of the Father manifest in all creation.

The power embodied in Him is the power that created the sun, moon, stars and earth **(D&C 88:7)**. He is the power by which worlds without number were created **(Moses 1:35)**. Not only is He the creator of all that is "out there," but also all that is "in here" (our own physical bodies [**Jacob 2:21**]), and He is the very power by which we each move and think and have our being **(Mosiah 2:21, D&C 88:48)**.

6. *"Believe that he has all wisdom, and all power, both in heaven and in earth"* (v. 9). Believe that we can counsel with Christ in all our doings—that no subject is too trivial or too intimate.

Christ is the spirit and author of all truth, no matter where, or in what field. How wise we would be to take Him as our guide no matter what our need for knowledge. We are told that He knows **"the end from the beginning" (Abraham 2:8)**. We must also realize that He knows the middle—where we are right now. We must remember that He is not only **"Alpha and Omega" (D&C 61:1)**, but He is the **"way" (John 14:6)** between the two.

It is He to whom we should direct all our thoughts **(Alma 37:36)**, the unworthy as much, if not more, than the worthy. He is the one who can direct our anger, unravel our frustration, and still our fears, if we will only come unto Him. How foolish we are to turn away from God in those very moments we need Him most.

7. **"Believe that man doth not comprehend all the things which the Lord can comprehend"** (v. 9). *Always* remember to give credit to God, not yourself, for your success in any area.

The degree of self-mastery prophets achieve is not a reflection of any extraordinary ability of their own to comprehend anything, but of the power of the Master to whom they surrender in all things **(2 Nephi 4:19–20)**. We will not achieve true self-mastery until we are willing to turn our "selves" over to the Master.

If we would always remember, even as they, that it is His grace that is **"sufficient for [us]"** **(Moroni 10:32)** and not our own "unprofitable" efforts **(Mosiah 2:21)**, then **"in nowise** [could we] **deny the power of God"** **(Moroni 10:32)**.

8. **"Repent of your sins...and humble yourselves before God"** (v. 10). Realize that humility and repentance are the key principles in Christ's plan, not perfection and pride.

This humility and repentance must be thorough and complete, of the "fine-tooth comb" variety. Only when we "come down in the depths of humility," realizing that we are "fools" **(2 Nephi 9:42)** compared to God, will we be willing to do the degree of soul-searching that breaks and lays open our hearts **(2 Nephi 2:7)**. And if the heart is not opened and cleansed, no amount of perfection on the outside will mask it before God **(1 Samuel 16:7)**. This degree of soul-searching and soul-surrendering will make "prophets" of us all (**Numbers 11:29**; see "prophet" in the Bible Dictionary). Having once accomplished this act of surrender, the gifts of the Spirit will pour into our lives until we have finally realized the greatest gift of all— His own promise of our place with Him (Ehat and Cook, *The Words of Joseph Smith*, p. 4).

9. **"Ask in sincerity of heart that he would forgive you"** (v. 10). Seek Christ's personal administration of His atoning sacrifice and grace in your life.

I have come to realize that somewhere in the process of repenting unto a complete remission of sins we must ask Christ specifically to apply His atonement in our behalf **(Alma 36:18)**. It is, after all, His sacrifice, His price, His blood. It is His gift. It is His wings that would gather us **(3 Nephi 10:5)**, His arms that would encircle us **(D&C 6:20–21)**.

The truth is that He employs no servant there at the final gate of that straight and narrow way **(2 Nephi 9:41)**, for it is the channel of rebirth and awakening **(Alma 5:7)**, and He is both the delivering physician and the Father of those so born. When a person comes to receive a remission of sins it will be administered to him personally, by the Lord Himself (Ehat and Cook, **The Words of Joseph Smith**, p. 5). His peace is unmistakable, His comfort undeniable. His presence and power, His voice, and eventually, in His own time, His face, will be ours **(D&C 88:68)**.

Enos experienced this moment when, after an extensive effort at prayer motivated by an intense hunger to know the truth for himself, he heard a voice come into his mind that said, **"Enos, thy sins are forgiven thee, and thou shalt be blessed"** (Enos 1:5).

Alma the Younger left us an even more plain account of coming to this One-to-one consciousness of Christ's own personal administration.

> **Now, as my mind caught hold upon this thought,** [the atonement of one Jesus Christ (v. 17)], **I cried *within my heart*: O Jesus, thou Son of God, have mercy on me, who am in the gall of bitterness, and am encircled about by the everlasting chains of death.**
> **And now, behold, when I *thought* this, I could remember my pains no more; yea, I was harrowed up by the memory of my sins no more.**
> **And oh, what joy, and what marvelous light I did behold; yea, my soul was filled with joy as exceeding as was my pain! (Alma 36:18–20, emphasis added)**

10. *"Always retain in remembrance...your own nothingness and his goodness"* (v. 11). Remember the goodness of *God*, and our own nothingness comparatively.

Even after Nephi had become a great prophet, he retained in remembrance his own **"wretchedness" (2 Nephi 4:17)**, giving God credit for his support **(v. 20)**. He acknowledged plainly that it was **"the robes of** [the Lord's] **righteousness" (v. 33)** and not any power or worthiness of his own that made him a free man. Though it flies in the face of all modern humanistic philosophy, let us consider what we, like Moses, "had never before supposed"—that "man is nothing" without the glory of God **(Moses 1:10)**.

It will never be *who* we are, but rather *whose* we are that makes the difference.

11. *"Calling on the name of the Lord daily"* (v. 11).

Not only should we call on the Lord daily but even *continually* **(Alma 13:28)**. Through his servant Alma, Christ has invited us to **"counsel with** [Him] **in all** [our] **doings" (Alma 37:37)**. President Ezra Taft Benson bore second witness to the all-encompassing application of that entreaty when he wrote:

> The *constant* and most recurring question in our minds, *touching every thought and deed of our lives,* should be, "Lord, what will thou have me to do?" (First Presidency Message, *Ensign,* Dec. 1988, p. 2.)

While Christ Himself would counsel us to go before our Father in Heaven in prayers of praise, honor, and appreciation, the Father would, in turn, direct us to hear His Beloved Son, in whom He is well pleased **(Joseph Smith History 1:17)**. In our need, puzzlement, sinning and suffering, He is, through the administration of the Holy Spirit, the source of our guidance. There is nothing in which we cannot turn to Him.

Every day will bring relapses into "sin," into thoughts, words or actions that distance us from God and others. If we are to *retain* what we have *obtained*, we must keep our relationship with Him explicitly honest and continue to seek His atoning intercession with the Father **(Hebrews 7:25)**.

I have found that if I neglect my relationship with Him, within two days I am an hungered and athirst, and within three I have started to slip back into that spiritual wilderness **(Alma 37:42, 45)** from which only He can deliver me **(Mosiah 23:23)**.

12. *"Standing steadfastly in the faith of that which is to come"* (v. 11). Benjamin's immediate promises, as well as future glorious events.

While it is true that one of the things "which is to come" and in which we must stand steadfast is the glorious second coming of the Lord, I believe that this admonition can also be applied to the promises that Benjamin is about to rehearse to us.

As we begin to experience some of the promises listed on the right side of the model **(Mosiah 4:12–16)** we will find ourselves not able to keep them perfectly. We will have to be satisfied with consistency, not constancy. Standing steadfast in hope for ourselves and faith in Christ, we must realize that it takes time to rid ourselves of the "old ways." Our nature has been changed, not our past. Neither have our bodies been changed. We are still subject to hunger, fatigue, etcetera. We must give ourselves allowance for these imperfections and be willing to admit them and accept them.

When we relapse we must not get discouraged or despair that these principles do not work. We must keep trusting in God, realizing that often His pattern is to ease our burden before relieving our bondage altogether **(Mosiah 24:14)**. Even Nephi, at the height of his role as a prophet, said of himself, **"I am encompassed about, because of the temptations and the sins which do so easily beset me" (2 Nephi 4:18)**.

If our hearts are changed we can be absolutely certain that we will see that change begin to manifest itself outwardly, albeit gradually. Celestial glory will continue to increase in us as we continue to turn to it **(D&C 88:40)**. We *must* surrender ourselves to the kind of relationship with God as described by Benjamin (and outlined on the left side of the model) before we can expect the results he promises (as outlined on the right side).

GUARANTEED SUCCESS

And finally we come to the promises—to the guaranteed results of focusing on the preceding twelve adjustments of perspective and priority. As we cover them in order you will notice that the first five are internal changes. God's changes **always** begin within. As President Benson has stated: **"The Lord works from the inside out. The world works from the outside in. The world would take people out of the slums. Christ takes the slums out of people"** **(First Presidency Message, *Ensign*, July 1989, p. 4).**

These first five promises are: "Ye shall"—

1. *"Always rejoice"* (v. 12).

    How often will we feel a feeling of joy? *Always,* and under all circumstances.

I experienced this transcendent miracle just this past summer. Through the sudden and potentially devastating experience of opening my door to a highway patrolman bearing the news of my oldest daughter's sudden death in an automobile accident, through her funeral at which He gave me strength to speak, I was suspended in a state of joy, not shock, as most people thought.

Why? Because I have come to know of God's goodness and benevolence. I know for myself, and not by anyone else's witness, that not even a sparrow falls **(Matthew 10:29)** without His divine consciousness, and that **"all things work together for good to them that love God"** **(Romans 8:28)**. I know that my daughter loved God. And I know that I love Him, and that I trust Him enough to be **"willing to submit to all things which the Lord seeth fit to inflict upon [me], even as a child doth submit to his father"** **(Mosiah 3:19)**.

2. *"Be filled with the love of God"* (v. 12). A two-way love—His for you and *yours for Him.* It is absolutely essential that it be two-way.

Today, I am "filled with the love of God"—not just His love for me, but even more important, my love for Him. His love had patiently stood at the door and knocked, but it wasn't until my love finally answered that the essential two-way connection was made that has changed my heart **(Jacob 6:5)**. It wasn't until I began to see His intervention everywhere, in every coincidence, that I became filled to overflowing with love for Him.

3. *"Always retain a remission of your sins"* (v.12).

As I have become humble and honest enough in His presence to share even my worst mistakes, I have watched in amazement as those very mistakes are consecrated unto my gain by His charity and power. Today, I do not have a past that I regret. Instead I have only a glorious history of lessons—finally learned.

I have found, however, that the hour I cease to retain in my remembrance this relationship with Him, I lose that peace that passeth understanding. In other words I lose the remission of the "dis-ease" of sin. I find myself relapsing into a state of fear, guilt and resentment. I regress into a **"natural man,...an enemy to God" (Mosiah 3:19)**. (Mainly because in that condition I am an enemy to everyone—especially myself.)

4. *"Grow in the knowledge of the glory of him that created you...of that which is just and true"* (v. 12). We will increase in our ability to receive personal revelation.

In other words we will grow in the gift of personal revelation borne to us through the medium of the Holy Ghost. It was because of this promised blessing that I knew from the moment I heard of my daughter's death that it was all right; it was just and true.

I know that such a degree of conscious contact with God and with His glory and purposes comes only through recognizing and acknowledging His comprehension of all things, which I cannot comprehend unaided.

5. *"Ye will not have a mind to injure one another"* (v. 13). Our natures will be changed.

Our dispositions will be changed. We will have no desire to do evil (to ourselves or others) but will desire to do good continually **(Mosiah 5:2)**. It was this change that brought me to a place where I did not have to count calories, or restrain a voracious appetite. As long as I put God first, I simply had no more desire to hurt myself with food; I ceased to overeat and thus lost weight.

It is only because of these five internal, heart-deep changes that I have experienced the external, observable results, and that they have been consistent and genuine. Other results have come, including all those that Benjamin promised. We need to remember that these are only examples. Our personal realization of results will be tailored to our personal needs and will extend into every facet of our lives. Anywhere we have had a weakness, we will find it transformed into a strength **(Ether 12:27)**.

6. *"Ye will not suffer your children that they go hungry or naked* [either emotionally or physically]*"* (v. 14).

As my need to *appear* perfect disappeared, my strict, cold, "letter of the law" brand of parenting did also. I found myself spending far more time loving and sharing with my children and far less time criticizing and judging them. Their hunger for my attention and their "nakedness" to my misdirected frustration and anger was relieved.

7. *"Neither will ye suffer that they transgress the laws of God, and fight and quarrel one with another"* (v. 14). And this because you will have a *"mind to...live peaceably"* with them and *"render to* [each of them] *according to that which is* [their] *due"* as children of God (v. 13).

As I became a **"peaceable follower[s] of Christ" (Moroni 7:3)**, I found myself more naturally inclined to love and accept, to listen and understand my children's feelings and needs.

8. *"Ye will teach them to walk in the ways of truth and soberness"* (v. 15). You will have the natural ability to teach, especially through example. *Your* nature will be such that *you* will be able to walk in ways of truth and soberness, calmness and faith. They will thus learn it deeply. It will be something you *are*—not just something you say.

As I changed, my children began to change. My ability to **"walk in the ways of truth and soberness"** (v. 15) caused them to become more honest and "sober" also. Their excesses of misbehavior began to diminish even as mine did. How humbling it has been to see that much of the confusion and contention in them had been a reflection of my behavior.

9. *"Ye yourselves will succor those that stand in need of your succor"* (v. 16). You will become more selfless, completely so— and in the best ways. You will not even fear financial insecurity. You will have a feeling of *abundance*, not scarcity, in all areas of your life.

Viewing everyone as equal before God, we will become **"no respecter of persons"** (D&C 38:16). We will continue to progress in Christlike qualities, and our faith and charity will begin to affect our dealings with others. The fear of being too generous will leave us (v. 16).

In fact, fear of anything will begin to fade because we will have come to **"know in whom [we] have trusted"** (2 Nephi 4:19). We will have come to believe His assurance that while there are numberless ways to sin **(Mosiah 4:29)**, **"[His] grace is sufficient for all men that humble themselves before [Him]"** **(Ether 12:27)**. We will be able to enter into His rest **(Matthew 11:28)**, knowing that it is **"not requisite that a man should run faster than he has strength"** and that what God requires can be accomplished if **"all these things are be done in wisdom and order" (Mosiah 4:27)**.

SUMMARY

In summary may I repeat **"that** [we] **are eternally indebted to** [our] **heavenly Father,"** and that we should **"render to him all that** [we] **have and are" (Mosiah 2:34)**. He has sent His Beloved Son into the world that we might **"hear Him" (Joseph Smith History 1:17)**, and more than just hear Him, that we might become like Him **(Moroni 7:48)**. Is that God's charge to us? No, it is His promise. Do we have power in ourselves to accomplish it? No. The power is in Christ **(Moroni 10:32)**. Will self-sufficiency achieve it? No. We are not sufficient **(Mosiah 2:20–21)**. Will church activity alone accomplish it? No. Keeping the **"law...availeth nothing" (Mosiah 3:15)**. While it is true that **"the Lord is bound when we do [what] he say[s]" (D&C 82:10)**, it is a transcendent truth that it is the motive and intent of the heart that God considers **(1 Samuel 16:7)**. Even though **Doctrine & Covenants 130:20–21** informs us that blessings are predicated upon obedience to law, it is only ourselves and God who can know whether that outward display of obedience is indicative of our compliance with the lower law of performances or the higher law of love. We as individuals and as a people are in severe danger if we do not acknowledge and admit to ourselves that Christ's scathing words to Joseph, **"They draw near to me with their lips, but their hearts are far from me", (Joseph Smith History 1:19)**, could just as easily apply to us, when we place our efforts above His.

We must remember that **"there shall be *no other name* given nor any other way *nor means* whereby salvation can come" (Mosiah 3:17, emphasis added)** than by Christ. So do we have a thousand things to do today to be worthy? No. We have only one work today and that is to love God the Father, and to come unto His Son, who is also beloved of the Father.

President Benson asserted that we must be **"convinced that Jesus is the Christ, choose to follow Him, be changed for Him, captained by Him, *consumed in Him*, and born again"** (First Presidency Message, *Ensign*, July 1989, p. 5; emphasis added).

CONCLUSION

In conclusion I would like to say what a privilege it has been to participate in this symposium. Nowhere on any earth is there a gathering of people addressing a more powerful or important subject than we are here today.

May I take this opportunity to add my personal witness of the *Book of Mormon* to that of our beloved prophet, President Benson. Oh, how beautiful he is and how valiantly he is attempting to lead us out from under the condemnation of vanity and unbelief **(D&C 84:55)**! He is, in Christ, worthy and capable of his position and calling.

While the *Book of Mormon* is and always will be the most powerful instrument in bringing nonmembers into the Church, I know today that *that* is *not* its fullest purpose or potential. Its greatest purpose is to bring the already baptized, confirmed, endowed member unto Christ—into the fellowship of Christ **(D&C 88:133)**, into the **"church of the Firstborn" (D&C 88:4–5)**, to make of us not just His servants, but His *friends* **(D&C 93:45–46)**. It is to invite us to learn the principles by which we can establish a relationship with Him so intimate and tender that we may even come to refer to Him as *"my Jesus"* (*2 Nephi 33:6*).

The preceding article was given as an address by Colleen C. [Bernhard] Harrison on February 5, 1990 at the Book of Mormon Symposium, Brigham Young University, Provo, Utah. The model (chart) on page A–24, which is referenced several times during the address, was a handout at the symposium.

Benjamin's Promises
(Mosiah 4)

Outlined below are the fundamental principles we must surrender to in order to establish a relationship with God that will give us the ability to experience the results listed on the other side of this chart. (The points of relationship and the list of results are not represented as lining up one to one.) It is only through this relationship—one of mutual love and "cleaving" **(Jacob 6:5)**—that we will find a source of power far greater than our own that can transform us from the inside out.

Relationship

1. *"Salvation might come to him that should put his trust in the Lord."* (v. 6) Recognize and trust the Lord Jesus Christ specifically.

2. *"Salvation, through the atonement...for all mankind."* (v. 7) Accept and apply the atonement of Jesus Christ to all mankind, including myself.

3. *"There is none other salvation save this."* (v. 8) Acknowledge that all salvation (improvement) from any source comes (though anonymously) from Jesus Christ.

4. *"Believe that he is."* (v. 9) Believe that Jesus Christ is a living entity, available to each of us personally this very day and hour, through both the light of Christ and the Holy Ghost.

5. *"That he created all things."* (v. 9) Believe that Christ created all things, and that he is the instrument of the Father manifest in all creation.

6. *"Believe that he has all wisdom, and all power, both in heaven and in earth."* (v. 9) Believe that we can counsel with Christ in all our doings—that no subject is too trivial or too intimate.

7. *"Believe that man doth not comprehend all the things which the Lord can comprehend."* (v. 9) Always remember to give credit to God, not yourself, for your success in any area.

8. *"Repent of your sins...and humble yourselves before God."* (v. 10) Realize that humility and repentance are the key principles in Christ's plan, not perfectionism or pride.

9. *"Ask in sincerity of heart that he would forgive you."* (v. 10) Seek Christ's personal administration of His atoning sacrifice and grace.

****

Acting on these principles will bring us to a place of remission of sins, a mighty change, as described in verse 11. In order to retain that condition we must:

10. *"Always retain in remembrance...your own nothingness, and his goodness."* (v. 11) Remember the goodness of God and our own nothingness comparatively.

11. *"Calling on the name of the Lord daily."* (v. 11)

12. *"Standing steadfastly in...that which is to come."* (v. 11) Benjamin's promises as well as future glorious events.

Listed below are some of the results we are promised if we will allow the correct perspective and understanding of our relationship to God to permeate the deepest places of our hearts. It is by no means a complete list. The total list could not be represented because it is personal and singularly appropriate for each of us. The first five will be the same for all—the rest will be tailored to each of us personally and uniquely.

Results

1. *"Always rejoice."* (v. 12)

2. *"Be filled with the love of God.* (v. 12) A two-way love—His for you and yours for Him. It is absolutely essential that it be two-way.

3. *"Always retain a remission of your sins."* (v. 12)

4. *"Grow in the knowledge of the glory of him that created you…of that which is just and true."* (v. 12) We will increase in our ability to receive personal revelation.

5. *"Ye will not have a mind to injure one another."* (v. 13) Your nature will be changed.

****

Because of these five internal changes you will see external results.

6. *"Ye will not* [have to] *suffer your children that they go hungry or naked* [either emotionally or physically]." (v. 14)

7. *"Neither will ye* [have to] *suffer that they transgress the laws of God, and fight and quarrel one with another* (v. 14) (And this because you will have a *"mind to…live peaceably"* with them and *"render to* [each of them] *according to that which is* [their] *due"* as children of God [v. 13].)

8. *"Ye will teach them to walk in the ways of truth and soberness."* (v. 15) You will have natural ability to teach, especially through example. Your nature will be such that you will be able to walk in ways of truth and soberness (calmness and faith). They will thus learn it deeply. It will be something you *are*—not just something you say.

9. *"Ye yourselves will succor those that stand in need of your succor."* (v. 16) You will become more selfless, completely so—and in the best ways. You will not even fear financial insecurity. You will have a feeling of *abundance*, not scarcity, in all areas of your life.

THE POWER OF HIS EVERLASTING WORD
(Alma 5:5, 7)

THE HONEST LIGHT OF TRUTH

These two verses from the *Book of Mormon*, **Alma 5:5** and **7**, disclose the key to getting out of bondage—whether that bondage be to Lamanites, or a destructive habit, or to a dysfunctional past. In any of those cases, being free—free to grow and shine and become one's own fullest potential self—in this life and in the next hangs squarely on recognizing, acknowledging, and embracing (internalizing) **"the power of his** [everlasting] **word."**

Let us examine then, just what this power is by searching the symphonic nature of several scriptures:

In **John 1:14** we are told that the "Word" is the Lord Jesus Christ Himself. Thus we are led to understand that **"the power of his** [everlasting] **word"** is the power of Jesus Christ.

In *Doctrine and Covenants* **84:45** the transposition is plainly stated: **"For the word of the Lord is truth, and whatsoever is truth is light, and whatsoever is light is Spirit, even the Spirit of Jesus Christ."** So now we have the understanding opened to us that **"the power of his** [everlasting] **word"** is synonymous with the power or Spirit of Christ, which is synonymous with truth.

Next, we find in *Doctrine and Covenants* **84:46** that Christ is the light that lighteth every man who comes into the world. So thus we understand that every man and woman has the potential, at least, to be in conscious contact with truth, and that conscious contact is the power that will lead them out of bondage. This is true of everyone—member or non-member.

So at its most basic level, a level available to all, the light of Christ is a source of truth that functions even anonymously if necessary. In other words even agnostics and atheists have it, if they live by a standard of truth and honesty. We would do well to realize there are likely some "agnostics" even among active Latter-day Saints—people who, *if they would be true and honest* and who fear (respect) God, whose standard is truth, more than they do man (their family and societal expectations), would have to admit, "I don't *know* if there is a God or not…at least a God who is *personal to me*."

So where and how do we begin to let this respect for truth enter our lives? We begin by accepting the challenge to recognize, acknowledge and embrace *honestly* what our conscience tells us is *true* about our past and present choices.

THE KEY IS WRITING

Writing is the key to this honest look within. Keeping a notebook that we can use to write down our inner thoughts or feelings is essential. A very wise person once said, "How can I know what I think until I see what I say?" Writing tends to solidify our focus, cutting through the inner turmoil of all the "voices" we hear within; the "old tapes" that were imprinted in us by the influence of parents and significant others (siblings, extended family, close friends, etc.).

Besides using writing to keep up with current "events," a second writing project is unavoidable if a person desires the privilege of "graduating" from the basic level of conscience, the light of Christ, to the realization of the gift of the Holy Ghost. This writing project is the exercise of doing a fearlessly honest moral inventory of our past. This must be done because even though we might clean up our storefront, so to speak (picture a little old-fashioned country store), or in other words, our current life—if we do not go back into the storeroom (our past) and check every box and barrel stored there as thoroughly as we consciously can, we will still be plagued with "rotten smells" that will drive others away. And the most significant "other" our stored-up garbage will drive away will be the Holy Spirit. And since we need His "patronage" in our little store (His power in our life) in order to continue our progression in living by personal revelation, we would be wise to do all we can to cultivate His constant attendance with us. He is, after all, the First Comforter who can in His own time and in His own way prepare us to receive the Second Comforter, even Jesus Christ Himself.

A THOROUGH HOUSECLEANING

And so let's begin this inventory process. Visualizing that country store might prove helpful. We could even visualize it with a big sign stretched across the front that says "Temporarily Closed for Inventory," and we could take a couple of days and just work on the project. Most of us, however, find that we have to keep the "store" of our life open for business as usual while we conduct this inventory work in our spare time, drawn out over a longer stretch of time—a month or so for instance. This can be a pretty taxing time in either case, but it is worth it. A fullness of the Holy Spirit's companionship is our desire and will be our reward. His gifts are beyond comprehension—the greatest being the gift of revelation, which begins with the sure witness of Christ. Not just your witness of Him either, but even more important—His witness of *you*. Oh, what a small price to pay—to do this fearless and searching moral (honest) inventory.

It will take a great deal of faith and maybe some false starts to get people to attempt this effort, though, for the substance of its promise is only hoped for and not yet seen. And after all, their hesitancy is understandable because (1) this is going to be hard work on their part—no quick fix from a priesthood blessing or a counseling session; this is the **"working out one's own salvation" (Mormon 9:27)** part of the process of humbling themselves; (2) there are some pretty scary things back there in that storeroom of the past—boxes and bundles, for instance, marked "From Mom (or Dad) with Love" that stink to high heaven. How do people clean those out without offending their parents—whether living or dead? These are real concerns and need to be met with patience and the assurance that it's worth it.

The bottom line, as always, for each of us individually is to what length we are willing to go in order to obtain the promised results of such a thorough "housecleaning," to have the fullness of whatever degree of spiritual guidance we have been ordained to receive. For those of us who have received the ordinances of baptism and confirmation, that fullness is of the Holy Ghost, which fullness brings the gifts of the Spirit, the greatest of which is the spirit of revelation. That gift will eventually, in God's time, introduce each of us individually to the reality of our true eternal heritage and identity. We will have the privilege of receiving the mysteries of the kingdom of heaven, to have the heavens opened unto us, and to commune with our eternal family **(D&C 107:19)**. Thus will all the **"rivets"** that hold the **"creeds of** [our] **fathers, who have inherited lies,"** be loosed; and the **"confusion"** and **"corruption"** in our personal lives will be removed **(D&C 123:7)**. Our hearts will be changed and we will have no more desire to do evil, but to do good continually. Our dispositions will be changed **(Mosiah 5:2)**. Do you hear that? Do you realize what it means? A person who is **"in the midst of darkness"** (negativity) can be **"illuminated" (Alma 5:7)!**

THE MECHANICS

And what are the mechanics of the process? I can only share what has worked for me. Keep in mind that everyone is different, and the light of truth in each person might lead to personalizing this procedure.

A. Get a notebook. Label several pages in five- or ten-year increments.

B. Now turn to the highest power you can *honestly* acknowledge— even if it be only your own inner desire to be free of the bondage (the bad habit, etc.) you admit you're in. (**Alma 32** tells us that even a desire is sufficient for a beginning and can work in us.)

Draw upon that highest power in you, either by praying (if you can visualize a personal Higher Power, such as a Heavenly Father or Savior) or by picturing that desire to get well, to be free, as a spark of light—a candle or flashlight—held in your hand as you venture into the past; just as long as you see and feel your source of light as "illuminating" **(Alma 5:7)**.

C. Now begin by listing any and every negative memory you have. (By focusing on the negative I do not begin to imply ignoring the positive. If it helps you, keep a separate list of positive memories, but know that doing so will extend the length of time the inventory process will take.)

What you're looking for is any memory of a person, place, thing or situation in your past that still makes you feel any degree of negative emotion. Following is a sample of the form I used, with some hypothetical examples at different age levels.

Person, place, thing or situation	Negative emotion the memory causes (fear, guilt, anger, resentment, bitterness, etc.)	Why does it make me feel that way?
0–5 years Little girl that stole my doll	1) anger, 2) guilt	1) because she stole it 2) I hated her & my mom told me that was bad
5–10 years stealing money from my mom's purse	1) guilt, 2) resentment	1) I knew it was wrong 2) I blamed her because she wouldn't give me money
10–15 years Uncle John babysat me.	1) fear, 2) guilt, 3) resentment	1) He always tickled me. I feared him/it. 2) He told me not to tell my mom 3) I felt helpless

Just reading those examples might give you a feeling for how the process could help a person begin to develop a relationship with complete truth and honesty. No more pretending that it didn't happen, or that it didn't hurt. No more pretending that we don't feel the way we do. Thus the roots from which our present-day defeating and even destructive behaviors spring begins to come to light.

THE REST OF THE PROCESS

When the inventory is done, and we have left no box, bag, or barrel unopened (to continue our storeroom metaphor) up to the present time, we come to the next step. This is a big one, so brace yourself! Using this written inventory as a guide, we must admit the "exact nature" of our "wrongs" to ourselves, to God, and to another person.

Before you panic, look back at your list. The exact *nature* of your wrongs are not the things listed in the first column—those are just the outward circumstances, the symptoms of the underlying heart-deep problem. The "exact" nature of your wrongs—the spiritual roots of those outward behaviors—are revealed in the middle column. For instance, if you go back and run your eyes down that center column and find the word "fear" listed over and over again, you can see clearly the truth about yourself—that you are a person who (even though you might be very active—even anxiously active—in the Church) has a real faith deficit. Or as another example, if you find a lot of guilt-type words showing up in that center column, you now know that you are a person with a tendency to refuse the atonement of Christ in your own behalf. If you find a lot of words such as "anger," "bitter," "resentful," it reveals your heart-level rejection of the atonement of Christ *for others*. (One way or the other, Christ and His atonement are what we've been underutilizing, or we wouldn't have been in bondage to begin with.)

After this process we must turn to Christ consciously and deliberately **(Alma 36:18; Alma 38:8)** and ask Him to apply His atoning power to our hearts, to purify them of those character traits that cause us to resist His gracious offer of cleansing—to give us a "remission of our sins." He will then burn through our inner unconscious selves—cleansing us and revealing to us all that we've missed. We will find ourselves awakening to (sometimes gradually, sometimes abruptly) and enjoying the ever-increasing companionship of the Holy Spirit.

Note, however, the Lord's choice of the word *remission* of our sins. What we have obtained (this cleaned-out storeroom of life) must be *retained* by taking frequent, even daily inventories, and when we find ourselves tempted to store away a fear or an anger, etcetera, we must promptly admit it to ourselves, to God and to another trusted person. For example, a quick call to a close trusted friend to admit "I was just tempted to lie to Sister Jones about why I couldn't teach her primary class, but then I consciously reached out to the Lord (remember He's the Light of Truth) and found the courage in His Spirit to be honest." When we not only *feel* tempted but actually give into a temptation, we need to promptly admit it to ourselves, to God, and to that trusted other person—and not hide in denial or rationalization. (**Note: If any of our past situations or current ones involve moral transgressions, the "trusted third person" needs to be our bishop.)

ONE "LAST" THING

We also have not finished the process until we make amends to anyone we might have harmed. The only condition under which we would avoid making amends is if to do so would deeply injure or disrupt someone's current life. Making amends for current inventory issues is the equivalent of the old adage that we should never let the sun set on a trouble between us and another person.

When we pursue this course to the best of our ability, relying continuously on the guidance of a loving Heavenly Father and Elder Brother, as communicated to us through the administration of the Holy Spirit, we cannot help but be filled with an ever-increasing degree of consciousness of that guidance. The very gifts of the Spirit begin to pour out in such abundance that we can hardly contain them and we know that He is our "constant companion"—even as our confirmation promises us. Life becomes an adventure, not a chore and a challenge, not a trial. Our journey to find Him, even the Spirit of Truth, begins with aligning ourselves with the truth—past and present. In this willingness to become honest is the power of truth, the power of Christ, the power of His everlasting word.

DISCUSSION ON OPPOSITION
(2 Nephi 2:11–13)

2 Nephi 2:11—

> For it must needs be, that there is an opposition in all things. If not so, my first-born in the wilderness, righteousness could not be brought to pass, neither wickedness, neither holiness nor misery, neither good nor bad.

Once again, as with "the ends of the atonement" in verse ten, there is one little phrase in this verse that must be understood to make it all fit together. It's like a jigsaw puzzle piece that just needs to be turned around and looked at from a little different direction, and suddenly not only does it fit, but it pulls a big part of the puzzle together. The phrase is "brought to pass."

At first glance a person reading by the "letter" and not the "spirit" of the message would get the impression that God is arbitrarily applying "opposition" to us to "bring to pass" (or cause) both good and bad, as if He is wielding some arbitrary despot-like decision over us, like pawns on a chessboard. This couldn't be further from the truth.

The truth is that God, as we observed earlier , works by rules that are older and more sovereign than even He is—eternal principles that no one "made up." These *facts*, these *truths*, just are. They are not arbitrarily fashioned by our particular Father's fancy. We need to realize that there is not another unit of creation where, if we dropped something it would fall *up*, or if we lied we would find happiness.

In these words of explanation of a wise father to his child (Lehi to Jacob), you can almost hear the voice of our Heavenly Father, trying to explain to each of us, as soon as we're willing to listen, the following:

> You see, child, I must allow opposition, or in other words, at least *two* choices to exist, even though this brings to pass much wickedness and misery. In fact, child, if you could only see from my perspective, you would realize that wickedness and the resulting misery it causes are exactly what I'm trying to discover in my children's hearts. I allow opposition to exist among my children in order to prove them; and I could not *not* allow it—for it would take away their chance to exercise their agency. That cannot be done.

If there were no opposition, no opportunity to be exposed to evil, there would be no opportunity for us to choose, and it is by our choices that we demonstrate and maintain our valiancy. I add "maintain" because I have come to feel deeply that there is never a time when a person no longer has to exert a conscious exercise of will to maintain his or her position. I feel that even our Heavenly Father, for instance, consciously and deliberately maintains His allegiance to eternal truth at all times. If the ability to choose differently had ever been literally removed from Him, even at this late date, He would find Himself and His actions null and void—without meaning or import—because of a lack of choice. I have come to realize that God does not function in a void of neutrality any more than you or I do. That thought may alarm those who entertain the old Protestant idea that God and "heaven" are free of the challenge of choices.

Lest I alarm any one who would quote our apostles and prophets, who state that God could never fall, let me add my most emphatic witness to that. *We never have to worry about God choosing a negative or "evil" choice;* thus He will never fall. This is not because He lives in an environment void of choices, but *because of His personal perfection*—which He obtained in exactly the same way He asks us to—by discovering any *self-will, self-pity, and self-righteousness* in ourselves and presenting it to Christ, the great physician, for removal. He is devoid of these characteristics, even as He asks us to demonstrate our desire to be. He can *always* be trusted to act sanely, moderately, correctly, and *functionally*, as expressed in Twelve Step language.

To believe that God acts the way He does, chooses as He does, because He lives in an environment free of choices, is to do to Him exactly what we have dysfunctionally wished to do to ourselves. It is to place the reason or cause for one's behavior *outside* of oneself. It's a manifestation of the old "If things could just be perfect *around* me, *then* I could be perfect" mode of thinking. God is perfect because His integrity is *within* Him, not because of His environment.

Let us consider the last portion of this verse and listen to the very witness of God, given through His prophet's voice.

2 Nephi 2:11 (continued)—

> **Wherefore, *all* things must needs be a compound in one** [have the option of at least two choices]**; wherefore, if it should be one body** [just having one option] **it must needs remain as dead** [having no agency]**, having no life** [the result of positive choices] **neither death** [result of negative choices]**, nor corruption nor incorruption, happiness nor misery, neither sense nor insensibility.** [These are just more *results* of the alternatives we are *always* free to choose from.] **(emphasis added)**

Notice the first words of this portion, the ones that say, **"Wherefore, *all* things must needs be a compound in one."** When are we, collectively and individually, going to stop just believing *in* God and start *believing* God? He just said that *all* things must needs be a "compound"—in other words, have two options. How explicitly does He have to state it? Maybe the next verse will show us.

2 Nephi 2:12—

> **Wherefore, this thing** [lack of opposition] **must needs** [would] **destroy the wisdom of God and his eternal purposes, and also the power, and the mercy, and the justice of** *God.* (emphasis added)

What an alarming, exclamatory thing to say! God be destroyed or any part of Him, even?!

Yes.

If there were no opportunities to make choices, even on His level; if He were functioning in a vacuum, devoid of options, then His wisdom, His mercy, His justice, His power, and all His eternal purposes would be for naught—just empty actions, demonstrating nothing. It is no demonstration of integrity to be honest, merciful, wise, or just when one has no options. To paraphrase an old saying, "It's what you choose to do when you can do *anything* you want that proves your character."

The next verse gets even more specific.

2 Nephi 2:13—

> **And if ye shall say there is no law** [no uncreated absolutes], **ye shall also say there is no sin** [opportunity to choose contrary to those absolutes]. **If ye shall say there is no sin, ye shall also say there is no righteousness** [opportunity to choose actions based on and in conformity to those absolutes]. **And if there be no** [chance to choose] **righteousness there be no** [chance to feel] **happiness** [because "happiness" is the direct result of choosing righteousness and comes *no other* way]. **And if there be no righteousness nor happiness there be no punishment** [natural consequences of choosing contrary to those uncreated absolutes] **nor misery** [the feeling that is *unavoidably* linked to those negative consequences].

And here's where Lehi, speaking for God, for truth, gets rigorously honest about it:

2 Nephi 2:13 (continued)—

> *And if these things are not there is no God.* (emphasis added)

There would be "no God" if "these things" (opposite choices, opposite consequences, opposite feelings) did not exist. First, if these things did not exist, He *Himself* could not have been proven and purified long ago, when it was His turn to be mortal.

Let us be like Him. Let us see the need and the actual blessing of opposition, realizing that on the influence of opposition we mount up, *if we so choose*, to our eventual place with our Father in Heaven. We can either do that, as He did, or we can choose to feel one of three other ways—I don't *want* it this way (self-will); I don't *like* it this way (self-pity); or I don't *need* it this way (self-righteousness).

Second, God is not—even now, even at this late date—if these things *are* not. Listen to the present tense of the verbs in Lehi's plain, straightforward statement. God has not come to a place of cessation of agency, of lack of choices. He made choices to get where He is, and *He is consciously making choices to stay where He is.* By the act of His own free will He serves all His creations and all His children. The force of *His* faith maintains the order in all things:

> **By this we understand that the principle of power which existed in the bosom of God, by which the worlds were framed, was faith; and that it is by reason of this principle of power existing in the Deity, that all created things exist; so that all things in heaven, on earth, or under the earth exist by reason of faith *as it existed in Him.***

> **Had it not been for the principle of faith the worlds would never have been framed neither would man have**

been formed of the dust. It is the principle by which Jehovah works, and through which Jehovah works, and through which he exercises power over all temporal as well as eternal things. Take this principle or attribute—for it is an attribute—from the Deity, *and he would cease to exist.* (Joseph Smith, *Lectures on Faith,* pp. 8–9, emphasis added)

To end our discussion, let us give Lehi the last word—a sobering word at that. Listen to him tell you what would also cease to exist if God our Father, our link with the eternal family before Him, ceased to have faith. Listen, and realize that even at this very moment His active exercise of His own choice, of His own free will, sustains you and all that you see. And why? *Because He loves you.*

2 Nephi 2:13 (continued)—

And if there is no God we are not, neither the earth; for there could have been no creation of things, neither to act nor to be acted upon; wherefore, *all things must have vanished away.* (emphasis added)

The Origin of the Twelve Steps as Reflected in the Gospel of Jesus Christ

In April 1939 a man by the name of Bill W. in association with a number of other people officially published to the world the Twelve Steps and Twelve Traditions of Alcoholics Anonymous. The fact that these people were even alive, much less sober and able to publish a book (*Alcoholics Anonymous*), was one of the greatest miracles of modern times. The medical world was amazed, left without an explanation for this unprecedented restoration to normal, sane living, totally relieved of the need to drink. What had Bill and his associates done? What answer had they found? It was simply this: They had found God.

Believing they could do the impossible if it were God's will, they set about to form a fellowship based on spiritual principles. Principles so universal and true that they could be applied by anyone who had even the smallest amount of willingness to believe in a benevolent God, leaving each free to define God as they best understood Him.

It worked.

Little did anyone realize that in that humble effort by a bunch of previously hopeless, derelict drunks was the beginning of the single most powerful program for overcoming self-destructive behaviors that has ever been introduced to the world. No efforts by medical science or modern psychology has ever duplicated their success.

Latter-day Saints should not be surprised at the success of these Twelve Steps. The Prophet Joseph Smith taught that with correct principles people can learn to govern themselves. It should also be no surprise that principles so profoundly effective as the Twelve Steps would be in complete harmony with the scriptures and with the gospel.

In the years since their introduction, these principles applied in this order, have been found to overcome any form of addiction, behavioral as well as chemical. It is in the overcoming of behavioral addiction that Latter-day Saints are finding Joseph's words fulfilled in these steps.

On the following page, you will find the Twelve Steps only slightly adapted from AA's originals. Under each of these you will find the scriptural equivalent accompanied by references.

These principles are correct. These steps are sure. They can "restore us to sanity," put our lives in balance, and give us the ability to "govern ourselves." Why? Because they turn our hearts to God. Nothing less than a personal relationship with Him can give us the power we need.

Excerpted from the pamphlet, "The Twelve Steps of Heart t' Heart." Reprinted with permission from Heart t' Heart.

The Twelve Steps
as Reflected in the Gospel of Jesus Christ

1. **We admitted we were powerless over compulsive addictive behaviors*—that our lives had become unmanageable.** *Admitted that we of ourselves are powerless, nothing without God. (Mosiah 4:5; Alma 26:12)*

2. **Came to believe that a Power greater than ourselves could restore us to sanity.** *Came to believe that God has all power and all wisdom and that in His strength we can do all things. (Mosiah 4:9; Alma 26:12)*

3. **Made a decision to turn our will and our lives over to the care of God as we understood Him.** *Made the decision to reconcile ourselves to the will of God, offer our whole souls as an offering unto Him, and trust Him in all things forever. (2 Nephi 10:24; Omni 1:26; Mosiah 3:19; 2 Nephi 4:34)*

4. **Made a searching and fearless moral inventory of ourselves.** *Made a searching and fearless written inventory of our past in order to thoroughly examine ourselves as to our pride and other weaknesses with the intent of recognizing our own carnal state and our need for Christ's Atonement. (Alma 15:17; Mosiah 4:2; Jacob 4:6–7; Ether 12:27)*

5. **Admitted to God, to ourselves, and to another human being the exact nature of our wrongs.** *Honestly shared this inventory with God and with another person, thus demonstrating the sincerity of our repentance, and our willingness to give away all our sins that we might know Him. (Mosiah 26:29; Alma 22:18)*

6. **Were entirely ready to have God remove all these defects of character.** *Became humble enough to yield our hearts and our lives to Christ for His sanctification and purification, relying wholly upon His merits, acknowledging even our own best efforts as unprofitable. (Helaman 3:35; 2 Nephi 31:19; Mosiah 2:20–21)*

7. **Humbly asked Him to remove our shortcomings.** *Humbly cried unto the Lord Jesus Christ in our hearts for a remission of sins that through His mercy and His grace we might experience a mighty change of heart, lose all disposition to do evil, and thus be encircled about in the arms of safety because of His great and last sacrifice. (Alma 36:18; Alma 38:8; Moroni 10:32; Mosiah 5:2; Alma 34:15–16)*

8. **Made a list of all persons we had harmed and became willing to make amends to them all.** *Made a list of all persons we had harmed and*

became willing to make restitution to all of them (even those we had harmed in what we might have considered righteous anger), desiring instead to be peacemakers and to do all that we could to come unto God by being first reconciled to others. (3 Nephi 12:9; 3 Nephi 12:24; 3 Nephi 12:44–45)

9. **Made direct amends to such people wherever possible except when to do so would injure them or others.** *Made restitution directly to those we had harmed, confessing our own wrongdoing in each instance except when to do so would further injure them or others. (Mosiah 27:35; 3 Nephi 12:25; Mosiah 26:30)*

10. **Continued to take personal inventory and when we were wrong promptly admitted it.** *Realizing that the weakness to be tempted and to sin is a part of the mortal experience, we continued to take personal inventory and when we were wrong promptly admitted it, being willing to repent as often as needed. (2 Nephi 4:18; 2 Nephi 10:20; Mosiah 26:30)*

11. **Sought through prayer and meditation to improve our conscious contact with God as we understood Him, praying only for knowledge of His will for us and the power to carry that out.** *Sought through prayer and meditation to improve our conscious contact with God, seeking the words of Christ through the power of the Holy Ghost that they might tell us all things that we should do, praying only for a knowledge of His will for us and the power to carry that out. (2 Nephi 32:3; Alma 37:37; Helaman 10:4)*

12. **Having had a spiritual awakening as the result of these steps, we tried to carry this message to others still suffering from the effects of compulsive behaviors and to practice these principles in all our affairs.** *Having experienced a mighty change and having awakened unto God as a result of our sincere repentance demonstrated in taking these steps, we were willing to become instruments in carrying this message to others and to practice these principles in all our affairs. (Alma 5:7; Mosiah 27:36–37; Moroni 7:3)*

*Any problem may be inserted here, in place of "compulsive addictive behaviors."

Permission to use the Twelve Steps of Alcoholics Anonymous for adaptation granted by A.A. World Services, Inc.

Excerpted from the pamphlet, "The Twelve Steps of Heart t' Heart." Reprinted with permission from Heart t' Heart.

The Original Twelve Steps from Alcoholics Anonymous

1. We admitted we were powerless over alcohol—that our lives had become unmanageable.

2. Came to believe that a Power greater than ourselves could restore us to sanity.

3. Made a decision to turn our will and our lives over to the care of God as we understood Him.

4. Made a searching and fearless moral inventory of ourselves.

5. Admitted to God, to ourselves and to another human being the exact nature of our wrongs.

6. Were entirely ready to have God remove all these defects of character.

7. Humbly asked Him to remove our shortcomings.

8. Made a list of all persons we had harmed, and became willing to make amends to them all.

9. Made direct amends to such people wherever possible, except when to do so would injure them or others.

10. Continued to take personal inventory and when we were wrong promptly admitted it.

11. Sought through prayer and meditation to improve our conscious contact with God as we understood Him, praying only for knowledge of His will for us and the power to carry that out.

12. Having had a spiritual awakening as the result of these steps, we tried to carry this message to alcoholics, and to practice these principles in all our affairs.

The Twelve Steps are reprinted with permission of Alcoholics Anonymous World Services, Inc. Permission to reprint the Twelve Steps does not imply affiliation with this program. A.A. is a program of recovery from alcoholism—use of the Twelve Steps in connection with activities which are patterned after A.A., but which address other problems, does not imply otherwise.

The Twelve Traditions of *Heart t' Heart*

1. In *Heart t Heart* individual recovery depends on the loving, supportive fellowship of the group. Without acceptance and unity there can be no fellowship and thus no recovery.

2. In *Heart t Heart* there is only one ultimate authority—a loving God who manifests His will for each group in our prayerful group conscience. Our leaders are but trusted servants, they do not govern.

3. The only requirement for *Heart t Heart* membership is a desire to stop participating in compulsive addictive behaviors.

4. Each *Heart t Heart* group is autonomous within the guidelines of the steps and the traditions, encouraged only to practice these principles in all its decisions.

5. Each *Heart t Heart* group has but one primary purpose—to carry its message of recovery from compulsive addictive behavior to those who still suffer.

6. A *Heart t Heart* group ought never endorse, finance or lend the *Heart t Heart* name to any outside publication or enterprise, lest problems of copyrights, money, property or prestige divert us from our primary purpose.

7. Every *Heart t Heart* group ought to be fully self-supporting through voluntary donations from members only.

8. *Heart t Heart* should remain forever non-professional, but our world service center may employ special workers.

9. *Heart t Heart*, as such, ought never be organized. We may, however, create service boards or committees directly responsible to those they serve.

10. *Heart t Heart* has no official opinion on any outside issue. Neither is its intent to promote any doctrine or policy contrary to the Church of Jesus Christ of Latter-day Saints. Hence, the *Heart t Heart* name ought never be drawn into any controversy, the opinions expressed being simply those of the individuals who share them.

11. Our public relations policy is based on attraction, rather than promotion. We need always maintain the spiritual foundation of personal anonymity, acknowledging that all recovery comes through dedication to the principles of the program.

12. Personal anonymity is the spiritual foundation of all our traditions—ever reminding us that this program is focused on principles and not personalities.

Permission to use the Twelve Traditions of Alcoholics Anonymous for adaptation granted by AA World Services, Inc.
Excerpted from the pamphlet, "The Twelve Steps of Heart t' Heart." Reprinted with permission from Heart t' Heart.

The Original Twelve Traditions from Alcoholics Anonymous

1. Our common welfare should come first; personal recovery depends upon A.A. unity.

2. For our group purpose, there is but one ultimate authority – a loving God as He may express Himself in our group conscience. Our leaders are but trusted servants; they do not govern.

3. The only requirement for A.A. membership is a desire to stop drinking.

4. Each group should be autonomous except in matters affecting other groups or A.A. as a whole.

5. Each group has but one primary purpose – to carry its message to the alcoholic who still suffers.

6. An A.A. group ought never endorse, finance, or lend the A.A. name to any related facility or outside enterprise, lest problems of money, property and prestige divert us from our primary purpose.

7. Every A.A. group ought to be fully self-supporting, declining outside contributions.

8. Alcoholics Anonymous should remain forever non-professional, but our service centers may employ special workers.

9. A.A., as such, ought never be organized; but we may create service boards or committees directly responsible to those they serve.

10. Alcoholics Anonymous has no opinion on outside issues; hence, the A.A. name ought never be drawn into public controversy.

11. Our public relations policy is based on attraction, rather than promotion; we need always maintain personal anonymity at the level of press, radio and film.

12. Anonymity is the spiritual foundation of all our traditions, ever reminding us to place principles before personalities.

The Twelve Steps are reprinted with permission of Alcoholics Anonymous World Services, Inc. Permission to reprint the Twelve Steps does not imply affiliation with this program. A.A. is a program of recovery from alcoholism – use of the Twelve Steps in connection with activities which are patterned after A.A., but which address other problems, does not imply otherwise.

Traditional Guidelines for Individual Participation in Twelve Step Meetings

ANONYMITY is absolutely vital to the survival of a group. This concept should constantly remind us that we are not in these meetings to learn juicy facts about others. There must be absolutely no gossip in this fellowship. We come together to help bear one another s burdens, not to increase them with judgement or backbiting.

Often in sharing we feel a need to express the hurts and fears we keep inside, to free ourselves from the blame and shame that are often carry-overs from the past. Anonymity gives us the freedom to do that.

CROSS TALK/SIDE TALK is discouraged in group meetings. This means we neither interrupt nor engage in dialogue with another speaker. Twelve step meetings are not designed to be encounter groups or advice giving sessions of any sort. Commenting or giving advice discourages the individual s own ability to hear the Truth as spoken to their hearts directly by the spirit. (2 Nephi 32:3)

SEVENTH TRADITION COLLECTIONS are the sole support of most Twelve Step groups. Traditionally a cup or basket is passed at every meeting, inviting but not requiring donations.

PRAYER IN MEETINGS has been a tradition since the beginning of AA. Twelve Step meetings generally use set memorized prayers, such as the Serenity Prayer. These prayers were chosen because of their acceptability to the general public. In our group meetings we are free to open and close our meetings in the manner we are familiar with personal, spontaneous prayer guided by the Spirit.

Suggested Tools for Recovery

As a help in working the Twelve Steps and twelve traditions, participants in other Twelve Step groups have found the following tools to be of great assistance in their recovery. To be useful, a tool must be picked up and used. Not every recovering person uses every tool listed below. Those who do use them, do not always use each of the tools every day. However, we have found that the more tools we can use on a consistent, daily basis, the greater our potential for staying in recovery. Remember, the tools are not a replacement for the principles found in the Twelve Steps.

ABSTINENCE

Abstinence, simply defined, is the action of refraining from our compulsive behaviors, whatever they may be. Abstinence is a personal matter between ourselves and God. It will differ from person to person, even if their compulsions are the same.

Abstinence has been said to be both a *tool* of the program and a *result*. To be "physically" abstinent, to abstain from our compulsive behavior, is a tool because it helps us to honestly face our feelings, rather than resort to our compulsion to distract or comfort us.

There is also a dimension of abstinence that goes far beyond the physical realm. This is the *spiritual gift* of a complete loss of our *desire* to do our compulsive behavior. This gift comes as a result of applying the steps and their underlying principles in our lives. For some of us this gift comes quickly, and for others, it comes more slowly, but it does come to all.

CONFIDENTIALITY (ANONYMITY)

In many Twelve Step programs, confidentiality (or anonymity) is called the spiritual foundation of a recovery program. This tool reminds us that the focus in our recovery is on the principles and NOT the people in the group.

Confidentiality assures us safety in the freedom of expression of our innermost thoughts and feelings without the worry of gossip or retaliation. We come together in our support groups to bear one another's burdens, not to increase them with judgement or back-biting. Our sharing must be received with respect and kept in confidence.

Confidentiality does not mean that we cannot share the ideas and principles discussed in the meetings, only that identities not be attached to them.

Confidentiality also reminds us that all are equal in these groups. There are no prescribed leaders or "gurus" within the group and outside status makes no difference. We all gather here to acknowledge our common humanity.

LITERATURE AND MUSIC

Literature is used to help us more fully understand our path to recovery and to reinforce the use of the Twelve Steps. It gives us the ability to have a meeting with just ourselves when we are not able to reach out and connect with others in recovery. We especially recommend the daily use of the scriptures, as demonstrated in this workbook, *He Did Deliver Me from Bondage.* Some people have also found other Twelve Step program literature helpful.

It has been said that music is a powerful way to speak God's language, to praise Him and to express our deepest feelings to God and to others. It can be felt inside our hearts or performed aloud for others to enjoy. Listening to inspired music is both comforting and healing to our souls.

Hymns can be particularly healing. According to the 1985 LDS Church hymn-book, "hymns invite the Spirit of the Lord... move us to repentance and good works, build testimony and faith, comfort the weary, console the mourning, and inspire us to endure to the end" (p.ix). These attributes correlate directly to Twelve Steps principles.

MEETINGS

Meetings are an opportunity to come together to share our experience, strength, and hope. It is a way of providing ourselves with the fellowship of others who have finally decided to acknowledge personal powerlessness over one or more compulsive addictive behaviors in their own life or the life of a loved one, and who are seeking a God-centered solution.

PRAYER AND MEDITATION

Prayer and meditation are two sides of the same coin and are probably the most vital to recovery of all the tools. The whole focus and purpose of the Twelve Steps is to bring us closer to God. Communication between parties is critical to establishing a two-way relationship, and no relationship is more important than the one we have with our Savior, Jesus Christ. In honest prayer we share the *intimacies* of our heart. In quiet, sincere meditation He shares His will for us.

SERVICE

Service is a way of getting out of our compulsive behavior and into recovery. Sharing the message of recovery through faith in Jesus Christ and the application of the Twelve Steps is the most obvious form of service we can perform. However, any act of service will move us further into recovery. Going to meetings, sharing, listening to others share, talking to newcomers, and telephoning between meetings are all acts of service that will enhance our recovery.

SPONSORING

When a person goes to a foreign country, they will often be met by a sponsor – someone who knows the customs and practices of the country and will assist the new person in getting oriented. Sponsoring in *Heart t Heart* works the same way. A sponsor is someone who is living the Twelve Steps to the best of his or her ability. Sponsors generally have more experience in the program and have maintained some level of recovery.

It is recommended that we ask someone to be our sponsor soon after coming into the program. We listen to the sharing and to the Spirit and then choose someone with whom we feel we share a common bond. Or we take down the name and phone number of someone who has checked the sponsor column on the "We Care" list. Sponsoring may develop into a long term friendship or it may be temporary. It is perfectly acceptable to have more than one sponsor at the same time so that we can be sure of reaching someone when we are in need.

TELEPHONING

In other Twelve Step groups, we are encouraged to use the telephone as a means of breaking through our isolation and getting back on the road to recovery. Using the telephone to call others has been compared to having a meeting between meetings. It's a tool we can use any time we need to talk about our feelings and experiences, whether it be before, during, or after engaging in our compulsive behavior.

We encourage you to begin building a personal phone list that you can keep in a convenient place and use to reach out to others. A page has been provided at the back of this book for that purpose (A–57).

WRITING

Those who are most successful in recovery use the tool of writing frequently. Unspoken, unacknowledged feelings, whether positive or negative, are often the source of our need to "use"—the reason we begin our compulsive addictive behaviors. Writing is a way of bringing our feelings to the surface and exploring them. Many people find that they do not realize what their true feelings really are until they see them in front of them in black and white. Once on paper, these thoughts and feelings can be acknowledged, and a solution to the problem can be found.

Writing can also be used as a means of communicating with God, as we write the prayers of our hearts and then record what we feel the Spirit reveal to us.

Excerpted and adapted from the pamphlet, "The Nine Tools of Heart t' Heart." Reprinted with permission from Heart t' Heart.

To the Family and Loved Ones of the Addict:
Understanding "Codependency"

Early in the study of alcoholism it was dis-covered that family members of alcoholics often manifest a number of dysfunctional characteristics of their own, usually as a result of living with addiction. Their fear *for* the addict or *of* the addict can twist and distort a loved one's thinking and cause a ripple effect throughout the entire family system. While the addict is "hung up" on drugs or alcohol, loved ones can become "hung up" on the addict. Many people refer to this phenomenon as codependency.

Even after the addict becomes sober, loved ones may still be trying to deal with their own reactions to the trauma they experienced during the fearful years. Thus loved ones often need to do some recovery work of their own. The following thoughts might prove helpful to those who have lived or still live with addiction.

Many of us deal with feelings of unworthiness and emptiness that began in a difficult or abusive relationship with a practicing addict. Some of us were raised in families where addictive compulsive behaviors were manifest in alcoholism, drug addiction, workaholism or perfectionism. In some families the addiction was compulsive spending, gambling or raging. Some of us experienced sexual abuse, the result of another's most hideous compulsion. Others of us were subjected to the effects of these same addictive compulsive behaviors during our adulthood by either a spouse or a child.

In reaction to these circumstances we have learned to *endure* life rather than to *live* life. We have developed personality characteristics which act as coping mechanisms. These mechanisms, while at one time protective, prove to be detrimental to forming healthy relationships. Some of these characteristics are:

1. We assume responsibility for other's feelings and/or choices.
2. We have difficulty identifying our own feelings: happiness, pain, anger, joy, sadness, loneliness, etc.
3. We have difficulty expressing our feelings in healthy ways.

4. We tend to fear that our feelings or needs will be belittled or rejected by others.

5. We tend to minimize, alter or even deny the truth about our feeling or needs.

6. We tend to put other's feelings and needs ahead of our own, not allowing there to be a healthy balance with our feelings and needs.

7. Our fear of other's feelings (especially anger) determines what we say and do.

8. Our serenity and attention is determined by how others are feeling or by what they're doing.

9. We do not realize that feelings are not good or bad, that they just are.

10. We question or ignore our own conscience, our own values, in order to connect with significant others—trusting and obeying their feelings or opinions more than our own.

11. Other people's actions or desires tend to determine how we respond or react.

12. Our sense of self-worth is based on other/outer influences instead of on our personal witness of God's love and esteem for us.

13. We have difficulty making decisions and are frightened of being wrong or making a mistake.

14. We are perfectionistic and place too many expectations on ourselves and others.

15. We are not comfortable acknowledging good things about ourselves and tend to judge everything we do, think, or say as not being good enough.

16. We do not know that it is okay to be vulnerable and find it difficult, almost impossible, to ask for help.

17. We do not see that it is okay to talk about problems outside the family, thus we leave ourselves and our families stranded in the troubles they are experiencing.

18. We are steadfastly loyal—even when that loyalty is unjustified and often personally harmful to us.

19. We have to be needed in order to have a relationship with others.

Applying the principles found in the Twelve Steps to our daily lives and relationships can bring us a sense of balance and sanity and free us from these destructive characteristics. Each of us is growing at our own individual rate as we learn to relate correctly with our Heavenly Father and Savior. In recovery, we have come to realize that our relationship with God is the most important one of all and must be functioning well before any other relationship will function.

No matter how traumatic your past or despairing your present may feel, there is hope in these principles for a new way of life. Through living these principles and concepts, we guarantee you will find the strength within to be what God intended you to be—precious and free.

"Fearing [Others] More Than God"
An Ancient Problem

"Fearing man more than God" is a universal malady. Many people who are successfully recovering from addiction have discovered that this tendency to depend on other fallible mortals—parents, spouses, children—for validation and comfort was actually the root of their need to practice their addiction.

Down through the ages the prophets have counseled us repeatedly to "fear"—respect, need, or rely on—God before anyone else. President Ezra Taft Benson stated this concept very clearly:

"We should put God ahead of *everyone* else in our lives." (*Ensign*, May 1988, p. 4. Italics original.)

Three years later, Elder L. Tom Perry made another plain statement of this true principle:

"If we increase our dependence on anything or *anyone* except the Lord, we will find an immediate decrease in our freedom to act." (*Ensign*, November 1991, p. 65. Emphasis added.)

Scripture study shows that reliance on man rather than God is actually a confusion of agency, or as some people say, "boundaries." Where does our stewardship or responsibility for another person end and their stewardship or responsibility begin? Just whose salvation do we have the power or ability to "work out?"

The following is a partial list of scriptures which examine these issues and support this concept:

Fearing Man More Than God:

Psalms 3:1-3	Psalms 27: 1,3	Jeremiah 1:8
2 Nephi 8:7	D&C 3:7	D&C 5:21

Confusion of Boundaries:

Matthew 13:21	Gal. 6:4-5	Alma 29:4
Helaman 14:30-31	Ether 12:37	D & C 1:11

Traditions of Our Parents:

Psalms 27:10	Matthew 19:29	Alma 30:25
Helaman 16:20	D & C 123:7	Moses 6:54

Excerpted from the pamphlet, "Speaking Heart t' Heart on Codependency." Reprinted with permission from Heart t' Heart.

Twelve Step Programs for the LDS Community

Heart t' Heart is a 12-step program dedicated to helping LDS people overcome the effects of compulsive addictive behaviors in their lives or in the life of a loved one. With permission of AA World Services, Inc., *Heart t' Heart* adapted the 12 steps to reflect *Book of Mormon* references and LDS principles.

Heart t' Heart believes a behavior can be considered an addiction or compulsion when the person doing the behavior desires desperately to stop but has found no permanent way to do so. As such, *Heart t' Heart* meetings are open to individuals desiring to recover from behaviors such as codependency, eating disorders, workaholism, gambling, compulsive spending, perfectionism, as well as alcohol, drug and sex addictions. *Heart t' Heart* groups are available in the United States. For information on current *Heart t' Heart* groups, contact them at: *Heart t' Heart*, P.O. Box 247, Pleasant Grove, UT 84062, or on the internet at: www.heart-t-heart.org

*Heart t' Heart produces a supplement for this workbook which contains pamphlets and information on leading a Twelve Step group.

LDS Family Services Substance Abuse Recovery Services (SARS) Groups are sponsored by LDS Family Services. Generally, LDS Family Services does not provide direct professional services for alcohol and drug problems because of the long term nature of rehabilitation and specialized training required. They may offer some sponsorship of programs they feel are appropriate. Support groups may be started in an outlying area with the assistance of the local LDS Family Services representative. For more information, contact the LDS Family Services Agency in your area.

"We Care" List

Using the telephone to call others is a means of breaking through our isolation and getting back on the road to recovery. It has been compared to having a meeting between meetings. We encourage you to use this page to begin building a personal phone list that you can use to reach out to others.

Name	Phone

INDEX

– Quotes Index –

Notes

Notes

Notes

Notes

Notes

Notes

About the Author

"Drugs, alcohol, food, work, perfectionism, spending money, gambling, destructive sexual behaviors, you name it, we're addicted to it. Being mortal and being addicted are almost synonymous," so says Colleen Harrison, a self-acknowledged recovering junk food addict, maintaining a weight loss of over 140 pounds for the last ten years. During these ten years of recovery, Colleen, mother of twelve children, has survived the death of her oldest daughter and the loss of her first marriage to addictive behavior. Drawing on the power (grace) of Jesus Christ, Colleen has completed a B.A. and an M.A. in English at Brigham Young University. While at BYU, Colleen combined courses in psychology, human development and creative writing to create a uniquely LDS version of narrative therapy. "Writing—in a journal, on the back of an envelope, anywhere—is one of the cheapest and most powerful forms of therapy a person can use to recover from addiction, compulsion, or any other earth-life challenges," Colleen maintains.

Currently, Colleen is pursuing a Ph.D. in Family and Human Development at Utah State University, in Logan, Utah. "Family and human development—that's what the restored gospel of Jesus Christ is all about—Eternal Family and Eternal Development." Strongly committed to both, Colleen continues to maintain the recovery the Lord has blessed her with through consistent, daily application of the Twelve Step principles as they correlate with the Book of Mormon and the gospel of Christ. In this book she has attempted to capture in a very personal style the process of spiritual awakening in these twelve principles. They have truly given her a hope in Christ that is her strength and her light as the last days strike close to home.

Colleen lives with her husband, Phil Harrison. They have a combined family of 17 children, 18 grandchildren, 3 cats and a dog. You may write to Colleen c/o Windhaven Publishing and Productions, P.O. Box 282, Pleasant Grove, UT 84062.

WINDHAVEN

PUBLISHING & PRODUCTIONS
PO BOX 282, PLEASANT GROVE, UT 84062

Order Form

To Order Additional Copies of *He Did Deliver Me from Bondage*, send this order form along with check or money order in US dollars to the address above.

Code	Item	Price	X	Qty.	=	Total
1002	*He Did Deliver Me from Bondage* (8.5" x 11"; softbound; ISBN: 1-930738-00-5)	$14.95*	X	_____	=	_____
1004	*He Did Deliver Me from Bondage* (5.5" x 8.5"; softbound; ISBN: 1-930738-01-3)	$12.95*	X	_____	=	_____

SUBTOTAL _____

Sales Tax: _____
Please add 6.25% for books shipped to a Utah address.

Shipping: $2.00 per book U.S./$4.00 per book Canada. _____
Overseas, call for rates.

TOTAL ENCLOSED _____

PLEASE PRINT:

Date: _____

Name: _____

Address: _____

City, ST, ZIP _____

_____

Phone: (_____) _____

List additional Ship-To addresses on back. Credit card orders may be place on-line at www.rosehavenpublishing.com or by phone or fax.

*Prices subject to change without notice.

VOICE: 801.785.8002 TOLL-FREE 877.785.8002 FAX: 801.796.0923

WWW.WINDHAVENPUBLISHING.COM WINDHAVEN99@HOTMAIL.COM